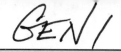  GEN1 W9-BRI-561

 ™

References for the Rest of Us

PROGRAMMING BOOK SERIES FROM IDG

Are you baffled and bewildered by programming? Does it seem like an impenetrable puzzle? Do you find that traditional manuals are overloaded with technical terms you don't understand? Do you want to know how to get your PC to do what you want? Then the . . . *For Dummies* programming books from IDG are for you.

The . . . *For Dummies* programming books are written for frustrated computer users who know they really aren't dumb but find that programming, with its unique vocabulary and logic, makes them feel helpless. The . . . *For Dummies* books use a humorous approach and a down-to-earth style to diffuse fears and build confidence. Lighthearted but not lightweight, these books are a perfect survival guide for first-time programmers or anyone learning a new environment.

IDG BOOKS

Millions of satisfied readers have made . . . *For Dummies* books the #1 introductory-level computer book series and have written asking for more. So if you're looking for a fun and easy way to learn about computers, look to . . . *For Dummies* books to give you a helping hand.

ACCESS PROGRAMMING FOR DUMMIES™

ACCESS PROGRAMMING FOR DUMMIES™

Rob Krumm

IDG BOOKS

IDG Books Worldwide, Inc.
An International Data Group Company

San Mateo, California ◆ Indianapolis, Indiana ◆ Boston, Massachusetts

Access Programming For Dummies

Published by
IDG Books Worldwide, Inc.
An International Data Group Company
155 Bovet Road, Suite 310
San Mateo, CA 94402

Library of Congress Catalog Card No.: 94-75908

ISBN: 1-56884-091-8

Printed in the United States of America

10 9 8 7 6 5 4 3 2 1

1B/TQ/QZ/ZU

First Printing, September, 1994

Distributed in the United States by IDG Books Worldwide, Inc.

 is a registered trademark of IDG Books Worldwide, Inc.

About IDG Books Worldwide

Welcome to the world of IDG Books Worldwide.

IDG Books Worldwide, Inc., is a subsidiary of International Data Group, the world's largest publisher of business, and computer-related information and the leading global provider of information services on information technology. IDG was founded over 25 years ago and now employs more than 5,700 people worldwide. IDG publishes over 195 publications in 62 countries. Forty million people read one or more IDG publications each month.

Launched in 1990, IDG Books is today the fastest growing publisher of computer and business books in the United States. We are proud to have received three awards from the Computer Press Association in recognition of editorial excellence, and our best-selling *...For Dummies* series has over 10 million copies in print with translations in more than 20 languages. IDG Books, through a recent joint venture with IDG's Hi-Tech Beijing, became the first U.S. publisher to publish a computer book in the People's Republic of China. In record time, IDG Books has become the first choice for millions of readers around the world who want to learn how to better manage their businesses.

Our mission is simple: Every IDG book is designed to bring extra value and skill-building instruction to the reader. Our books are written by experts who understand and care about our readers. The knowledge base of our editorial staff comes from years of experience in publishing, education, and journalism — experience which we use to produce books for the 90s. In short, we care about books, so we attract the best people. We devote special attention to details such as audience, interior design, use of icons, and illustrations. And because we write, edit, and produce our books electronically, we can spend more time ensuring superior content and spend less time on the technicalities of making books.

You can count on our commitment to deliver high-quality books at competitive prices on topics you want to read about. At IDG, we value quality, and we have been delivering quality for over 25 years. You'll find no better book on a subject than an IDG book.

John Kilcullen
President and CEO
IDG Books Worldwide, Inc.

For More Information...

For general information on IDG Books in the U.S., including information on discounts and premiums, contact IDG Books at 800-434-3422 or 415-312-0650.

For information on where to purchase IDG Books outside the U.S., contact Christina Turner at 415-312-0633.

For information on translations, contact Marc Jeffrey Mikulich, Foreign Rights Manager, at IDG Books Worldwide; FAX NUMBER 415-286-2747.

For sales inquiries and special prices for bulk quantities, write to the address above or call IDG Books Worldwide at 415-312-0650.

For information on using IDG Books in the classroom, or for ordering examination copies, contact Jim Kelly at 800-434-2086.

The ...*For Dummies* book series is distributed in the United States by IDG Books Worldwide, Inc. It is distributed in Canada by Macmillan of Canada, a Division of Canada Publishing Corporation; by Computer and Technical Books in Miami, Florida, for South America and the Caribbean; by Longman Singapore in Singapore, Malaysia, Thailand, and Korea; by Toppan Co. Ltd. in Japan; by Asia Computerworld in Hong Kong; by Woodslane Pty. Ltd. in Australia and New Zealand; and by Transworld Publishers Ltd. in the U.K. and Europe.

IDG Books Worldwide, Inc. is a subsidiary of International Data Group. The officers are Patrick J. McGovern, Founder and Board Chairman; Walter Boyd, President. International Data Group's publications include: **ARGENTINA'S** Computerworld Argentina, Infoworld Argentina; **AUSTRALIA'S** Computerworld Australia, Australian PC World, Australian Macworld, Network World, Mobile Business Australia, Reseller, IDG Sources; **AUSTRIA'S** Computerwelt Oesterreich, PC Test; **BRAZIL'S** Computerworld, Gamepro, Game Power, Mundo IBM, Mundo Unix, PC World, Super Game; **BELGIUM'S** Data News (CW) **BULGARIA'S** Computerworld Bulgaria, Ediworld, PC & Mac World Bulgaria, Network World Bulgaria; **CANADA'S** CIO Canada, Computerworld Canada, Graduate Computerworld, InfoCanada, Network World Canada; **CHILE'S** Computerworld Chile, Informatica; **COLOMBIA'S** Computerworld Colombia, PC World; **CZECH REPUBLIC'S** Computerworld, Elektronika, PC World; **DENMARK'S** Communications World, Computerworld Danmark, Macintosh Produktkatalog, Macworld Danmark, PC World Danmark, PC World Produktguide, Tech World, Windows World; **ECUADOR'S** PC World Ecuador; **EGYPT'S** Computerworld (CW) Middle East, PC World Middle East; **FINLAND'S** MikroPC, Tietoviikko, Tietoverkko; **FRANCE'S** Distributique, GOLDEN MAC, InfoPC, Languages & Systems, Le Guide du Monde Informatique, Le Monde Informatique, Telecoms & Reseaux; **GERMANY'S** Computerwoche, Computerwoche Focus, Computerwoche Extra, Computerwoche Karriere, Information Management, Macwelt, Netzwelt, PC Welt, PC Woche, Publish, Unit; **GREECE'S** Infoworld, PC Games; **HUNGARY'S** Computerworld SZT, PC World; **HONG KONG'S** Computerworld Hong Kong, PC World Hong Kong; **INDIA'S** Computers & Communications; **IRELAND'S** ComputerScope; **ISRAEL'S** Computerworld Israel, PC World Israel; **ITALY'S** Computerworld Italia, Lotus Magazine, Macworld Italia, Networking Italia, PC Shopping, PC World Italia; **JAPAN'S** Computerworld Today, Information Systems World, Macworld Japan, Nikkei Personal Computing, SunWorld Japan, Windows World; **KENYA'S** East African Computer News; **KOREA'S** Computerworld Korea, Macworld Korea, PC World Korea; **MEXICO'S** Compu Edicion, Compu Manufactura, Computacion/Punto de Venta, Computerworld Mexico, MacWorld, Mundo Unix, PC World, Windows; **THE NETHERLANDS'** Computer! Totaal, Computable (CW), LAN Magazine, MacWorld, Totaal "Windows"; **NEW ZEALAND'S** Computer Listings, Computerworld New Zealand, New Zealand PC World, Network World; **NIGERIA'S** PC World Africa; **NORWAY'S** Computerworld Norge, C/World, Lotusworld Norge, Macworld Norge, Networld, PC World Ekspress, PC World Norge, PC World's Produktguide, Publish& Multimedia World, Student Data, Unix World, Windowsworld; IDG Direct Response; **PAKISTAN'S** PC World Pakistan; **PANAMA'S** PC World Panama; **PERU'S** Computerworld Peru, PC World; **PEOPLE'S REPUBLIC OF CHINA'S** China Computerworld, China Infoworld, Electronics Today/Multimedia World, Electronics International, Electronic Product World, China Network World, PC and Communications Magazine, PC World China, Software World Magazine, Telecom Product World; IDG HIGH TECH BEIJING'S New Product World; IDG SHENZHEN'S Computer News Digest; **PHILIPPINES'** Computerworld Philippines, PC Digest (PCW); **POLAND'S** Computerworld Poland, PC World/Komputer; **PORTUGAL'S** Cerebro/PC World, Correio Informatico/Computerworld, Informatica & Comunicacoes Catalogo, MacIn, Nacional de Produtos; **ROMANIA'S** Computerworld, PC World; **RUSSIA'S** Computerworld-Moscow, Mir - PC, Sety; **SINGAPORE'S** Computerworld Southeast Asia, PC World Singapore; **SLOVENIA'S** Monitor Magazine; **SOUTH AFRICA'S** Computer Mail (CIO), Computing S.A., Network World S.A., Software World; **SPAIN'S** Advanced Systems, Amiga World, Computerworld Espana, Communicacoes World, Macworld Espana, NeXTWORLD, Super Juegos Magazine (GamePro), PC World Espana, Publish; **SWEDEN'S** Attack, ComputerSweden, Corporate Computing, Natverk & Kommunikation, Macworld, Mikrodatorn, PC World, Publishing & Design (CAP), DataIngenjoren, Maxi Data, Windows World; **SWITZERLAND'S** Computerworld Schweiz, Macworld Schweiz, PC Tip; **TAIWAN'S** Computerworld Taiwan, PC World Taiwan; **THAILAND'S** Thai Computerworld; **TURKEY'S** Computerworld Monitor, Macworld Turkiye, PC World Turkiye; **UKRAINE'S** Computerworld; **UNITED KINGDOM'S** Computing /Computerworld, Connexion/Network World, Lotus Magazine, Macworld, Open Computing/Sunworld; **UNITED STATES'** Advanced Systems, AmigaWorld, Cable in the Classroom, CD Review, CIO, Computerworld, Digital Video, DOS Resource Guide, Electronic Entertainment Magazine, Federal Computer Week, Federal Integrator, GamePro, IDG Books, Infoworld, Infoworld Direct, Laser Event, Macworld, Multimedia World, Network World, PC Letter, PC World, PlayRight, Power PC World, Publish, SWATPro, Video Event; **VENEZUELA'S** Computerworld Venezuela, PC World; **VIETNAM'S** PC World Vietnam

About the Author

Rob Krumm began working with computers in 1979 as a math teacher in Downingtown, Pennsylvania. In 1981 he started a school in Walnut Creek, CA dedicated to teaching people how to use personal computers and software. He published his first book, *Understanding and Using dBASE II,* in 1983. It was based on teaching materials he developed for his dBASE II courses at Walnut Creek. Since then, he has written more than forty books and many articles on computer hardware and software.

Rob's primary interests include the impact of changing technology on standard academic curriculum and teaching. He is currently writing a computer program to help his daughter's elementary school track their library books.

Credits

Vice President and Publisher
Chris Williams

Editorial Director
Trudy Neuhaus

Brand Manager
Amorette Pedersen

Manuscript Editor
John Pont

Editorial Assistant
Berta Hyken

Production Director
Beth Jenkins

Associate Production Coordinator
Valery Bourke

Pre-Press Coordinator
Steve Peake

Copy Editor
Deb Kaufmann

Production Staff
Tony Augsburger
Paul Belcastro
Linda M. Boyer
Mary Breidenbach
J. Tyler Connor
Kent Gish
Sherry Dickinson Gomoll
Angela F. Hunckler
Drew R. Moore
Mark C. Owens
Carla Radzikinas
Dwight Ramsey
Patricia R. Reynolds
Gina Scott

Indexer
Liz Cunningham

Book Design
University Graphics

Cover Design
Kavish + Kavish

Dedication

To everyone that has ever tried to write a computer program, I say the following:

"What's miraculous about a spider's web?" said Mrs. Arable. "I don't see why you say a web is a miracle — it's just a web."

"Ever try to spin one?" asked Dr. Dorian.

Charlotte's Web, E.B. White

Acknowledgments

A long overdue thanks to Chris Williams, whom I first met at the 1983 West Coast Computer Faire. Back then, I carried my manuscript from booth to booth looking for a publisher.

(The publisher would like to give special thanks to Patrick J. McGovern, without whom this book would not have been possible.)

Contents at a Glance

Cartoons at a Glance
by Rich Tennant

page 1

page 6

page 9

page 83

page 183

page 339

page 349

Table of Contents

Introduction

*Y*ou've made two smart choices: choosing Access and buying this book. Access provides a rich environment that encourages you to create *smart* tools — tools that are as much fun to use as they are to design. More important, these tools allow you to help other people (who are a lot less familar with Access than you) become more productive by taking advantage of the power of Access.

The 5th Wave   By Rich Tennant

"I JUST DON'T THINK THIS NEW SALES KID IS GONNA WORK OUT."

How to Use This Book

The best way to use this book is right along with your computer. Load up Access and start working with the examples and techniques presented in every chapter.

Once you get the hang of a technique, you'll probably want to do some experimenting. Go ahead! There's no reason to try to learn the whole program in one gulp. In Access programming, each new technique or trick you learn opens up a lot of possibilities.

> When you see shaded lines of code (like these), type them as one line, not two.

When you're ready for more or you can't quite get Access to do what you want, move on to the next example. Remember, even though a program doesn't work the first time, it may lead to a valuable discovery.

About This Book

This book shows you how both Access and the applications you create with it can be shaped and customized to fit your needs. In this book, you'll find:

- Explanations written for nonprogrammers who need to customize Access

- The key concepts, techniques, and tricks of the trade that you need for using Access to its full potential

- A step-by-step approach that guides you easily through each key area so that you can quickly start to see results

- Lots of pictures and diagrams — in programming, a picture is often worth a thousand lines of code

- Examples that are clearly related to one another, so you can see how each new technique is related to the previous examples

About You

In writing this book, I've made a few assumptions about you. Here's a brief summary of the concepts I'm assuming you're comfortable with:

- **The Windows interface.** You should know how to load programs; open, close, and size windows; and use drop-down menus, dialog boxes, and shortcut keys.

✔ **Files and directories**. You should have a basic understanding of DOS filenames and the DOS directory system, including rules for filenames, directory names, and paths.

✔ **Tables.** You should have a basic understanding of how to define fields, the different data types, and default values.

✔ **Queries.** You should also have basic understanding of how to use a query form to generate sets of data.

✔ **Forms.** You should be comfortable with creating a form and using it to enter data into a table; adding, or moving controls on a form, and using property sheets for controls.

✔ **Reports.** Finally, you need to know how to create and print a report, and understand both the use of the Print Preview window and the process of printing under Windows.

Chapter 1 provides an overview of the key points about tables, queries, forms, and reports that are required to create Access programs.

Why You Will Succeed with Access

I anticipate that some of the people who read this book will bring with them unhappy experiences with such highly touted tools as dBASE III or IV, Paradox 3 or 4, or FoxPro for DOS or Windows. Although these programs are a significant advance over the dark ages of computer technology, they still have a long way to go in terms of bringing custom programming to the average computer user. Many database jobs started by nonprofessional programmers are never finished. It isn't their fault. The tools available simply aren't good enough.

Access provides computer users with a tool they can learn and use to build attractive, understandable, easy-to-use applications that do exactly what they're supposed to.

Here are ten important reasons why Access is the best tool for building an application:

✔ **The Windows interface.** The Windows interface — menu bars, drop-down menus, dialog boxes, and so on — provides Access with a look and feel that have already proven to be comfortable to a broad range of computer users.

✔ **Mouse operation.** Selecting items with the mouse is easier, faster, and more accurate than keyboard entry. Creating a database application that minimizes standard data entry and maximizes mouse-oriented selection is the key to creating useful applications.

✔ **Color and graphics**. Even the best DOS-based database can display only 2000 characters on the screen at one time. Windows allows you to place much more information on the screen, including fonts, colors, drop shadows, lines, 3D effects, icons, and images. These features allow you to design displays that clearly and effectively communicate with the user.

✔ **Forms**. A *form* is a window that is used to present information on the screen and interact with the person using the program. Forms can include all of the Windows interface elements, including graphics, menus, and mouse operations. You can design forms to use the most basic as well as the most advanced features of Access, including Access Basic programs.

✔ **One file**. Access eliminates the need to keep track of dozens of files containing the tables, forms, reports, programs, and macros that are related to an application. Instead, Access stores all the items related to an application in a single file. This also makes it easy to copy and back up an application.

✔ **Wizards**. Although you can choose to customize every aspect of an Access application, you can also use the Access Wizard to quickly set up sections of the application, such as forms, reports, selection queries, and even groups of buttons on a form. Anything created by the Wizard can be modified just like any item that you create from scratch. For example, it's often easier to create a custom report by starting with a Wizard report form and then adding and deleting elements.

✔ **Event-based programming.** This is the most important item in this list. An *event* is some action that a user takes when working with a program — for example, clicking a button or entering an amount. In Access, you link your programs directly to the items you see on the screen, and then you define what should happen when a particular action is taken. Instead of writing long lists of commands that are meant to cover a wide range of actions, you insert small segments of instructions along with the button, entry box, or other item that appears on the screen.

✔ **Easy testing**. Access provides tools that make it easy to test the expressions, macros, and Access Basic code you create. Because Access doesn't need to create a separate compiled version of your program, you can quickly change the code until you get the desired results.

✔ **SQL**. Structured Query Language is a method by which blocks of data can be requested for use. In Access, you can use SQL statements in expressions, macros, and Access Basic as a shorthand way to obtain data. Although many people shy away from SQL, I believe that once you get the hang of SQL, you'll find that it is an effective way to integrate data into any application.

✔ **OLE/DDE**. Object Linking and Embedding and Dynamic Data Exchange are Microsoft's names for Windows programs that allow you to store different types of information in any application. For example, an Access database can contain a spreadsheet created with Excel or a sound recording made with the Windows Sound Recorder.

How This Book Is Organized

This book has four major sections. Part I discusses the basic storage unit in Access — the table — and provides an introduction to Access expressions and SQL.

Part II discusses macros and Access Basic. You use these tools to perform arithmetic, manipulate text, a customize forms and reports in Access — in short, they are the means for building simple functions or entire applications.

Part III shows you how to apply expressions, macros, and Access Basic to customize and enhance your forms and reports.

Part IV shows you how to develop solutions to several common business problems.

"You" and "the User"

Throughout this book, I refer to *you* and sometimes to *the user*. Aren't they the same thing? In a book about word processing or spreadsheets, that would probebly be true. But when you are talking about programming a database such as Access, it's likely that you are creating something that someone else will use. After all, programs are usually written so that a person other than the programmer can accomplish something.

When I talk about *the user,* I'm referring to the person who will use your program. The art of programming involves anticipating what other people will or won't do. Writing a program is a bit like writing a book. You decide what to do based on your understanding of your audience. For this reason, I find it necessary to talk about both *you* — the person reading the book and writing the programs — and *the user* — the person who will use the program.

Icons Used in This Book

This icon signals technical information. You might want to skip these sections your first time through the book. ▪

This icon indicates useful information or helpful advice. ▪

This symbol means watch out — be careful with the information presented. ▪

And the little square after this sentence indicates the end of the technical stuff, tip, or warning. ▪

Where to Go from Here

The best part about programming in Access is that no matter what level you start on, you are almost certain to create fun, useful, and interesting programs. The more you learn, the more you can show off.

Even if you've never written a line of code or a macro command, jump right in. Before you know it, you'll have Access performing tricks that programmers working in old-fashioned languages might only dream about.

Part I
Getting Ready to Program

The 5th Wave By Rich Tennant

"IT'S AN INTEGRATED SOFTWARE PACKAGE DESIGNED TO HELP UNCLUTTER YOUR LIFE."

In This Part...

Database programs are often intimidating, difficult to understand, and hard to use — even by people who make their living writing programs. Access, however, is easy to use and has lots of built-in features that automatically handle tedious details. At the same time, it's powerful enough to manage almost any type of programming problem.

You don't need to be an Access expert before you can start writing programs. Part I covers the information you need if you are new to Access or just want a review. If you're familiar with Access, you still may want to give these chapters a quick look to make sure you understand the basics.

Chapter 1
Access Basics

● ●

In This Chapter

▶ How Access is organized

▶ The lowdown on Data Access

▶ The structure of Access tables

▶ Details about field properties, including those added for Version 2.0

● ●

*T*his chapter presents an overview of some of the basic elements in Access. For those who are familiar with basic Access operations such as creating a table or generating a form, the information in this chapter will serve as a useful review. For others, this chapter will give you a handle on the basics that are required for mastering the programming concepts covered in the rest of this book.

Names, Collections, and Containers

One of the most troublesome characteristics of databases is that they are made up of lots of parts. Unlike word processing, where you usually work on one document at a time, database operations involve several different parts working together.

One of the goals of Access is to simplify database operations by providing a single unified structure that includes all the parts of a database. Unlike almost all other database programs, Access stores all the various parts — tables, indexes, forms, reports, macros, and Access Basic program modules — in a single disk file with the extension MDB (Microsoft Data Base). As shown in Figure 1-1, when you open the MDB file, all the parts contained in the database are listed in a window called the *database window*.

The database window is a *collection* of *objects divided into six lists:* tables, queries, forms, reports, macro sheets, and Access Basic modules. The *tabs* on the left side of the window are used to select which list is displayed in the window.

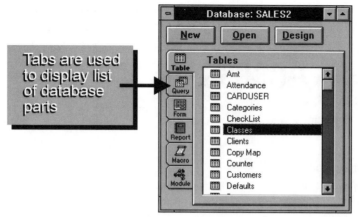

Figure 1-1: The database window lists all the different parts of your database.

Collections and objects

The lists displayed in the database window are a convenient way to look at the names of the parts in a database. They represent one aspect of a key concept in Access called a *collection*. In Access, a collection includes all the parts of a specific type. For example, the list of tables that appears in the database window represents the *table definition collection*. If you change the database window display to Forms, the list shown is the *forms collection*.

The individual parts in a collection are called *objects*. If the name *Inventory* appears in the Tables list, you can say that *Inventory* is an object in the table definition collection. A form named *Invoice* is an object in the forms collection.

Collections and objects in Access are not limited to the names in the lists in the database window. Objects such as tables, forms, and reports are composed of smaller parts. For example, a table must contain one or more fields. The fields included in a table fit the definition of a collection because they are a list of parts and they are all of the same type. In other words, inside each table object is a collection of fields. Similarly, a report contains one or more controls. This means that inside each report object is a collection of controls.

Using collections and objects, Access creates a single framework that you can use to define the relationships between any of the parts in a database system. For example, suppose you have a field called *Invoice Number* in a table called *Invoice*. Table 1-1 shows how Access views that field in terms of collections and objects. As shown on the first row of Table 1-1, *Invoice* is an object in the table definition collection of the open database. The field *Invoice Number* is an object in the fields collection of the *Invoice* table.

Table 1-1: Relationships between objects and collections

Object	*Collection*	*Part*
Invoice Number	Fields	Table Definition
Invoice	Table Definitions	Database

You might be wondering whether a table is an object or a collection. Remember that each object is included in a collection. Therefore, a table is an object that is included in a collection. The collection in turn is included in a larger object which Access calls the *container*. Containers are objects that *contain* collections of smaller objects.

Although the terms object and collection might seem similar, they express different relationships with regard to what they contain, as follows:

✔ **Object.** An object contains one or more collections. Each collection represents a *different* type of object. For example, a table definition contains a collection of indexes and a collection of fields.

✔ **Collection.** A collection consists of one or more objects of the *same* type. All of the items in the fields collection are, by definition, the same type of object — that is, fields.

The database engine
When you open an Access database file and display the database window, you tend to start thinking about lists of objects and collections. In terms of objects and collections, the top of the pyramid appears to be the database container.

This approach is fine if you are using Access manually. When writing Access programs, however, you will find that additional objects and collections exist above the level of the database:

✔ **DbEngine.** The *engine* is the top level in the hierarchy of collections and objects. The DbEngine is the part of Access that controls all basic database operations involving the storage and retrieval of data.

✔ **Workspace.** The DbEngine controls a collection of one or more workspaces. A *workspace* object contains all the open databases accessed by a user for one session. A session begins when a user logs into the Access DbEngine and ends when the user logs out.

If you are used to working with Access manually, you probably haven't needed to think about levels of objects above the current open database. Table 1-2 shows the relationships between the top level in Access, the DbEngine, and a specific database object. When you open a database, that object is part of the workspace collection, which is part of the DbEngine object.

Table 1-2: Relationships between higher-level objects and collections

Object	Collection
DbEngine	Workspaces
Workspaces	Databases
Users*	
Groups*	
Databases	Table Definitions

* These objects are used when Access security and permissions features to control multiuser access.

The DbEngine and data access

If you have worked with versions of Access earlier than 2.0, the concept of the DbEngine object will be new to you. As I mentioned, DbEngine is the part of Access that performs basic data storage and retrieval operations. That statement seems to leave open some questions: What other parts are there to Access? What do they do? Why bother to talk about the DbEngine as a separate part?

Beginning with the last question first, the DbEngine is more than just a part of Access. The DbEngine allows other programs to use Access databases directly. Visual Basic 3.0 and Excel 5.0 can use the same system of objects and collections to access data stored in MDB files. Microsoft hopes that other software manufacturers will include support for this engine in future releases of their programs. The parts of Access that are controlled by the DbEngine *are called Data Access* objects and collections.

How is Access different than Data Access? The operations controlled by Data Access are only part of what Access does. For example, forms and reports are Access objects but not DbEngine objects. In other words, forms or reports included in the same MDB file are not accessible by Excel. For that matter, they wouldn't make much sense in Excel if they were. Access objects and collections can be used only in Access. A Data Access compatible program such as Excel 5.0 can use the Data Access portion of a MDB file. The DbEngine object controls the objects and collections that can be shared with Data Access compatible programs.

One advantage of the Data Access concept is that once you learn how to write programs that store and retrieve data in any of the Data Access compatible applications, you can use the same techniques in other applications without having to learn a new system.

Naming objects

The hierarchical system used in Access makes it easy for you to identify any object. You form a complete *identifier* name by stringing together the names of the objects that contain other objects. Access uses a period or an exclamation point as a separator for each name. Figure 1-2 shows how the identifier name of a control on a form is created.

Figure 1-2:
Identifier
names
match the
system of
object
containers.

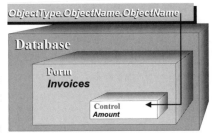

In this example, the *Amount* control on a form called *Invoices* would be addressed as **Forms![Invoices]![Amount]** or **Forms.[Invoices].[Amount]**. The word **Forms** indicates the type of object; **[Invoices]** and **[Amount]** refer to the specific form and the control.

You may wonder about the use of the period, exclamation point, and brackets. Periods are used to separate the names used in an identifier. You have the option of using an exclamation point before a name that is *user-defined*. Since the form in Figure 1-2 has a user-defined name, you can use an exclamation point or a period. The brackets are used to enclose user-defined names that may contain spaces. The grammar and syntax for identifier names are discussed in detail in Chapter 2. For now, you need to remember that identifier names in Access correspond to the hierarchical arrangement of objects in the Access system. As you will see, this can lead to identifier names that are real whoppers. The following identifier refers to a control on a subform (that is, a form contained in another form):

```
Forms![Invoices].Form![Parts Details]![Price]
```

What does it mean? Simply read the name from left to right, separating each segment of the identifier. First, **Forms![Invoices]** indicates a form named *Invoices*. *Forms* is the *collection* name and *Invoices* is the name of one member of that collection.

```
Forms![Invoices]
```   The name of a form

The **.Form** that follows the form name indicates that the identifer will include a reference to a subform contained in the named form. This means that **.Form** actually refers to a subform. I would have used something like **.Subform** in this situation to more clearly differentiate from Forms. Because **.Form** is a keyword (not user defined) it is preceded by a . (period).

```
Forms![Invoices].Form
```   *The name of a subform within a form*

Identifiers used with form or subforms can be confusing because the object names *Forms* and *Form* appear in the same name. *Forms* — with an *s* — refers to a form object. If you leave off the *s*, the *Form* object refers to a subform control. This is an unfortunate choice on the part of the designers of Access since most users miss the subtle difference between *Forms* and *Form*. Subforms are discussed in detail in Chapter 19. ■

Next, the actual name of the subform, **Parts Details**, is entered using ! to separate it form the **.Form** keyword:

```
Forms![Invoices].Form![Parts Details]
```

The final portion of the identifer is the name of the control on the subform, which in this example is called ***Price***. Once again, ! is used because ***Price*** is a user-defined name.

```
Forms![Invoices].Form![Parts Details]![Price]
```

Although it may take some time to get used to reading long identifer names, you will probably begin to appreciate the ability to express in a single name both simple and complex relationships among objects.

Fortunately, in most cases it isn't necessary to type in these full names. One of the big improvements in Access 2.0 is the inclusion of new Wizards and builders that eliminate the need to enter long names manually.

Tables and Fields

At the heart of all Access operations is information stored in a table. The table object is the only part of the Access system that actually stores data. All other objects, such as queries, forms, and reports, depend on data from *underlying tables*.

For most users, database operations begin with the creation of one or more tables. A *table* is a collection of data. But there's more to a table than just a bunch of data. The words on this page make up a set of data. What distinguishes a *table* from a page of text or numbers in a spreadsheet is its structure. The structure changes data into information. Figure 1-3 illustrates the difference between unstructured information and organized, structured information.

The structured information organized in a *table* is clearly easier to understand and read. But why?

> ✔ **Columns classify**. Each column in a table represents a distinct *classification*. In Figure 1-3, every item in the *Model* column is the name of a car model. Each item in the *Mileage* column is a numeric value for the number of miles.

> ✔ **Rows repeat patterns**.The classification pattern established by the columns repeats on each row. Each row represents information about some *thing* that exists, for example, a car, a person, a building, a financial transaction, or a date on a calendar.

These two factors make it easy to read table information because each row in the table is *predictable*. Think about how you usually read a table. First, you get a feel for the structure of the table and what each classification means by looking at the column headings and the first row. Then you usually scan a particular column to find a row of special interest. You know in advance that, all the information on that row will be related to the same person, place, or event.

This predictable structure allows computer programs to perform similar operations at much faster speeds and with greater accuracy than humans.

Unstructured Data
1993 Infinity G20, 742, 1993 Ford Explorer, 646, 1993 Ford Explorer, 101, 1989 Acura Integra, 76431, 1987 VW Jetta, 159240, 1993 Ford Explorer, 10, 1993 Ford Explorer, 373, 1993 Toyota 4Runner, 2408, 1993 Ford Explorer, 489

Figure 1-3:
Unstructured data versus structured information.

Structured Information

Year	Make	Model	Mileage
1993	Infinity	G20	742
1993	Ford	Explorer	646
1993	Ford	Explorer	101
1989	Acura	Integra	76431
1987	VW	Jetta	159240
1993	Ford	Explorer	10
1993	Ford	Explorer	373
1993	Toyota	4Runner	2408
1993	Ford	Explorer	489

Columns and rows, fields and records

All databases have a two-dimensional structure. If you think of the structure as a table, you would naturally use the terms *columns* and *rows*. However, you will find that Access, like most databases, also uses the terms *fields* and *records*. In general, *field* is synonymous with *column* and *record* is synonymous with *row*.

The terms *row* and *column* are useful when you are thinking about the physical layout of a table of information. *Field* and *record* refer to the logical relationship of data items because fields and records do not always appear in a row and column layout. For example, fields on a form all belong to one record even when the form does not have a row and column layout.

Although I'm much too young to remember, I'm told the term *field* goes back to the days when paper punch cards were used to record data that would be fed into old-fashioned mainframe computers. IBM punch cards had 80 columns. A *field* on a punch card was a set of adjacent columns. For example, columns 1 through 10 would be for the first name, and 11 through 25 for the last name. This method of allocating fields by counting columns is called *fixed length field* structure. It is used in many popular databases, including dBASE and FoxPro. Fixed length fields have some disadvantages. For example, if you have a first name longer than 10 characters, you have to drop the extra characters. If you enter a short last name, you waste the unused columns. ■

Fields refer to one classification of data that can be found in every record, such as a last name or date of birth. When you work with a field, you may be manipulating data from one or more records. For example, when you want to sort information, you select one or more fields to use as the sort keys.

A *record* contains all the information you have stored about a single person, place, or thing. For example, all the information you have stored about John Smith is contained in his record.

You will find that the terms row, column, field, and record are used in different areas throughout the Access system depending on the type of display mode you are working with. Don't get too hung up on the terms: what is important is the concept of database structure.

Creating a new table

Each Access database contains one or more tables of information. New tables are created by selecting the **New** button in the Database window when the **Table** icon is selected. This action opens the Table design window, which is shown in Figure 1-4.

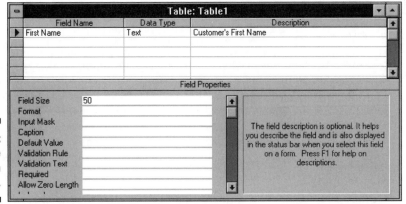

Figure 1-4:
The Table design window.

Each field you define has three parts:

- ✔ **Field Name**. This is the name by which the field is identified. Each field in the same table must have a unique name.

- ✔ **Data Type**. Access supports eight types of fields: text, memo, number, date/time, currency, counter, yes/no, and OLE object. The different field types are discussed in the next section of this chapter.

- ✔ **Description**. The description is a note you write indicating the purpose of the field. The note is optional and I usually don't bother filling it in. However, as a responsible author, I should point out that you may regret it if you don't fill in the descriptions. When you go back to this database a year from now, the meaning of the *date* field may not be as clear in your mind. Descriptions also help other people understand the structure of the table in ways that the field names alone may not do. Having said all this, I won't mention descriptions again.

There are a few issues to consider when thinking about field names. Access lets you use spaces in field names, so you can enter phrases such as, *Date of Birth* rather than an abbreviation such as *DOB*. Phrases have the advantage of more clearly identifying the meaning of the field. On the other hand, you may find it tiresome entering a phrase like *Date of Birth* in expressions or formulas. Abbreviations are much easier to enter but their meaning is less clear. People who use your applications may not immediately grasp what DOB stands for when it appears on forms or reports. The trick is to strike a balance between clarity and ease of entry.

You should also remember that spaces are tough to see when text is displayed in proportionally spaced fonts, as is the case with Windows. An extra space inserted in a field name can cause all sorts of havoc in an application. Instead of entering the field name *First 1*, for example, the user might enter *First 1* (with two spaces before the 1). One solution is to eliminate spaces by taking advantage of the fact that Access retains the case of character in field names. Instead of *Date of Birth,* you could use *DateofBirth*. This eliminates the potential problem of unwanted spaces. It also gets you used to the naming style used in Access Basic.

Access lets you define a Caption property for each field. The field's caption is automatically used instead of the field name to identify the field on forms and reports. This means you can use an abbreviation like *DOB* as the field name to make expression and formula writing simple, and use a caption like *Date of Birth* to more clearly label the field when it appears on forms and reports. (Properties are discussed in the next section.) ■

It Takes All Types of Fields

Fields can be one of eight types:

- **Text.** Text fields are used for storing text information up to 255 characters in length. The most common type of field, it is used for short text entries such as names and addresses.

- **Memo.** Memo fields are used for storing large blocks of text up to 32,000 characters (about 10 pages) in length. Use this type of field when you want to enter or import large blocks of text.

- **Number.** Number fields are used for numeric data that can be used in mathematical calculations. Access also has a Currency field type that is used for monetary values (for example, dollars-and-cents amounts).

- **Date/Time.** Values are entered into this field type in standard date and time formats, for example, 1/1/94 , 12:53:00 PM or 1/1/94 12:53:00 PM.

- **Currency.** Currency values provide accurate calculations of very large numbers. Specifically, this field type allows for the storage and precise calculation of numeric values to plus or minus 900 trillion.

- **Counter.** A counter field automatically provides a unique numeric value for each record added to a table, starting with 1 for the first record, 2 for the second record, and so on. Once a counter value is assigned to a record, it will never change or be used again in that same table. You cannot edit counter fields.

- **Yes/No.** This field type is used for recording logical yes/no or true/false values.

- **OLE Object.** This field type is related to the Windows 3.1 feature *Object Linking and Embedding* (OLE). The OLE Object field type enables you to store documents, spreadsheets, graphics, drawings, sounds, video, and other information created in Windows applications that support OLE.

You can store an entire document or spreadsheet using the OLE object type field. Remember that the source application (for example, the word processor or spreadsheet) must support OLE. ■

Field Properties

In addition to the three items (field name, type, and description) that every field can have, each field has a set of properties. A *property* is a characteristic of an object, such as its size, type, or name. Each different object in Access has its own set of properties.

Access has eleven properties (three are new in Version 2.0) that can be associated with a field. The properties available for a field depend on the field type. For example, only the Caption property is available for all fields. Also keep in mind that the choices available for properties vary with the field type. For example, both the Text and Number field types have a Format property. However, the format choices available are not the same because text and numbers logically are not treated in the same way. Table 1-3 shows which properties are available for the different field types.

Table 1-3: Properties by field type

	Text	Memo	Number	Date/ Time	Currency	Counter	Yes/ No	OLE Object
Field Size*	X		X					
Format*	X	X	X	X	X	X	X	
Input Mask**	X		X	X	X			
Decimal Places			X		X			
Caption	X	X	X	X	X	X	X	X
Default Value	X	X	X	X	X		X	
Validation Rule	X	X	X	X	X		X	
Validation Text	X	X	X	X	X		X	
Required**	X	X	X	X	X		X	X
Allow Zero Length**	X	X						
Indexed	X		X	X	X	X	X	

* Indicates that property options vary depending on the field type.
** New in version 2.0.

With the exception of Field Size and Format, the properties operate the same way for each of the field types. The different field properties are described in the following sections.

Field size

You can specify the field size for Text and Number field types.

Text field size is easy to understand. You simply enter a value that sets the maximum number of characters for the field, up to a limit of 255. The default is 50. Remember that a large field size, for example, 100, won't waste disk space if you enter fewer characters. Access, unlike dBASE , Paradox, and FoxPro, does not use fixed length fields, so only the characters entered into a field are stored on disk.

Number field size is more complicated because the choices involve math concepts related to the way decimal numbers (which are used by humans) are translated into binary numbers that the computer can manipulate. Most people are unaware that when computers or even pocket calculators perform basic arithmetic, they carry out a complicated process of converting from decimal to binary, and then back again. One result of this unseen process is that databases will allocate different amounts of memory according to the type of number you want to use. Table 1-4 summarizes the different types of field sizes that can be selected for Number fields.

Table 1-4: Number field size property settings

Property Setting	Value Range	Decimals	Precision	Memory Used
Byte	0 to 255	none	-	1 byte
Integer	-32,768 to 32,767	none	-	2 bytes
Long integer	-2,147,483,648 to 2,147,483,647	none	-	4 bytes
Single	-3.402823E38 to 3.402823E38	up to 7 places	6 digits	4 bytes
Double	-1.79769313486232E308 to 1.79769313486232E308	up to 15 places	10 digits	8 bytes

The default setting for Number fields is Double, and you can simply leave it at that in 99% of the cases. One exception will be discussed in detail when I describe linking tables. This exception involves linking a Number field to a Counter field in another table. In such cases, it is best to select Long integer as the field size, because all Counter fields are automatically assigned that field size.

Field formats

With the exception of OLE object fields, Access makes a distinction between the way data is entered and the way it is displayed. For example, if you enter the number 1100.0 in a field, you might want that number to be displayed as $1,100.00. This can be accomplished by selecting a field format that forces all entered data to be displayed in a common manner.

Formatted data is generally easier to read, especially in the case of numeric values, because items such as commas, dollar signs, and decimal places are consistent no matter how the data is entered. Formatting also eliminates the need to enter nonsignificant characters such as dollar signs or commas, which can be inserted automatically depending on the format.

Access provides a drop list of predefined formats for number, currency, and date fields. In addition, Access recognizes special codes that create user-defined formats. User-defined formats are discussed in Chapter [15].

Input mask

Input masks are used when the data entered in the field has a predefined structure. Examples are dates, social security numbers, part numbers, and phone numbers. The input mask serves two functions. First, it limits the entry to a specific length and type of character. Second, it can automatically insert fixed characters into the entry. A phone number field is a good example. The input mask consists of literal characters — the dashes and parentheses — and the # placeholders which holds a place for a number or space:

(###)-###-####

If you enter 5559991212, it will appear in the fields (555)-999-1212. There are many ways you can control data entry with input masks. The next example adds ! to change how the mask fills. It fills from the right rather than the left:

!(###)-###-####

This makes the area code optional. If you enter 9991212 the field will show ( )-999-1212.

You can also use the input mask to control whether the fixed characters in the mask are stored in the field. The ;1 added to the next input mask tells Access to store only the characters entered in the field. This means that if you enter 9991212, that is exactly what is stored in the field, even though it is displayed as ( )-999-1212:

!(###)-###-####;1

If you define both a Format and an Input mask property for a field, the format is used to display the field. The input mask is activated only when you are editing the field. The following example sets the format for the field as #, a plain numeric display, but uses !(###)-###-####;1 as the input mask. A blank record will display this field as a blank. When you place the insert point in the field, the mask ( )- - appears while you are entering the numbers. When you exit the field, the number is displayed as a plain number, for example, 9991212, until you edit the field again.

Format: #

Input Mask: !(###)-###-####;1

To help you select or create input masks, Access provides the Input Mask Builder, which is shown in Figure 1-5. You can select an input mask from a predefined list, or use the dialog boxes to create a new input mask.

If you enter *Password* as the input mask, Access displays an asterisk in the field

Figure 1-5:
The Input
Mask
Builder
dialog box.

for each character you enter. This type of mask is typically used with security passwords, since it prevents people from reading your input on the screen while you are editing. Remember that Password does not implement any type of password security. It simply suppresses the display of the characters as they are entered.

Decimal places

The Decimal places setting works with the format setting to control the number of decimal places displayed for a field. There are two points to keep in mind.

First, selecting Currency as the format does not automatically set the decimal place display to 2. To have a dollars-and-cents display, you must change decimal places from Auto to 2.

Second, like format, the decimal places setting controls how a field is displayed. It does not limit the entry itself. Suppose you set the decimal places property to 0 and enter values such as 1.25 and 2.25 in the field. The field will show 1 and 2 as the values. However, the full entries — 1.25 and 2.25 — are stored in the cell. When you edit the field, the full stored value will appear. Also, if you perform a calculation on the field, the results reflect the full entry into the field, not the displayed values (for instance, 1.25 + 2.25 = 3.5, not 1 + 2 = 3). If you want to limit the number of decimal places that can be input to a field, use an input mask (such as ###,###.##).

If you enter a user-defined format that contains a different number of decimal places than you specified in this property, Access gives priority to the decimal places property. If you set the format as #.0000 and decimals are zero, the field will show zero decimal places.

Caption

The caption property is a name, phrase, or description that is used as the default column heading or control label for the field. This property lets you use simple field names, for example, *DOB*, but have a more meaningful phrase, like *Date of Birth*, appear on datasheets and forms. Simple field names make it easier to write expressions, macros, and Access Basic programs.

Default value

Use the Default value property to enter a value that is automatically inserted in the field each time a new record is added. Default values are usually literals, such as zero for an *Amount* field or NY for a *State* field. You can use system functions such as Date( ) to insert the current date as a default.

A *literal* value is one that means exactly what it says. For example, 100 is a *numeric literal* and *"Joe Smith"* is a *text literal*. Numeric literals do not require any special formatting. Text literals are usually enclosed in quotation marks. In Access, date literal values are enclosed in the # symbol. For example #1/15/95# stands for January 15, 1995.

Remember that Access inserts the default value only once for each new record when it is first added to the table. If you delete the contents of a field, Access will leave the field empty. Access will not reinsert the default value.

Validation rule and validation text

Like input rules, validation rules are used to control the information entered in a field. The difference is that input masks control entry based on *structure* (such as the number or type of characters entered), but validation rules evaluate the *content* of the entry. For example, you might have a validation rule requiring that the entry is a # number between 0 and 100.

Validation rules are expressions used by Access to determine whether the item entered should be stored as the value of the field. The following expression limits the dates that can be entered into a field to 15 days before or after the current system date:

```
Between Date()-15 And Date()+15
```

The validation text is a message displayed in a dialog box when a user makes an invalid entry. If you do not enter validation text, Access displays the following generic message in a dialog box when invalid data is entered: *The value you entered is prohibited by the validation rule set for this field.*

Once you start to make an entry in a field with a validation rule, you may get stuck because Access won't let you move to the next field, close the table, or change to design mode while the entry is invalid. Press Esc to discard the entry and return to the last saved value, if any, for that field. This allows you to get unstuck from the validation rule. Note that if you press Esc a second time, you will also discard all changes made to the current record. ▪

You cannot use an expression as the validation text. This means that the validation text displayed for a field will always be the same, regardless of what is entered. This is often a limitation. If you use *Invalid Date Entered* as the validation text, users will know that they have entered a bad date. But the message doesn't tell them what a valid date would be. The alternative is to use an Access macro or Access Basic code to handle input validation. See Part II for details. ▪

In Version 2.0 of Access, you can set a table-level validation rule. A table-level validation rule is applied to all records that are added to the table, whether entry is made in the table's datasheet or a form, appended from another table, or imported from another database. Field validation rules apply only in the table's datasheet or in a control on a form bound to the field.

Because a table-level validation rule is not linked to any specific field, the expression you use must indicate which field is involved in the rule. For example, if you want to ensure that the *Date* field always contains the system date, you can use an expression like this:

```
[Date]=Date()
```

Required

The Required property forces the user to make an entry in a field. Access will not store a record if it contains a null value in any field for which the required property is *Yes*. A *null value* is a blank entry. In a numeric field, zero is not a null value and is considered a valid entry. In text fields, Access considers a space or a series of spaces as a null value. You must enter at least one visible character for a required entry.

Remember that Access does not enforce the required entry property until you attempt to save the record. It then displays a separate message box for each required field that has not been filled out. The message boxes are displayed in the order in which the required fields appear in the table structure. If you require an entry for the *First Name* and *Last Name* fields, Access will display a message box that tells users that *First Name* is required. Only after they have filled in that field will the message box for *Last Name* appear.

Allow zero length

The allow zero length setting allows entries of null values in text fields that can be distinguished from no entry. Suppose you have a field for a driver's license number. When that field doesn't contain any information, it can be interpreted to mean one of two things:

- **Empty.** An *empty* field means that you know that there is no driver's license number for this record.

- **Unknown or non-existent.** A *non-existent* field is one for which there may or may not be a driver's license number, so the entry has been skipped for the time being. This type of distinction can sometimes be made by entering a phrase such as *Unknown*.

In some cases, it may be useful or necessary to tell the difference between *empty* fields — there is definitely no information for this item — and *unknown* fields — there might be an entry later.

Normally, when the Allow Zero Length property is set to No, any records left blank are automatically assigned a null value. The field is treated as an *empty* field. If you want to indicate that a particular field represents an *unknown* value, you must enter *Unknown* or *None* into the field.

The problem with this approach is that users must always remember to enter the correct phrase: Unknown, None, NA, and so on. As an alternative, Access provides the Allow Zero Length property. When this properly is set to Yes, you can indicate an empty field by entering two quotation marks (" "), and indicate an unknown field by leaving it blank (that is, with a null value). You can use this approach with any text field without having to remember a special phrase for empty records.

You can later use specific criteria to select records for only empty or unknown values. The following example uses the *Is Null* operator to select unknown records:

Field: Driver's License

Criterion: Is Null

When you want to locate records that contain a specific empty value, you would use " " as the criteria:

Field: Driver's License

Criterion: " "

Indexed

When property is set to Yes, Access creates and maintains an index of the values entered into the Indexed field. An index is a sorted list of the contents of a field with a pointer value that indicates where each value is found in the table.

A table index is similar to an index in a book. The topics in a book usually aren't organized in alphabetical order, so most books include an alphabetical index at the back, listing each topic and the page on which it is found. The page number in the index is the *pointer* because it tells you the location in the book where the topic can be found. Using the index to locate a specific topic is much faster than reading through the entire book.

Access maintains two types of indexes:

- **Primary key index.** The *primary key* is a field or combination of fields that uniquely identifies each record. Every table should have a primary key defined. When you select a primary key, Access generates a *primary key index* that is used to determine the order in which records are displayed. If no primary key is defined for a table, the records appear in the order in which they were entered. The primary key index cannot contain duplicate or null values. If the field or fields you select for the primary key currently contain either duplicates or null values, you will not be able to set the primary key.

  Although Access doesn't require a primary key, it is strongly recommended. It speeds data retrieval and enables you to define default relationships between tables.

- **Field Index.** An indexed field is *not* used to determine the order of the records in the table. Field indexes come into play only when Access is required to sort or search records using the data in the specified field.

Setting primary key indexes

A table can have only a single *primary key* index. The primary key values determine the order in which records are displayed.

You can set a primarily key for a table in two ways in the table design mode by:

- ✔ **Key icon.** Select the field or fields you want to include in the primary key. Click the key icon. Access confirms that these fields are part of the primary key by displaying a key icon to the left of the field names.

- ✔ **Indexes dialog box.** The Indexes dialog box is displayed with the View Indexes command. The dialog box contains a datasheet with three columns: Index Name, Field Name, and Sort Order.

  Enter a name, a field, and an order for the first field you want in the primary index. The Index Name of the Primary index is usually *Primary*, but you may use any name you want. In this entry a primary index set the Primary property in the bottom half of the dialog box to *Yes*. Access places a key icon next to the Index Name.

  If you want to add more fields to the primary key, move to the next row in the dialog box. Do not enter an Index Name. Move to the Field Name column and select a field. Then select a sort order for the field. Access automatically places a key icon on this row. Note that no index properties are available for the additional fields.

The number of fields in the primary index affects how the Indexed property for the field is displayed. If the primary key for a table is a single field, its Indexed property is automatically set to *Yes, No Duplicates*.

On the other hand, if the primary key includes more than one field, the field's Indexed property remains *No*. Why? In a primary key, duplicate values can appear in any one of the fields in the key. However, two records cannot have the same value in all the fields in the primary key.

For example, look at the following five names:

First	Middle	Last
John	Q.	Public
John	H.	Smith
Susan	L.	Public
Alan	L.	Smith
John	M.	Smith

If the primary key index was set to any one field, such as Last, some records would be duplicates and need to be changed or removed before the primary index could be used. If the primary key included all three fields, First, Middle and Last, none of the record would be considered a duplicate.

Regardless of how you create the primary key, the properties of the primary key index can be modified in the Indexes dialog box. For example, you can us this dialog box to change a primary key from an ascending sort order (the default) to a descending sort order.

Setting field indexes

When you are working with relatively small tables (say, less than 1000 records), you can probably ignore the use of indexes. If you search or sort large tables, say 10,000 to 20,000 records, however, you'll be spending a lot of time watching the status line bar move from 0% to 100% while processing the table. If you find you are searching or sorting the same field over and over, speed up the operation by adding an index for that field. Two types of indexes are available:

- ✔ **No Duplicates**. This index operates like a primary key in that no duplicate or null values can be entered into the field.

- ✔ **Duplicates Allowed.** This option creates an index for the field but allows duplicate values, including nulls, to be stored in the field.

If the primary key for a table is a single field, its Indexed property is automatically set to *Yes, No Duplicates*. If the primary key includes more than one field, the field's Indexed property remains *No*. The properties of the primary key index are defined in the Indexes list.

When I use terms like *small table* or *large table*. I am trying to indicate a relative performance level. The speed at which a certain table is processed depends on the computer more than the number of records in the table. A *small table* is one that your computer can manipulate quickly enough that you don't notice a significant delay between the time you issue a command and the time that Access returns the answer. It's my guess that a 386-33MHz with 8MB of memory and a 19ms hard drive could handle a 1000 record table with a few dozen fields very quickly. A user with a 386-16MHz, 4MB, and a 28ms hard drive will find the same table *large* because the computer will process the data so much more slowly. In the current context, a table is large enough to require an index if it gets frustrating waiting for a query or an operation to sort or select records. With 10,000 to 20,000 records, most of today's computers will show a significant delay while the table is sorted or searched. ■

It is important to understand that there is no free lunch when you're trying to improve performance with field indexes. Access must take the time to maintain the index each time a new record is added to the table or an editing change alters the location of a record in an index. The more indexes you define for a given table, the more time it will take to add or modify records.

In general, you should maintain indexes only for fields that are frequently used for locating or sorting records. For example, if a table contains invoice information, the primary key is probably the invoice number. However, you may also need to locate invoices by customer name or date. Try adding indexes for those fields if you find those retrievals sluggish.

Multiple field indexes

An additional difference between the Indexed property and the primary key is that the primary key can include more than one field. You can create multiple field indexes by using the Indexes sheet in the table design mode. You open the Indexes sheet shown in Figure 1-6 by using the View | Indexes command or clicking the Indexes icon. The Indexes sheet lists all the indexes defined in the table, including the primary key and field indexes, if any.

When you create a field index with the Indexed property, the sort order is always ascending. You can change the order to descending by changing the setting in the Sort Order column. ■

Why create a multiple field index? The answer is the same as for a single field index :— improved performance during sorts and searches. The example in Figure 1-6 is a sort order for a table that contains vehicle information in three fields: year, make, and model. In this case, no single field contains sufficient information to identify a vehicle.

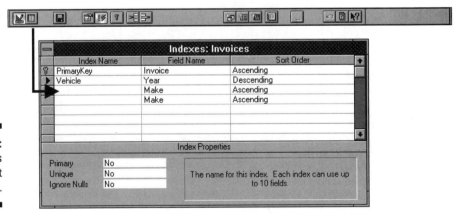

Figure 1-6:
The Indexes
sheet
window.

To create this multiple field index, a name, — *Vehicle* — is entered on the same line as the first field in the index, *Year.* Each additional field, such as *Make* and *Model,* is entered below that line. Note that the Index Name column for the additional fields is left blank. This tells Access that all the fields belong to a single index.

Remember that the sort order of each field in a multiple field index can be set independently. In Figure 1-6, the *Year* field is sorted in descending order while the other fields are sorted in ascending order. This means that the newest vehicles will be listed first while maintaining an alphabetical listing by make and model.

But when will Access use this index? Access automatically uses the index when an operation specifies the fields (and sort order) as designated in the index. Figure 1-7 shows a query that contains the three fields specified in the Vehicle index from Figure 1-6. Notice that not only are the fields the same, but the sort orders specified in the query (descending, ascending, and ascending) match the sort order of the index. When Access processes this query, it will automatically use the index to speed up retrieval of the records. If the table has a large number of records, there would be no delay while the *Running Query* bar was displayed. Records would be displayed almost immediately. If you went back to the source table and deleted the index, however, the same query would run much slower the next time it was processed.

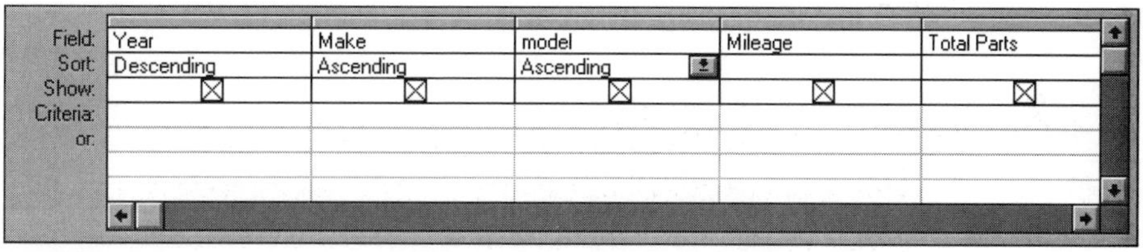

Field:	Year	Make	model	Mileage	Total Parts
Sort:	Descending	Ascending	Ascending		
Show:	☒	☒	☒	☒	☒
Criteria:					
or:					

Figure 1-7: The query will use the Vehicle index when processing.

The examples in Figure 1-6 and Figure 1-7 show that multiple field indexes are useful only when other operations, such as query processes, are specifically designed to use the index. This is not by accident. In most cases, the sequence of creation is just the reverse of the example — that is, you would create a multiple field index when a frequently used query is running too slow. Then you would use the query structure to indicate what sort of table index would speed things up.

Chapter 2
Expressing Your Ideas

• •

In This Chapter
▶ Building an expression tester
▶ Writing valid expressions
▶ Using functions and properties in expressions

• •

*T*his chapter provides an overview of the types of expressions that can be used in Access. You also see the kinds of tasks you can perform with these expressions. First, though, I need to answer one important question…

What Is an Expression?

Along with tables, fields, and records, expressions are one of the basic building blocks of Access. If you want Access to multiply the *Quantity* times the *Price* to arrive at the *Total,* you do so with an expression. If you've worked with spreadsheet applications such as Lotus 1-2-3 or Excel, you've written expressions during the creation of cell formulas.

Essentially, an *expression* is a statement the describes how one item is related to another. The simplest and most common type of expression is an *arithmetic* expression. These expressions use ordinary arithmetic operations such as addition, subtraction, multiplication, and division to define a relationship between two or more items. In spreadsheet programs, you use cell formulas to define relationships. In Access, the term *expression* is used instead of *formula.*

The following example is an arithmetic expression that calculates the value of *Total* by multiplying *Quantity* times *Price:*

```
Total = Quantity * Price
```

The exact meaning of *Quantity* and *Price* are not clear from looking at the expression. They might be the names of fields, controls on a form or report, or variables defined in an Access Basic program. Regardless of what the names stand for, the expression defines a relationship between them that Access can use to determine the value of *Total* — whatever that happens to be.

You may have noticed that the example expression does not contain any actual numbers. Instead it uses names such as *Total, Quantity,* and *Price,* which stand for some value. In Access, these names are called *identifiers* because they identify some item, such as a field or a control on a form that contains some information.

In Access you will find that expressions entered into property sheets have slightly different forms. The following expression seems to be incomplete because it lacks an identifier name in front of the equal sign. In this expression, how does Access know what *Quantity * Price* is supposed to equal?

```
= Quantity * Price
```

When an expression is entered into a property sheet its preceding relationship is determined by its context. For example, the preceding expression might appear in the Control Source property of a control on a report. To understand the relationship implied by the expression, you have to look at the Name property as well as the Control Source property:

Name: Total
Control Source: = Quantity * Price

When you put the two properties together, you get the full meaning of the expression: *Total = Quantity * Price.*

Although the most obvious examples of expressions deal with arithmetic, Access expressions also deal with text (also called *strings)* and dates. The following expression might look like normal arithmetic. However, in Access *BirthDate* and *Now* could be names that stand for dates, such as 7/15/94 or 9/13/51, rather than numbers. When Access calculates the value of the expression, *Age* will be the number of calendar days between the two dates:

```
Age = Now - BirthDate
```

In addition, Access provides many built-in *functions* that can be incorporated into expressions to perform special calculations. These functions add a wide range of capabilities to expressions. Some expressions can carry out operations that would require programming in less sophisticated programs. For example, the *DSUM()* function can calculate a total based on the contents of an entire table without requiring you to write any macros or Access Basic programs.

These built-in functions are actually mini programs written directly into Access. Many of these functions are also in other Microsoft applications that use expressions. For example, many Excel spreadsheet functions appear in Access.

In Access you can also create user-defined functions to use in place of, or in addition to, the built-in functions. (However, note that built-in functions execute faster than user-defined functions.) ■

The Elements of an Expression

Writing expressions is a creative endeavor, but there are some limitations. Expressions can include five elements:

- ✔ **Literals**. A literal is a specific value entered directly into an expression. A literal can be a numeric value, a block of text, or a date.
- ✔ **Operators.** An operator is a special symbol that indicates a relationship between any two items in an expression.
- ✔ **Constants**. A constant always has the same value no matter where in Access it is used.
- ✔ **Identifiers**. An identifier is a name that is inserted in an expression to hold the place for a value stored in some other part of Access.
- ✔ **Functions**. A function is a special name for a calculation or operation that is built into Access and can be integrated into an expression.

Literals

Literals are called literals because they mean exactly what you see. You use a special character called a delimiter before and after a literal to identify the type of data. Table 2-1 shows the types of literals that can be used in expressions and how they should be entered.

Table 2-1: How to enter literals in expressions

Type	*Delimiter*	*Example*
Number	none	123.7
Text	" or '	"Thank You!"
Date	#	#9/1/94#
Field or control	[ ]	[Date of Birth]

Operators

An operator is a special symbol that indicates a relationship between any two items in an expression. The most common ones, arithmetic operators, are shown in Table 2-2. Access also supports comparison and logical operators which are described later in this chapter in "True and False in Access."

Table 2-2: Arithmetic operators

Symbol	Operation
*	Multiplication
+	Addition
−	Subtraction
/	Division
^	Raise to a power

Another important operator is the ampersand (&) which is used to indicate concatenation. Concatenation — from the Latin word for *chain* — adds strings of characters into a single larger string. The & can be used to combine several items, such as field or control contents and literal text, to form a single phrase. Figure 2-1 shows how the & can be used to combine year, make, and model information — which is entered into separate boxes on a form — into a single phrase:

```
=[Year] & " " & [Make] & " " & [Model]
```

You may be wondering what the double quotes (" ") are for. They insert spaces between the year, make, and model. If you concatenated the data from the boxes using *=[Year] & [Make] & [Model],* you would end up with a phrase such as *1989AcuraIntegra.* Remember to add such characters as spaces, commas, and colons as part of the expression.

Wouldn't it be more convenient to enter and store the year, make, and model in a single field and eliminate the need for the complicated expression from Figure 2-1? Probably not! Entering each item in a separate field enables you to sort or select records easily by year, make, or model. For example, you may want the total number of cars by each make, ignoring the year or model. If you entered all three in a single field, you would have to do a lot of programming to get the desired result. As a general rule, it is best break up information into its *smallest logical components* in a table on a entry form.Then you can use expressions like the one in Figure 2-1 to reassemble the parts as needed. ■

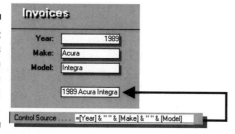

Figure 2-1:
The & is
used to
concatenate
items into a
phrase.

Constants

A *constant* always has the same value, no matter where in Access it is used. The
most commonly used constants are *Null, True,* and *False.* The following expression
assigns the logical value True to the *Is Taxable* field:

```
[Is Taxable]=True
```

A complete list of the constants supported by Access can be found in the declarations section of the Utility library's DataConstants module. ■

Identifiers

An *identifier* is a name inserted in an expression to hold the place for a value
stored in a field, a control, or a memory variable in Access Basic. An identifier is
the opposite of a literal. Identifiers enable you to create expressions that use
information stored in tables,
forms, and reports. In the following expression, the names *[Sales Tax]* and
[Sales Price] are identifiers that refer to some field or control:

```
[Sales Tax] = 1.065*[Sales Price]
```

Identifiers are usually enclosed in brackets, as shown in the example. However,
if the identifier is a single word such as *Tax* rather than a phrase such as *Sales
Tax,* you can leave out the brackets. Even though the brackets are missing in
the following expression, Access will recognize *Tax* and *Price* as identifiers:

```
[Tax] = 1.065*[ Price]
```

Functions

A *function* is a special name for a calculation or an operation that can be integrated into an expression. Access has several hundred built-in functions. Later in this book, you will learn how to expand that list by adding your own, user-defined functions to the Access system.

Sometimes Access is too helpful

When expressions are entered into property sheets, Access automatically tries to resolve what it sees as incorrect syntax in expressions. This is usually helpful, but not always. The following expression, which is meant to calculate the yearly quarter for the *Invoice Date,* contains a mistake. The letter **q** should have been entered as *"***q***"* (a text literal):

```
=DatePart(q, [Invoice Date])
```

However, Access isn't clever enough to figure this out. The syntax checking routine assumes that **q** refers to a field or a control. The routine isn't sophisticated enough to note that *q* is one of the literals supported by the DatePart() function. Access automatically encloses the item in brackets, changing the expression to read:

```
=DatePart([q], [Invoice Date])
```

The syntax is valid but it probably isn't what you had in mind. When correcting the expression, remember to delete the brackets when you add the quotation marks. Since you didn't enter the brackets in the first place, it's easy to overlook the fact that they were added to the expression and must be removed before you can get the correct syntax. In the following expression, the quotation marks have been added but the brackets aren't deleted:

```
=DatePart("[q]", [Invoice Date])
```

This won't work. The correct entry is

```
=DatePart("q", [Invoice Date])
```

All function names are followed by a pair of parentheses. The parentheses are used to enclose the *argument* or *arguments* required by the function. For example, the *Day( )* function extracts the day number from a full date. In the following expression, the argument for the *Day( )* function is the identifier *[Date of Birth]*:

```
=Day([Date of Birth])
```

In some cases, you can use the result of one function as the argument of another function. The next example uses the *Day( )* function to extract the day number from the *Date( )* function. *Date( )* returns the date from the system clock calendar. Placing a function within the parentheses of another function is called *nesting*. In the next example, *Date( )* is nested inside *Day( )*. When functions are nested, Access begins its calculations starting with the innermost function. In the following example, Access first calculates the value of the *Date( )* function and then uses that value to figure out the value of *Day( )*:

```
=Day(Date())
```

Functions may require or optionally permit more than one argument. The *DiffDate( )* function shown in the next example calculates the number of weeks between July 4th and Christmas 1994. The function requires three arguments — *"w"*, *#7/4/94#,* and *#12/25/94#* — inside the parentheses. A comma is used to separate each argument.

```
=DiffDate("w", #7/4/94#, #12/25/94#)
```

There are a few exceptions to the rule that functions always end with parentheses. For example, the *Date, Now,* and *Time* functions, which return values from the system clock calendar, can be used with or without parentheses. This means that *=Date* and *=Date( )* are both valid expressions that return the current date from the system clock calendar. A pair of parentheses with nothing between them is called a *null argument*.

To avoid confusion, it is probably best to use the null argument — *( )* — with functions like *Date*, because *Date* is often used as a field name. If you enter the expression *=Date* in the Control Source property of a control, Access will interpret it as a field identified and converted to *=[Date]*. If you use *= Date( )*, you avoid this problem. ▨

Three Rules for Writing Expressions

You can combine the five elements that are used in expressions in an almost unlimited number of ways. However, there are a few rules that limit the way you can put these items together to form valid expressions. These rules will help you avoid some of the more common mistakes that can occur when you write expressions.

Rule 1: Operators equal items minus 1

Any expression is composed of a series of *items* linked together by *operators*. Every item, except the first, must be preceded by an operator. This means that the number of operators in an expression is one less than the number of items. In the following expression, there are five items: two identifiers and three literals, including the period at the end. This means there must be four operators in the expression. It is quite common to forget an & in a long concatenation expression. Use 1 rule to check expressions for this error.

```
="Pay" & [Amount Due] & " before " & [Date] & "."
```

Rule 2: Use the correct delimiters

The expression in the next example looks like a chronological calculation that finds the number of days between today and 1/1/95:

```
=1/1/95-Date()
```

However, Access doesn't treat 1/1/95 as a date because it is not surrounded by #. Instead, Access assumes a numeric literal expression that divides 1 by 1 and then by 95. Here's the correct expression:

```
=#1/1/95# Date()
```

Rule 3: Use brackets to enclose identifiers that contain spaces

Because Access allows you to use names that contain spaces, for example, *Date of Birth* or *Parts Inventory*, you need to use brackets when such names occur in an expression.

Also keep in mind that on some screens (those running at high SVGA resolutions, such as 1024 x 768), it's hard to see when an extra space is inserted. If you look carefully at the following expression, you can see that an extra space is inserted between *Date* and *of*. This might not be so easy to spot on a 14-inch screen because the characters are so small:

```
=Month([Date of Birth])
```

One way to avoid these problems is to use the Access Basic naming style for your identifiers. Instead of *Date of Birth,* for example, you would use *DateOfBirth.*

Exploring and Testing an Expression

What happens if you enter an expression incorrectly? Depending on the exact mistake, you might see **#Name?** or **#Error** in place of the number, date, or text that you expected. In some cases, you can find the problem simply by looking at what you entered or by using the on-line help.

Other problems can't be deciphered by simply staring at the expression. A useful method of debugging an expression is to create a form and set up controls that help you test the various parts of the expression. This technique is also useful when you want to explore the results of an expression or a function to help you determine if your approach to problem solving is correct.

One simple method of exploring expressions is to create an *Expression Tester* form. An example of this type of form is shown in Figure 2-2. The form allows you to enter an expression into a text box. The *Results* box shows the value of the expression, and the *Data Type* box shows a number from 1 to 8 that represents the type of data. Table 2-3 lists these values and the corresponding data types.

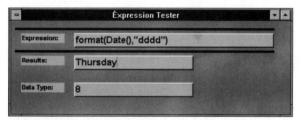

Figure 2-2: Expression Tester form.

In the example shown in Figure 2-2, the expression *format(Date(),"dddd")* is tested. The result is *Thursday*, that is, the name of the day of the week that is extracted by the *Format()* function when *dddd* is specified. The data type is 8, text.

The value of the Expression Tester is that you can quickly alter all or part of the expression and immediately see the results. For example, if you delete a *d* from the format string, the result will change to *Thu*, that is, a three-character weekday name. With a function like *Forrmat( )* that has a large variety of options, a form similar to the one in Figure 2-2 can help you explore the possibilities more quickly than you could in any other way. I find that playing around with a function in the Expression Tester form gives me a much better idea of what the thing actually does than simply reading about it.

Table 2-3: Data type values

Value	Data Type
0	Empty
1	Null
2	Integer
3	Long
4	Single
5	Double
6	Currency
7	Date
8	String (text)

You can save some typing by using the **Edit Copy** and **Edit Paste** commands to copy the expression from the Expression Tester form to a property sheet, a macro sheet, or an Access Basic module. ■

Creating the Expression Tester

You create the Expression Tester form pictured in Figure 2-2 by adding three text box controls to a blank form. Figure 2-3 shows the structure of the Expression Tester form. The properties for the controls are listed in Table 2-4. The *Expression* control is simply an *unbound* control. Unbound controls do not have a field or an expression specified for their Control Source property. When you first open the form, the other controls show **#Error** until you enter a valid expression.

Figure 2-3:
The
structure
of the
Expression
Tester form.

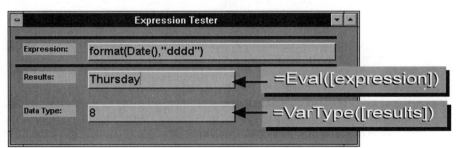

Access classifies all of the controls that appear on a form or report as either bound or unbound. A *bound control* is either linked to a field in one of the tables or it is calculated by an expression. An *unbound control* is not linked to any formula or field. Any data entered is discarded as soon as the form is closed. When you first open a form with an unbound control, it is automatically assigned a null value unless you use the Default Value property to insert some other initial value. ▪

Table 2-4: Expression Tester form controls

Property	Value
Control Name:	Expression
Control Name:	Results
Control Source:	=Eval([expression])
Control Name:	Data Type
Control Source:	=VarType([results])

The Eval ( ) Function

The text you enter into the unbound control on the Expression Tester form is treated simply as text. To make the Expression Tester work, Access must evaluate the text you enter into the unbound control as if it were an expression.

The solution is the *Eval( )* function used in the Results control. *Eval( )* is probably the most difficult Access function to understand because, unlike most functions, it is not designed to help you manipulate data or perform a calculation. Its purpose is to help you create more flexible expressions. (Some authors might be wary of tackling this topic in Chapter 2. However, this is as good a place to start as any. And it will help make you well prepared to write some elegant expressions and programs later.)

Usually, the word *elegant* conjures up pictures of candlelit dinners or opening night at the opera. To a programmer (romance aside), *elegant* refers to simple expressions or a small series of commands that do a lot of work and can be used over and over. In contrast, a *clunky* expression or block of code uses a lot of commands to do one thing and can be used only in a specific situation. ▪

Eval( ) works in a manner similar to the Find and Replace commands found in word processing programs. When Access encounters an expression that contains one or more *Eval( )* functions, it changes the way it usually calculates the expression's value. Instead of immediately trying to determine the meaning of the expression, Access pauses to *find* all of the Eval( ) functions and replace them with certain text stored elsewhere in the Access system. In other words, when Eval( ) is used, the expression that Access actually evaluates is different from the one you entered.

Figure 2-4 shows how this process takes place, step by step, in a form designed along the lines of the Expression Tester from Figure 2-3. In step 1, a control named *Results* contains the function *Eval([expression])*. The function refers to the contents, if any, of another control or field called *Expression*. Before Access tries to determine the value of *Results*, it replaces the entire function *Eval([expression])* with the text in *Expression*.

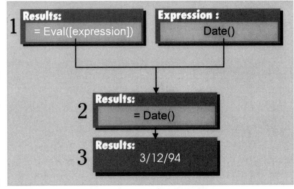

Figure 2-4:
How
Access
processes
the Eval( )
function.

When the replacement is made in step 2, you end up with *=Date( )*. The equal sign is left over from the original expression entered into *Results*. It is combined with the text *Date( )*, which comes from the *Expression* control referenced in the *Eval( )*.

In step 3, Access evaluates the expression *=Date( )* and displays the current system date on the form, that is, 3/12/94.

The power of *Eval( )* lies in the fact that Access will perform the replacement every time the original expression, *=Eval([expression])*, is calculated. This means that the contents of the expression can change each time the text in the *Expression* control changes. This is exactly what allows the Expression Tester to work.

Interesting trick — but what does it do? The answer is that *Eval( )* allows you to write an expression or program that can literally change the structure of its commands as it runs. For example, suppose that a program allows the user to select the sort order for a report from a list of fields. That's easy to do if you know in advance the names of all the fields in the table. However, *Eval( )* makes it possible to create a program that would work with any table, no matter what fields it contains. Later in this book, you will see how to build Access Basic routines to do exactly that.

Performing Basic Math with Expressions

The simplest and most easily understood expressions are arithmetic expressions that perform such basic tasks as addition, subtraction, multiplication, and division. Most of this stuff is straightforward, but two areas can cause problems if you aren't experienced with expression writing.

When you write expressions that use addition or subtraction operators with multiplication or division operators, you may encounter unexpected results because of something called the *order of operations,* or *order of precedence.* Arithmetic is not performed according to the order in which the expression is written — from left to right. Instead, Access, like most applications, scans the entire expression and calculates all the multiplication and division operators (* and /) first. The program then makes a second scan and calculates all the addition and subtraction operators (+ and -) to arrive at the final value of the expression. Table 2-5 lists the order of operations used in Access.

Table 2-5: Order of operations

Order	*Operator*	*Symbol*
First	Change order	()
Second	Raise to a power (exponentiation)	^
Third	Negation	-
Fourth	Multiplication and division	*, /
Fifth	Integer division	/
Sixth	Modulo arithmetic	Mod
Seventh	Addition and subtraction	+, -
Eighth	Text concatenation	&

When an expression or a section of an expression enclosed in parentheses contains more than one + or - operator, the operators are calculated from left to right. The same is true for * or / operators in the same expression or parentheses.

The form in Figure 2-5 illustrates the significance of the order of operations. The form is used to calculate the percentage gain or loss for an investment. The purchase price of the stock is entered in a control called *Buy*. The current market value of the stock is entered into *Current*. To calculate the percentage gain or loss, two additional controls — *Expression A* and *Expression B* — are added to the form. Each of these controls uses the same basic formula: subtract *Buy* from *Current* and divide by *Buy*. However, they produce different results. Why?

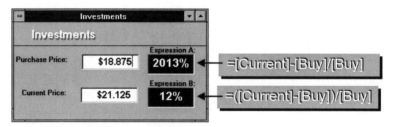

Figure 2-5: Parentheses change the order of operations.

The answer lies in the seemingly minor fact that *Expression B* includes a pair of parentheses. Without the parentheses, Access calculates *Expression A* according to the order of operations in Table 2-5. First, *Buy* is divided by *Buy*. Then the result is subtracted from *Current*, yielding the wrong value for percentage gain or loss. The parentheses in *Expression B* change the order of calculation so that Access first subtracts *Buy* from *Current*, and then divides the result by *Buy* to arrive at the desired result.

Keep in mind that not every expression requires parentheses to get the correct results. The order of operations is significant when you mix certain operators in the same expression. For example, you need to be careful when + or - operators are used in the same expression with * or /.

True and False in Access

Calculating values is only one use for expressions. Expressions can be used also to evaluate the relationship between two or more items. Such expressions use *comparison* operators and always result in a value of true or false.

Figure 2-6 illustrates the use of a comparison expression. The expression uses the less than operator, <, to determine if the mileage is below 150. Any car with less than 150 miles is considered a new car. The following expression results in either a true or false value, depending on the value stored in the *Mileage* field:

```
=[Mileage]<150
```

Figure 2-6:
A comparison expression displayed on a form.

The form in Figure 2-6 also reveals something interesting about what *true* and *false* mean in Access. The form has two controls that use the same comparison expression. However, one control shows -1 and the other shows the word *Yes*. In Access, true and false are expressed as numeric values. Any comparison expression that evaluates as false has a numeric value of zero. Any expression that evaluates as true has a nonzero value, -1 by default. This is why the first comparison expression shows -1.

Showing 0 and -1 for true and false is a bit obscure since they look like ordinary numbers. Access solves this problem with display *formatting,* which lets you show True/False, Yes/No, or On/Off rather than the numeric values. The second example shows *Yes* instead of -1 because the Yes/No format was applied to that control. The result is a display that clearly expresses whether or not the car is new.

Use of the True/False and Yes/No formats is not limited to fields and controls that express logical true and false values. You can apply these formats to any numeric field or control. The format shows false if the value is zero and true for any other value, positive or negative. For example, if you apply a Yes/No format to a numeric field such as *Mileage,* it will show No for zero mileage and Yes for any nonzero value. This fact will be useful when you use the If Then/and End If statements in Access Basic programs. ■

Table 2-6 lists the comparison operators in Access. I always have trouble remembering if the *less than or equal to* operator is <= or =<. Fortunately, Access recognizes either form . The same applies to >= and =>.

Table 2-6: Comparison operators

Operator	*Meaning*
<	Less than
<=, =<	Less than or equal to
>	Greater than
>=, =>	Greater than or equal to
=	Equal to
<>	Not equal to

Compound Expressions

A *compound* expression is two or more comparison expressions joined with a *logical* operator. Compound expressions enable you to create expressions that evaluate more than one comparison at a time. Using the example in Figure 2-6, suppose you used the following two values to determine whether a car should be classified as new:

  ✔ The mileage is less than 150.
  ✔ The year is 1994.

You can combine two or more expressions into a single compound expression using the logical operators listed in Table 2-7.

Table 2-7: Basic logical operators

Operator	Meaning
And	True only when all parts are true
Not	Reverse true and false
Or	True if any part is true

Figure 2-7 shows a modified form that uses a compound expression to determine whether the displayed vehicle is new. The mileage is below 150 but the year is 1993, so the car is judged to be not new. With the **And** operator, each individual expression must be true for the entire expression to be true. The **And** operator is called an *exclusion* operator because requiring more conditions makes it harder for a record to qualify.

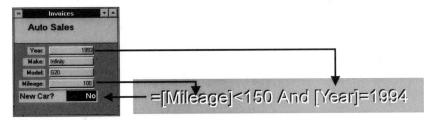

Figure 2-7: The And operator combines two comparisons into a single expression.

When you create a compound expression, make sure that each individual expression is complete. For example, suppose you want to select for mileage between 150 and 1000. The following expression is incorrect because the section following the And operator is incomplete. There is nothing to compare the *<=1000* to:

```
=[Mileage]>=150 And <=1000
```

The correct expression is shown in the following example. Even though both expressions relate to the same field or control — *Mileage* — the identifier must appear in both segments of the compound expression:

```
=[Mileage]>=150 And [Mileage]<=1000
```

The **Or** operator is called an *inclusion* operator because the compound expression is true if any of the individual expressions are true. The following expression allows a vehicle to qualify if either the mileage is low or the year is 1994:

```
=[Mileage]<150 Or [Year]=1994
```

Expressions with Properties

Most of the information in this chapter also applies to writing expressions and formulas in other applications, in particular spreadsheets and databases. The concept of *properties*, however, is a bit different.

Access is constructed out of data *objects*. Like objects in the real world, objects in Access have *qualities* or *properties,* such as length, width, color, location, and a name.

When you use an identifier in an expression, Access assumes that you are interested in the value of the object to which the name refers. The following expression refers to the value of the *Price* and *Quantity* fields, which are multiplied to get the value of the expression:

```
=[Price]*[Quantity]
```

In addition to the current value of a field or a control, Access allows you to refer to a property possessed by the object. For example, Figure 2-8 shows a text box control called *Example*. The box in the lower part of the form contains a series of controls that display information about the *Example* control: its font, size in points, height, and width.

When you want to refer to a property rather than a value, you use a period to attach the property name to the identifier:

```
Identifier.Property
```

For example, to obtain the name of the font used to display text in the *Example* control shown in Figure 2-8, you would use the expression:

```
=Example.FontName
```

How do you know that the property is called *FontName* and not just *Font*? In many cases, you can use the name that appears in the property sheet as a guide. If the name contains a space, drop the space to arrive at the property name. For example, the *Default Value* of the *Example* control would be referenced as *Example.DefaultValue.* To be absolutely sure about what the property is called, however, you might need to refer to the Access documentation or a help screen.

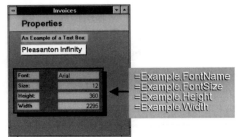

Figure 2-8:
Expressions can refer to the properties of a control on a form.

Remember that you can set the value of properties using macros or Access Basic, and they can be set manually in the design mode. This means you can modify the appearance of forms and controls automatically. For example, you can make some controls visible and others invisible depending on entries made by the user. In version 2.0 of Access, you can change some properties (that were not available in versions 1.0 and 1.1) for instance, the width of a control . ∎

What's a Twip?

In Figure 2-8, the values returned for the width and height measurements are expressed in *twips*. Simply defined, a *twip* is a unit of measurement equal to 1/1440 of an inch. But why would you want to use this unit? After all, the measurements you enter into Access are in terms of inches. Why get involved with this twip thing?

I first encountered twips a half-dozen years ago in Microsoft's Word for DOS, version 1.0. Microsoft came up with this unit of measurement to bridge the gap between typographers and computer users. This was pretty insightful, because Word 1.0 was released well before anyone used the term *desktop publishing*.

Printers, typesetters, and others who deal with printing have traditionally measured distances in units called *points* and *picas*. An inch is composed of 72 points, and a pica is ⅙ of an inch.

Today, almost every Windows user knows something about *points* because that's the measurement used to select the size of text fonts. Each line of 12-point text is 12/72, that is, 1/6 inch in height. At the same time, however, most other measurements are expressed in inches. For example, the default page size for reports is 8.5 in. by 11 in., not 612 points by 792 points.

Microsoft uses the twip unit because it can be evenly divided by common typographical units (points and picas) as well as by fractions of an inch. Table 2-8 lists some common conversions.

Table 2-8: Converting twips to other measurements

Unit	Twips
1 inch	1440
.1 inch	14
1/8th inch	180
1/6th inch	240
1/16th inch	90
1 point	20
1 pica	240

When writing expressions, remember the 1440 value. The following expression calculates the width of the *Example* control in inches:

```
=Example.Width/1440
```

By measuring in twips, Access ensures a high degree of accuracy for the alignment of items on the screen or the printed page. The standard VGA screen has a resolution of 75 dots per inch. The standard laser printer uses 300 dots per inch. Because Access can measure in increments as small as 1440 per inch, you should have no problems with the alignment of items displayed or printed from Access. ■

Chapter 3
The SQL Story

*I*n the computer business, everyone likes standards — as long as it's their standard. SQL, which stands for *Structured Query Language*, was designed to be the standard language for database operations.

SQL is designed to be both hardware and software independent. When using SQL, you don't need to know anything about the actual database software or hardware involved in an operation. All you need to know is the standard SQL method of requesting information, which ought to be the same on all SQL systems.

You use SQL operations when you work with Access but the prgram usually hides the SQL language from you. For example, all query operations are performed using SQL, but all you see is the query form grid that holds your specifications and the datasheet that is generated when the query is processed.

You can be very productive in Access without knowing anything about SQL. A basic understanding of SQL, however, will significantly enhance your use of Access.

Working with Sets

The major advantage of SQL is that, to a large degree, it frees you from writing procedural instructions when you need to retrieve data. *Procedural instructions* tell the program to take an action. For example, the following series of commands is written in a dBASE-type language:

```
Open File CUSTOMER.DBF
Set Index To LASTNAME.IDX
Set Filter To LastName="Smith"
List All AreaCode, Phone
```

The purpose of these commands is to display the area code and phone number for a customer named Smith. You might not be able to tell this by reading the commands because each instruction deals with the mechanics of the process — opening files, setting indexes, and so on. With procedural languages, if you add a command or rearrange commands, you will not get the desired result. More significantly, this specific sequence of commands works only in dBASE type program groups. Another application would require a different group of commands to produce the same result.

A SQL command, called a *statement*, is *set* oriented. Essentially, a SQL statement describes the set of data you want to retrieve. The following statement is the SQL equivalent of the previous example. The main command is *Select*, and the words in **bold** are SQL keywords called *clauses:*

```
Select AreaCode, Phone From Customer Where LastName="Smith";
```

There must be a semicolon at the end of every SQL statement. Always check to see that you have included it. ■

All SQL operations are conducted with a single statement that contains a full description of the required information. When writing a SQL statement, you are not concerned with how the data gets retrieved but only with the contents of the data set. This is the major benefit of the SQL approach. In many Access operations, you can use SQL statements in place of normal expressions to insert a data set into an object. For example, all forms and reports have a Record Source property. This property is usually the name of a table or query, but it can also be a SQL statement.

Writing SQL statements can be a tedious, error-prone process. Access solves this problem with the SQL display window, which is available when you work in the query design mode. Figure 3-1 shows a query form that performs the same task as the SQL statement in the previous example. The SQL icon on the button bar lets you change from the query form display to a window that shows the equivalent SQL statement. Selecting the design icon changes the display back to the query design form.

The SQL statement and the query form display are dynamically linked; any change you make to one automatically flows through to the other. When designing a complex query form, you may find that some changes are easier to make in the SQL display than in the query form display. For example, all of the elements in the query are listed as a single block of text, so you can edit them like any other text using **Copy Cut** and **Paste**. ■

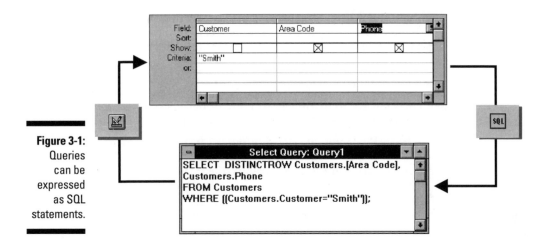

Figure 3-1:
Queries
can be
expressed
as SQL
statements.

Remember that SQL is not a product like MS-DOS or Access, but a general standard for database query expressions. Although most SQL versions share the
same basic elements, they are not identical. Access SQL uses some keywords
that you won't find in other versions of SQL. For example, Access automatically
inserts the **DISTINCTROW** keyword into SQL statements. Access SQL also
includes the keyword **TRANSFORM,** which is used to create cross-tabulation
data sets that are not part of the standard set of SQL operations.

Cheating with the SQL Window

Reading the statements in the SQL window might be interesting, but the real
value of this feature is that it enables you to use SQL without writing any SQL
statements. The window is a sort of cheat sheet that gives you ready-to-run SQL
statements. You can copy statements from the SQL window and paste them
into a property sheet, a macro argument, or Access Basic program (be sure to
check the next warning).

If you paste a SQL window statement into an Access Basic program, you will
encounter a formatting problem because the SQL window breaks up the SQL
statement into several lines. That's okay for property sheets and macro arguments, but Access Basic requires that you enter each command on a single line.
You can correct this problem by deleting the line breaks after you paste the
text into the Access Basic window. This may take a few moments, but it sure
beats trying to write these things from scratch. ■

Suppose you want to copy the SQL statement shown in Figure 3-1 into the
Record Source property of a form. Here are the steps you would follow:

1. **Highlight the SQL statement.** You can speed this process with keyboard shortcuts. Press Ctrl-Home to place the insert point at the beginning of the window, if it isn't already there. Press Ctrl-Shift-End to highlight the entire statement.

2. **Copy the statement**. The shortcut key is Ctrl-c.

3. **Find the new location**. Navigate to the property sheet, macro argument, or Access Basic module where you want to insert the SQL statement.

4. **Paste the SQL statement.** The shortcut is Ctrl-v. If you already have an entry in the property sheet, you can replace it by highlighting the existing entry (with Ctrl-Shift-End) and then pasting the new entry.

Most of the editing shortcut keys in other Microsoft Windows products, such as Word for Windows or Works for Windows, work also in Access text editing modes. ∎

The SQL statement that you paste is comprised of multiple lines of text, but only one line at a time appears in the property or argument box. If you need to display or edit the SQL statement after it has been pasted, use the Zoom window. To open the Zoom window, press Shift-F2.

Why bother with this technique? Why not just save the query and use the query name as the Record Source? In many cases, that would work just as well. The advantage of this method is that you reduce the number of queries you need to store in the database window. This makes the query list easier to read, and you don't have to make up a query name every time you want to specify a data set.

In many cases, you will also find it easier to modify a SQL statement directly rather than opening and editing a separate query form every time you adjust the contents of the data set. This is especially true in Access Basic programs.

The SQL cheat sheet works in both directions. For example, suppose you encounter a SQL statement — entered by another user — that you don't understand but need to change. You can simply reverse the query form to SQL method:

1. Copy the SQL statement into the Clipboard.

2. Create a new query.

3. Select **New Query** when the Wizard comes up.

4. Select the Close button without selecting a source for the query.

5. Open the SQL window by clicking the SQL icon.

6. Access automatically inserts SELECT DISTINCTROW in the window. Delete that text, including the semicolon.

7. Paste the SQL statement from the Clipboard.

8. Return to the design display by clicking the Design icon.

You now have a query setup that matches the SQL statement. ■

Reading and Writing SQL

Even though the SQL window eliminates the need to write full SQL statements — you can simply copy and paste — it's still useful to understand how to compose these statements. For example, you can make adjustments in the data set produced by the statement without going back to the query form. It's a handy skill and usually easy to learn.

When Access generates a SQL statement, it uses the full identifier name for any fields in the statement, using the form *TableName.FieldName*, (for example, *customers.phone*). If you are writing or editing a SQL statement, remember that you need to enter the full identifier name only when there is ambiguity about field names. This ambiguity arises only when two or more tables contain identical field names. ■

A SQL statement consists of SQL *keywords* and Access *identifiers* and *expressions*. The most important keywords in SQL follow:

- ✔ **SELECT** is the first word in all SQL statements that retrieve data from one or more tables in the database. SELECT is followed by the name of each field (including calculated fields) you want to include in the resulting data set. You can automatically include all the fields in the source table by using ***** after SELECT.

- ✔ **DISTINCT** eliminates duplicate values from a field in the set of records retrieved by the SQL statement. DISTINCT is different from DISTINCTROW. DISTINCTROW eliminates a record from the data set only if the entire record is a duplicate. DISTINCT judges duplicates based only on the fields selected by the statement.

- ✔ **FROM** indicates which table or tables contain the desired fields.

- ✔ **JOIN** specifies a link between records stored in different tables. JOIN is used with the keywords INNER, LEFT, and RIGHT to indicate the type of link established between the tables.

  ✔ **WHERE** specifies the criteria to be used to select records for inclusion in the data set. WHERE is followed by a comparison expression. The resulting data set will include only records for which the expression is true.

  ✔ **ORDER BY** specifies the sort order for the data set.

  ✔ **GROUP BY** causes SQL to return one record for each unqiue value in the specified field.

In SQL terminology, SELECT is a *command*. FROM, ORDER BY, WHERE, and GROUP BY are *clauses*. DISTINCT is called a *predicate*. JOIN is called an *operation*.

The most common reason for writing a SQL statement is to fill in a Row Source property of a list or combo box controls on a form. Row Source lists seldom involve complicated operations such as joins, so you can quickly enter a SQL statement instead of creating a query to generate the desired listing. For example, suppose you want to list the company names in the Customers table:

```
Select Company From Customers;
```

If you want to make sure that the list doesn't contain any blank names, you add a WHERE clause to the statement:

```
Select Company From Customers Where Company Is Not Null;
```

Use the DISTINCT predicate to eliminate duplicate Company names:

```
Select Distinct Company From Customers Where Company Is Not Null;
```

Note that adding the DISTINCT predicate to the statement has the additional effect of sorting the Company names in alphabetical order. This effect is a byproduct of the process used to eliminate the duplicate records.

You can use expressions in SQL statements to return lists of calculated values. The following example returns the result of a text expression that combines the Last Name and First Name fields:

```
Select [Last Name] & ", " & [First Name]
From Customers
Order by [Last Name], [First Name];
```

Adding new lines to SQL statements

The SQL statement in the preceding example was typed on several lines. Starting a new line before each SQL keyword is considered good form. It also makes it easier to read the SQL statement. You aren't required to add extra lines to a SQL statement — a single line statement is perfectly valid — but you will probably want to break up long statements into several lines.

When you enter text in a property or macro argument box, you can start a new line with Ctrl-Enter. You can also use Ctrl-Enter in the Zoom window, which is opened with Shift-F2.

Remember to end the last line of the SQL statement with a semicolon.

SQL Operators

One nice feature of SQL is the special operators used for writing comparison expressions. You can use these SQL operators in any Access expression, whether or not the expression is included in a SQL statement. Three of the most useful operators are

- Like
- In
- Between...And

The Like operator

The Like operator lets you use wildcard logic in expressions. Wildcards are used to select groups of files in DOS command file specifications and in Windows File Selector dialog boxes.

The Like operator is followed by a pattern string. The pattern can contain any sequence of characters plus the wildcards *, ?, and #. The * lets you match any group of characters. The ? matches any one character, and # matches any one digit.

The following example uses the pattern *Hamilton*. This pattern matches any item that contains *Hamilton*, for example, *Jones & Hamilton*, *Joe Hamilton's Fish Store*, or *Hamilton Air & Gas*:

```
=[Company] Like "*Hamilton*"
```

The Like operator is often used with dates. The following expression matches dates in December of 1994:

```
=[Date] Like "12/*/94"
```

The In operator

The In operator is used to determine whether an item is in a list of values. The following expression is true if the City is one of the three included within the In operator:

```
=[City] In("New York", "Philadelphia","Washington")
```

The In operator is not affected by the order of the items inside the parentheses.

The Between...And operator

The Between...And operator is useful when you want to select values that fall within a range of values. For example, the following expression is true if the Amount is between 100 and 500:

```
=[Amount] Between 100 And 500
```

Because you only enter the identifier name once, this is simpler than writing a comparable Access compound expression:

```
=[Amount]>=100 And [Amount] <=500
```

Expressions That Summarize

In Access, you can write an expression that includes a summary of data stored in a table or query. When you use an identifier in an expression, it typically refers to the *current* record, which is usually the record displayed on the form or datasheet, or printed on the report.

Expressions that summarize go beyond this limitation by accessing information stored in an entire set of records. For example, the form in Figure 3-2 displays records from a table that contains sales information: the invoice number, the date, the category for the sale, the amount of the sale, and the tax. At the bottom of the form, the total sale amount for the displayed record is calculated (using the expression *=[Sale]+[Tax]*).

What if you want to enhance this form with information from the other records in the table? For example, you might want to know how many sales have been entered into the sales log, andthe total for all the sales.

You can include this type of summary information by adding controls that use expressions containing summary functions. The following expression calculates the total value entered into Tax for all the records in the table:

```
=Sum([Tax])
```

Figure 3-2: The form displays data from a single record.

But what exactly does that expression mean when it is used on a form? Which records from what table are used to compute the sum? Access has two groups of summary functions that provide different methods of determining which record set is used to calculate a summary.

Access uses the term *aggregate* instead of *summary* when referring to functions that summarize information. *Aggregate* indicates that the function operates on the contents of a data set rather than on a single record. ■

SQL Aggregate Functions

The SQL aggregate functions listed in Table 3-1 automatically operate on the currently established set of records for a query, form, or report. Recall that every query, form, or report can be linked to a record source that is either a table or a query. The SQL aggregate functions use the records in that record source as the source of their calculations.

The name *SQL aggregate functions* is a bit misleading because you don't need to know anything about SQL to use the functions. All you need to remember is that when you use functions like *Sum( )* or *Avg( )*, the record source for the function is the record source for the query, form, or report in which the expression appears. This means that you can't use SQL aggregate functions in any part of Access that does not have a specific record source defined, such as in macro actions or in Access Basic.

There is a way to indirectly use a SQL aggregate function in Access Basic. The function must be included in a full SQL statement inside an Access Basic command that uses SQL statements. Examples of this are shown later in this book. ■

Table 3-1: SQL aggregate functions

Function Name	Operation
Avg( )	Arithmetic average of the values
Count( )	Number of records
First( )	Value of the first record in the set
Last( )	Value of the last record in the set
Min( )	Smallest value in the set
Max( )	Largest value in the set
Sum( )	Total of all records
STDev( )	Standard deviation (nonbiased)
StDevP( )	Standard deviation (biased)
Var( )	Variance (nonbiased)
VarP( )	Variance deviation (biased)

Figure 3-3 shows how SQL aggregate functions were used to create an expanded version of the Sales Log form in Figure 3-2. The expanded form includes a section that summarizes all the records. This summary information will always be the same no matter which record is displayed because its source is the entire record set linked to the current form.

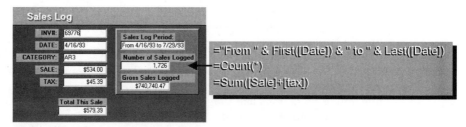

Figure 3-3: SQL aggregate functions can be used to place summary values on a form.

The expressions in Figure 3-3 provide useful examples of SQL aggregate functions. The first expression uses the *First( )* and *Last( )* functions to create a text display that shows the range of dates included in the table. The & operator connects the text items and the function values into a single phrase:

```
="From " & First([Date]) & " to " & Last([Date])
```

In this example, I chose to write an expression that combines text and function values (rather than create separate controls for each function to display a value). Access makes it easy to write these types of expressions because it automatically converts all the values to text when the & operator is used. In this example, the date values returned by the functions are combined with literal text without the need for any conversion. Other applications are not so permissive; they generate a *type mismatch* error when you try to combine dates (which are a special form of numeric value) with text.

The previous expression is based on an assumption about the table that may not be valid. It assumes that the records are entered into the table in chronological order. Sales information is usually but not always entered in the order in which the sales are made. It might be more accurate to use the *Min( )* and *Max( )* functions instead, because they locate the smallest (earliest) and largest (latest) dates, regardless of the order in which the records were entered:

```
="From " & Min([Date]) & " to " & Max([Date])
```

The second expression in Figure 3-3 uses the *Count( )* function. Instead of an identifier name as the argument, * was used. The * in SQL indicates *all fields*. When you count records, it doesn't make any difference what field you are counting, assuming that the field does not contain null values. The following expression counts all records that contain non-null values:

```
=Count([Date])
```

If you substitute * for a specific field name, you get a count of all records, including those with null values:

```
=Count(*)
```

The last expression in Figure 3-3 uses *Sum( )* to calculate the total of an expression, *[Sale]+[Tax],* rather than a single field. The value of *[Sale]+[Tax]* is calculated for each record, and then that value is added to the overall total:

```
=Sum([Sale]+[Tax])
```

Domain Aggregate Functions

Domain aggregate functions differ from SQL functions not in what they do — for example, sum or count — but with regard to which set of records they use to calculate summary values. As you saw in the previous section, SQL aggregate functions depend on the query, form, or report to define the record source for the calculation. The operation of domain functions is independent of their context. In other words, a domain function contains all the information needed to both define a record set and perform a summary calculation. These functions specify not only a calculation such as sum or average, but the record set — the *domain* — within which the summary takes place. The domain aggregate functions are listed in Table 3-2.

Table 3-2: Domain aggregate functions

Function Name	*Operation*
DAvg()	Arithmetic average of the values
DCount()	Number of records
DFirst()	Value of the first record in the set
DLast()	Value of the last record in the set
DMin()	Smallest value in the set
DMax()	Largest value in the set
DSum()	Total of all records
DSTDev()	Standard deviation (nonbiased)
DStDevP()	Standard deviation (biased)
DVar()	Variance (nonbiased)
DVarP()	Variance deviation (biased)

All of the domain aggregate functions share the same structure and syntax. In its simplest form, the domain functions use the following syntax:

```
DFunction(expression, record source)
```

The *expression* specifies the value you want to summarize. It can be as simple as the name of a field, or it can be an expression, for example, *[Sale]+[Tax]*. The expression argument in a domain function is identical to the arguments used with SQL aggregate functions. The *record source* is the name of a table or query.

Suppose you want to calculate the sum of the *Tax* field in the Sales table. You can use the *DSum()* function as follows:

```
=DSum("[Tax]","Sales")
```

Remember that this expression calculates the specified summary value regardless of where in Access it appears. Like SQL aggregate functions, domain functions can be used in queries, forms, and reports. They can be used also in macro actions, in Access Basic, or even in the property sheet of a table. Further, the value of the function is not affected by its context. This means you can calculate values from the Sales table in a control on a form linked to another table.

Domain aggregate functions also let you use an optional argument to set selection criteria that limit the records included in the summary calculation.

The following example adds a third argument that limits the records to those with a month value that matches the current month:

```
=DSum("[Tax]","Sales", "[Date] = Month(Now())" )
```

It's important to note that each argument used with a domain function should be entered as text. In other words, each items should be enclosed in quotation marks. The reason for this will be made clear shortly. This requirement can cause a problem, however, when you enter a comparison expression. For example, suppose the criteria you want to use in the domain function is:

```
Category="NOVA"
```

The expression itself contains quotation marks. If you simply inserted this into the overall domain function, you would end up with a syntax error:

```
=DSum("[Tax]","Sales", "Category="NOVA"" )
```

You can get around this problem by using single quotation marks in place of one of the sets of double quotation marks:

```
=DSum("[Tax]","Sales", "Category= 'NOVA' " )
```

The concept of domain aggregate functions is put to work on the form shown in Figure 3-4. In this example, a box on the form is used to display the following summary information: a count of records, a total for gross sales, and an average value for each sale. However, unlike the calculations performed with the SQL aggregate functions (see Figure 3-3), these summary values are based on a select group of records. Each of the domain functions uses a criteria expression that limits the records included in the summary to those that have the same category. For example, when you display a record that shows NOVA as the category, the totals in the summary box reflect only those records that match the category name NOVA.

Each time you display a record with another category, the values in the box will change to reflect the sales activity for that product. All of this happens without macros or Access Basic programming.

Using a Control Value as the Criteria

The criteria expressions in the domain functions shown in Figure 3-4 have an interesting feature that requires a change to the normal expression syntax. In each of the functions, the contents of the *Category* field are compared to the value of the *Category* control displayed on the form. If the currently displayed value in the *Category* control is NOVA, the domain functions should select only records that match that category.

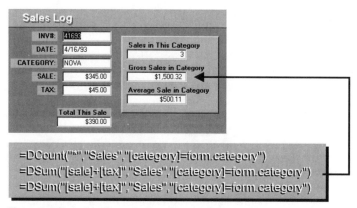

Figure 3-4: Domain aggregate functions are used to generate selective summary values.

Although this seems clear, it can be confusing because, in most regards, Access lets you treat a field and a control bound to that field as the same thing. As shown in this example, however, they are not identical (although they are closely related). When you refer to the *Category* field, you mean all of the category values in the data set. As Access processes the records, the value of the *Category* field changes for each record in the data set.

In the second instance, Category refers to the *Category* control on the form. This control has only one value at a time, and it doesn't change as Access processes the records in the data set.

On first thought, you might write a criteria expression that looks like this:

```
Category = Category
```

However, this won't work because Access has no way of knowing which Category is the field and which is the control. If a control on the current form and a field in the current data set have the same identifier name, Access assumes that any reference to the identifier refers to the field, not the control. You can refer to the control by adding the prefix *Form.* to the identifier. The correct way to write the expression is as follows:

```
Category=Form.Category
```

With this expression, Access compares the contents of each Category field to the current value of the *Category* control.

SQL and Domain Aggregate Functions

The syntax of the domain aggregate functions can be awkward. It seems more logical for the first argument to be the name of the record source. If so, the function would look like this:

```
=DSum("Sales", "[Tax]+[Sales]", "Category='NOVA' ")
```

There is a good and logical reason why this is not the case. If you read earlier in this chapter you may recognize that the domain aggregate functions are actually SQL statements using SQL aggregate functions. Look at the following SQL statement. This statement sums the *[Sale]+[Tax]* field in the Sales table for all records in which the *Category* field contains NOVA.

```
Select Sum([Sale]+[Tax])
From Sales
Where Category='NOVA'
```

Next, take a look at a domain aggregate function that performs the same calculation:

```
=DSum("[Sale]+[Tax]", "Sales", "Category='NOVA' ")
```

As shown in Figure 3-5, the arguments in the domain aggregate function are identical to the specifications in the equivalent SQL statement. Not only are they the same arguments, they are listed in the same order. This explains why the arguments in the domain functions are entered in a particularorder. Figure 3-5 shows that a domain aggregate function is simply a SQL statement entered in a different form.

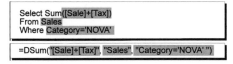

Figure 3-5: Domain aggregate functions are actually SQL statements in another form.

At first glance, Access seems to have lots of features that duplicate functions. From another point of view, however, you can see that Access follows the SQL model of database operations. The two types of summary functions — SQL and domain aggregate — are simply different forms of the same thing.

This also points out that the SQL window that is available when you are using the query form design mode also can be used to construct domain aggregate functions. Figure 3-6 shows how a summary type query can be changed to a SQL statement and then edited into a domain aggregate function.

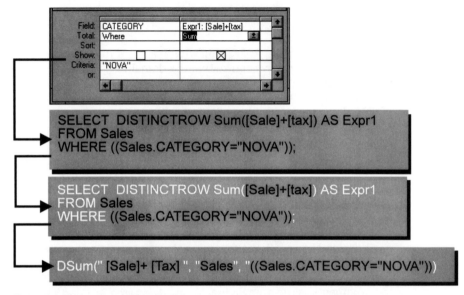

Figure 3-6: The evolution of a summary query to a domain aggregate function.

Changing the SQL statement into a domain aggregate requires only that you delete the SQL keywords and add the DSUM() function, leaving the specific expression, record source, and criteria arguments exactly as they appear in the SQL statement.

Chapter 4
Special Expressions

• •

• •

This chapter looks at some of the more unusual operations you can perform with Access expressions that contain built-in functions (supplied with Access).

Expressions That Find Data

One of the fundamental rules of application design is that the less typing required to enter data, the better the application. Throughout this book, you can see how Access features are applied to minimize the amount of data that a user has to enter. One strategy involves the use of codes or abbreviations. For example, instead of entering full city names such as San Francisco and Walnut Creek, the user enters abbreviations such as SF and WC.

The downside to this method is that you can't use the field contents to print addresses that everyone, including the post office, will understand. One solution is to create a table of the abbreviations and the corresponding full names. Figure 4-1 is an example of an abbreviation table that contains abbreviations for city names and the corresponding full name and zip code for each city.

To simplify matters, I've assumed that each city or town has only one zip code, something that isn't usually the case in metropolitan areas. I deal with this and similar situations in the next chapter, which describes the use of macros — in particular, the *Requery* action.

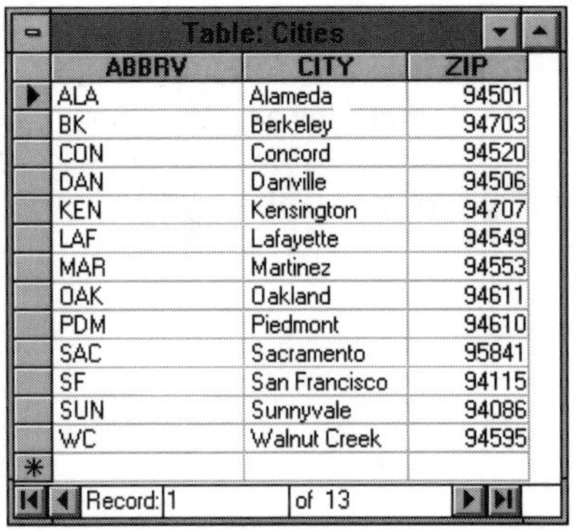

Table: Cities

ABBRV	CITY	ZIP
ALA	Alameda	94501
BK	Berkeley	94703
CON	Concord	94520
DAN	Danville	94506
KEN	Kensington	94707
LAF	Lafayette	94549
MAR	Martinez	94553
OAK	Oakland	94611
PDM	Piedmont	94610
SAC	Sacramento	95841
SF	San Francisco	94115
SUN	Sunnyvale	94086
WC	Walnut Creek	94595

Record: 1 of 13

Figure 4-1: An abbreviation table can be used to convert codes into city names.

When you want to display or print the full name, you can use *DLookup()* to locate the city name that matches the abbreviation. This function searches a specified data set for a particular value, and returns the value found in the *first* record that matches the specified criteria. The function has the following general form:

```
=DLookup(expression, record source, criteria)
```

The *DLookup()* function includes the following arguments:

- *Expression* is a field name or expression that you want to locate. In the example, the goal is to locate the full name of the city stored in the City field.
- *Record source* is the name of the table or query that will be searched.
- *Criteria* is a comparison expression that is used to pick out the record that contains the value you want to return.

For the city code example, you would create an expression like the following:

```
=DLookup( "City" , "Cities" , "Abbrv='WC' ")
```

This expression tells Access to look in the Cities table for the record containing WC in the Abbrv field and then return the contents of the corresponding city field. If you look closely at the syntax of the *DLookup()* function, you will notice that this function — like the domain aggregate functions discussed in the previous chapter — is really a SQL statement arranged in a different form. In the following SQL statement, the *First()* function limits the operation to returning a single value instead of a set of values (should the record source contain more than one record that matches the criteria):

```
Select First(City)
From Cities
Where Abbrv='WC';
```

Figure 4-2 shows how you can use this function in a form to convert an abbreviation to its full text. The top form shows what the user entered in the city field — the abbreviation WC. The bottom form includes a control with a *DLookup( )* function that uses the Cities table to convert the abbreviation to the full city name. It uses *DLookup( )* also to find the zip code of the city. (We assume that each city has only a single zip code.)

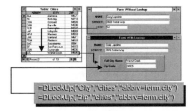

Figure 4-2: DLookUp() functions can be used to find the city name and zip code.

An interesting syntax issue is raised by the expressions in Figure 4-2. The criteria for the lookup operation is *abbrv=city*. To indicate that *city* refers to the contents of the city field displayed on the form, the *form* prefix is added to the expression:

```
=DLookup("City","cities","abbrv=form.city")
```

Why is this interesting? Because the contents of the city field don't appear on the form. The idea behind this technique is to display the full city name in place of the abbreviation that the user enters. If the city field isn't displayed on the form, how can you get away with the identifier *form.city*? This identifier works because Access reserves an identifier name for each field in the form's Record Source, even if you don't have a control bound to that field on the form. The *form* identifier prefix can be used to refer to a field that doesn't appear on the form but is included in the table or query that serves as the Record Source for the form.

Expressions That Contain Choices

You can use Access functions to create expressions that return values based on choices made by the user. Suppose you need to create a form with sales information that includes a sales tax calculation. However, the tax rate depends on the entry made in another field, such as the state or the city. For example, suppose you want to use an 8.25% tax rate if the state is CA, and a 0% rate otherwise.

To perform this calculation, the expression must evaluate a condition before it can return the correct numeric value for the tax rate. Two Access functions can evaluate a comparison expression before returning a value:

- ✔ **IIf()** allows you to enter a comparison expression followed by two alternative values.
- ✔ **Switch()** selects one value from a list of alternative values.

The IIf() funtion

With the IIF( ) function, you can have a comparison expression and two alternative values. If the comparison is true, the first value is returned. If false, the second value is returned instead. Figure 4-3 shows how this function works in the tax rate example. The first argument in the *IIf()* function is the expression *[State]="CA"*, which evaluates the contents of the *State* field. If this expression is true, the value entered as the second argument — .0825 — is returned. If the comparison is false, the third argument in the function — 0 — is returned as the value.

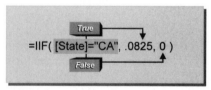

Figure 4-3: The IIf( ) function evaluates a comparison expression to determine which of the two values it returns.

The Switch () function

The *Switch( )* function lets you enter the equivalent of a table of values from which a value can be returned. For example, the following list shows tax rates that relate to various possible entries in the *State* field:

CA	.0825
NV	.04
OR	.05
Other	0

The items in the left column can be expressed as a series of comparison expressions such as *[State]=“CA”, [State]=“NV”*. To use the *Switch( )* function, you enter a series of pairs in which the first item is a comparison expression and the second is the value to return if the expression is true. The following expression shows how the table of values would look expressed as a *Switch( )* function:

```
=Switch([State]="CA",.0825,[State]="NV",.04,[State]="OR",.05,[State],0)
```

Note that it's possible to have more than one of the terms evaluate as true. In such cases, Access returns the first value in the table that evaluates as true, even though there may be other true items in the list.

The syntax of the *Switch()* function seems to imply that you can enter any type of expression in a given pair. This isn't actually the case. The comparison value is set by the initial expression. In the preceding example, the first expression — *[State]=“CA”* — establishes that all subsequent comparisons will be made to *[State]*. If you enter another type of comparison in the list — for example, *[Name]=“Walter LaFish”* — it is simply ignored.

Figure 4-4 shows a form that uses both the *IIf( )* and *Switch( )* functions to select the tax rate. On the left side of the form, the *IIf( )* function is limited to two choices for the tax rate based on whether or not the state is CA. The *Switch( )* function is more flexible because it can evaluate any number of alternative expressions and return a corresponding value. For example, the *IIf( )* function must return a tax rate of 0 for NV because that's the only alternative to the rate for CA. The *Switch( )* function can return a specific value for NV (4%).

With the *IIf( )* and *Switch( )* functions, you can define a value using a formula that contains more than one expression. When you use *IIf()*, you can store two different expressions — that is, two methods of calculating the value — in a single formula. Access selects the correct method based on the results of the comparison expression that you have included in the function. In other words, these functions give you a simple but useful level of decision-making capability for how various values are calculated in your queries, forms, and reports. This flexibility creates queries, forms, and reports that automatically adjust to differences in the source data.

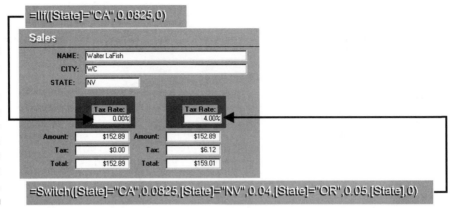

Figure 4-4:
IIf() and
Switch()
functions
are used to
select the
tax rate
based on
state.

Although *Switch( )* is potentially a very useful function, entering a long list of expression-value pairs can be tedious. If you have more than three or four alternatives, consider entering the items into a separate table in the database. Then you can use the *DLookup( )* function, which is discussed in the previous section, to obtain a value. The *DLookup( )* approach has the advantage of allowing you to easily add, delete, or modify items in the table without rewriting the expression.

Nesting IIf( ) functions

Ostensibly, *IIf( )* is limited to a simple choice between true and false. With nesting, however, you can use *IIf( )* to build more sophisticated logical structures. *Nesting* refers to entering one function as the argument for another function. For example, suppose that on July 1, 1994 the sales tax rate in California was increased (heaven forbid) to 8.5%. You need two levels of decision-making to handle this change:

Is the state CA? If not, the 0% tax rate is used. If the state is CA, you need to analyze the date of the transaction.

If the state is CA, is the date before 7/1/94? If so, apply the 8.25% tax. If not, apply the 8.5% tax.

Figure 4-5 illustrates the logical relationships involved in making the calculation.

We can convert he diagram in Figure 4-5 into the following expression. Notice that an entire *IIf( )* function is used as an argument in another *IIf( )* function:

```
=IIf([State]="CA", IIf([Date]<#7/1/94#, .0825,8.5), 0)
```

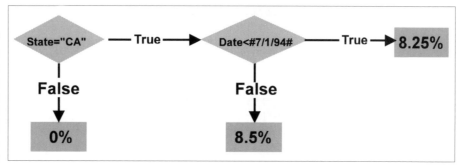

Figure 4-5:
This
flowchart
traces the
logic of
nested IIf()
functions.

It's important to understand the difference between nesting *IIf( )* functions and using a *Switch( )* function. When you use *Switch( )*, all of the expressions must be compared to the same value, which is specified in the first comparison expression. To make choices that involve different fields you can use nested *IIf( )* functions. In this example, the first choice involved *State*, and the second choice involved *Date*.

The *IIf( )* and *Switch( )* functions are expression-level equivalents of the If.../ Then.../Else and Switch.../Case structures available in Access Basic. ■

Generating Random Numbers

You will often find that you don't have any ready-made tables of data to use when you are developing an application. This can be a problem because it's often hard to see the consequences of an expression, a macro, or an Access Basic program if you don't have a modest amount of random data available.

You can solve this problem by using macros or Access Basic to generate records based on the use of the *Rnd()* function. This function generates a random number between 0 and 1 each time it is evaluated.

The *Rnd( )* function actually generates a *pseudo-random* number. The term *pseudo-random* is used because computers generate numbers in a strictly defined, mechanical way. Such a process cannot be truly random, as defined by the science of statistics. For practical purposes, however, this function generates data that is random enough to test an application. ■

The most common use of the *Rnd ( )* function is to generate an integer value within a specified range of numbers. For example, suppose you want to generate a series of whole numbers from 1 to 10. The general form of this expression is

```
Int((high - low + 1) * Rnd() + low)
```

In this expression, *low* stands for the beginning of the desired range and *high* is the upper end. The *Int( )* function produces an integer by truncating any digits to the right of the decimal point. For example, the expression *Int(9.75)* evaluates as 9. *Int( )* does not round decimals but merely drops them from the value .

If you are entering the high and low values directly into the expression, you can abbreviate the formula by calculating *high - low* + 1 yourself. For example, 10 - 1 +1 is 10. Therefore, to generate random numbers between 1 and 10, you would write this expression:

```
=Int(10*Rnd()+1)
```

To generate a lowercase letter in the range of *a* to *z*, you can combine *Rnd( )* with the *Chr( )* function. *Chr( )* returns characters based on their ASCII character value. In ASCII, the letters *a* to *z* are in the range of numbers 97 through 122. The expression that represents this is

```
=Chr(Int(122*Rnd()+97))
```

ASCII stands for the American Standard Code for Information Interchange. Although this data coding system is widely used in computers, it was designed for teletype machines. A number value was assigned for each character that could be sent or received by a teletype. The first 31 numbers in the code were special instructions for the teletype. Code 7, called bell, was used to ring a bell on the teletype. This bell alerted sleepy newspersons that an important story was coming over the teletype. The more important the story, the more bells, or code 7s, were sent. ASCII table names such as line feed, carriage return, and form feed also are carryovers from the days when information was sent via teletype.

Designers linked teletype machines with computers so that data could be sent and received without stacks of punch cards or paper tape. You can still see computers interfaced with teletypes in sci-fi movies from the 1960s and in the old "Outer Limits" shows. ■

You can use the *Rnd( )* function to locate random records in a table and return values from a field. For example, suppose as part of your testing of an application, you want a control on a form to randomly display a name from a list of 25 stored names . Figure 4-6 shows a table called People with two fields: *ID*, which is a counter field, and *First Name*.

The form control in Figure 4-6 uses a *DLookup( )* function to select one of the names in People at random and display that name in the form:

```
=DLookup("[First Name]","people","ID=Int(25*Rnd()+1)")
```

This expression uses the random number formula to generate a value to match the *ID* field.

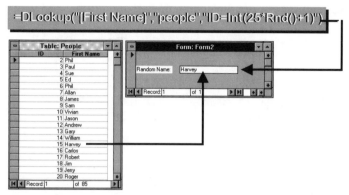

Figure 4-6: The Rnd() function can be combined with DLookup() to perform a random lookup of a name.

You might think that using a random-based expression in an update query is a quick way to fill in a field throughout an entire table of values. However, this won't work because Access will use the same random number for all of the records. To generate a full series of random numbers, you need to use Access Basic. ■

The Expression Builder

Nobody really likes writing expressions — including users of Access Versions 1.0 and 1.1. In response to their requests, Access 2.0 includes a special wizard called the *Expression Builder,* which is shown in Figure 4-7. Instead of writing expressions from scratch, you can use the buttons and panels in this dialog box to select various items that you want to include in an expression. Each selection inserts text into the expression window. You can manually edit the text in the expression window. When you have the desired expression, use the OK button to copy it into the property you are editing.

The Expression Builder is available from all property sheet items that can accept expressions, such as the Control Source property for a form or report control. As shown in Figure 4-8, you access the Expression Builder by clicking the button with the ellipsis icon. The drop-list button displays the list of available fields (assuming a control source has been specified for the form or report).

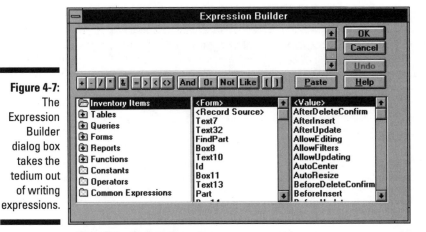

Figure 4-7:
The
Expression
Builder
dialog box
takes the
tedium out
of writing
expressions.

Figure 4-8: Buttons used to invoke the Expression Builder amd Field List.

The Expression Builder tries to assist your expression writing in several ways. For example, it automatically inserts an operator placeholder — *<<Ope>>* — between each literal, function, or identifier that you paste into the window. This will help you remember to follow the rule about entering operators between each item in an expression.

Such expression writing help can often be as awkward and cumbersome as it is useful. The real value in the Expression Builder is its list of identifiers. The *number one problem* for anyone writing simple expressions or full programs is remembering the names used for fields and controls in various tables, queries, and forms. The Expression Builder dialog box displays the names of all objects in the database, including tables, forms, reports, macros, and Access Basic modules. In addtion, when you select an object, the center panel of the Expression Builder dialog box lists each field or control contained in the object. The third panel lists the properties available for any field or control you select.

The Expression Builder can be worth its weight in gold when it is used to remedy the bane of many users: the plural *s*. For example, suppose you are creating a sales table. If the table contains invoice information, the natural tendency is to call the table *Invoices*. When you define the fields, you will probably use the name *Invoice* for the field that contains the invoice number. Later, however, you will be surprised at how many times you have to remember that the table name ends with an *s* but the field name does not. Display the Expression Builder, and you can quickly locate the table or query and get a full list of field names. Even if you don't write the expression in the Expression Builder dialog box, you can at least determine the correct name. This will eliminate many errors.

The Expression Builder also lists the names of macros stored in a group macro (*a group macro* is a single macro that has a number of named macros within it) and all of the Access Basic functions defined in a module.

Part II
Macros and Access Basic

The 5th Wave — By Rich Tennant

DOS OPERATING MANUALS PUBL.

"WAIT A MINUTE! THE MONSTER SEEMS CONFUSED, DISORIENTED. I THINK HE'S GONNA PASS OUT! GET THE NETS READY!!"

In This Part...

Access offers two ways to write programs: with macros and with Access Basic. My preference is to use Access Basic, but lots of people are content using macros. Some operations require that you use macros, so even the most advanced Access Basic programmer needs to use macros sometimes.

The following chapters introduce you to macros and Access Basic, show you how to write macros and Access Basic programs, and describe the good and bad points of each.

Chapter 5

How Macros Work

● ●

In This Chapter

▶ Defining the meaning of macros

▶ Setting values with macro actions

▶ Triggering macros with event properties

▶ Selecting arguments for macro actions

▶ Linking macros to events

● ●

*T*his chapter gives you a look at what the term *macro* means in Access, and shows you how to create Access macros.

A Term with Many Meanings

The term *macro* has been very badly treated — and mangled a bit — in the decade since Lotus 1-2-3 first appeared. Before discussing the main subject of this chapter, Access macros, it might be useful to clarify exactly what macros are.

Although the term *macro* has been around computing for a long time, many users encountered it for the first time with the advent of 1-2-3 for the IBM PC in 1983. 1-2-3 has a feature that allows you to enter the keystrokes used for a command or series of commands as text. You can then invoke that text as a command; that is, the program reads the text characters as if you entered them from the keyboard.

For instance, to save a spreadsheet, you have to type **/fs.** (The / means the display menu, f is for File, and s is for Save.) If you entered the text "/fs" into a cell, you could get 1-2-3 to read that text as a series of keyboard commands. Lotus called this feature a macro since it fit the macro concept, albeit in a broad way. A more accurate term for the feature would have been *keystroke macros* because the macros didn't actually invoke commands but fooled the program into thinking that someone was entering instructions from the keyboard.

Keystroke macros became one of the most popular features of Lotus 1-2-3 and helped drive it and the IBM PC to a dominant position in the microcomputer market. It is probably not too much of an exaggeration to say that 1-2-3 legitimized the personal computer as a business tool. Many people used macros to create what they called programs. Most programmers looked down their noses at these spreadsheets with keystroke macros, but these keystroke macro users were actually designing their own automated applications.

There are some problems with keystroke macros. In general, keystroke macros are

✔ **Hard to understand**. Most keystroke macros are indecipherable. To understand the contents and purpose of a keystroke macro, you must match each character with a menu option. Correcting an error in this type of macro can be maddening.

✔ **Sensitive to initial conditions.** Keystroke macros usually follow the menu structure of the application, so a macro usually works only if it is initiated at just the right point. If you start it at some other point (for example, when the menu is already open to a different command), the keystrokes won't produce the desired result.

✔ **Hard to structure.** Macros work best for linear tasks in which the macro is replayed straight through each time it is used. Creating macros that have optional segments, branches, or repeating loops is much more complex and inherently problematic.

Macro Actions

Access macros are not keystroke macros. Instead, Access macros consist of one or more actions. An *action* is a specific operation that can be performed on one or more objects in the database. Access macros overcome all the limitations of keystroke macros. In sophistication and structure, they come close to matching the capabilities of a programming language such as Access Basic. Unlike keystroke macros, Access macros are

✔ **Easy to understand**. Access macro actions have names that clearly indicate their function, such as SetValue or OpenForm. Any options, parameters, or arguments needed for the action are entered into a property sheet. In addition, each macro action has a description line that you can use to explain the purpose of the action.

✔ **Object oriented**. Because macro actions are directed at Access database objects, they aren't sensitive to initial conditions. Macros are not dependent on menu sequences. Instead, they are applied directly to the intended object.

✔ **Structured in their execution.** Each macro can have a unique name and a condition, in the form of an expression, that controls its execution. This structure enables you to build macro systems containing branch and loop structures like those found in languages such as Access Basic.

Events That Trigger Macros

Perhaps the biggest difference between keystroke macros and Access macros is the way that a macro is invoked. In programs such as 1-2-3 and WordPerfect, macros are executed when the user explicitly enters a command or a special key that starts the macro. For example, you might invoke a WordPerfect macro by entering Alt-x.

Although it is possible to execute a macro manually, the real power of Access macros is that they can be invoked automatically by a user's normal interaction with the Access interface. For example, Access macros can be invoked by such actions as opening a form, entering data into a control, or changing the displayed record.

An *event* in Access can be defined as the point in time when an action is performed on an object. For example, when you select the Open button in the Form list, you are performing the open action on a form object. Access records this as the OnOpen event for the form. Access keeps track of eight categories of events, as listed in Table 5-1.

Table 5-1: The categories of Access events

Event	*Description*
Window	Occurs when you manipulate objects on a form or report (e.g., open or close)
Data	Occurs when a field, control, or record is changed
Focus	Occurs when an object loses or gains focus
Keyboard	Occurs when you press any key on the keyboard
Mouse	Occurs when you click, double click, or move the mouse
Print	Formatting for print and printing information
Error	Occurs when Access produces an error
Timer	Occurs when a specific amount of time passes

Each object in Access maintains a list of events that can be associated with the execution of a macro or an Access Basic function. This chapter is concerned primarily with *data events*, which are triggered when a user enters or edits data on a form. These are not the only events that occur on forms but they are the most logical starting point for macro actions because they are triggered by the actions users normally take when entering data into a form.

Data events can be divided into two groups: events that are triggered by individual controls and events that are triggered by entire records. The event names are listed in Table 5-2.

Table 5-2: Data events may be triggered by entire records or by individual controls

Event	Record	Control or Field
OnCurrent	Yes	No
BeforeInsert	Yes	No
AfterInsert	Yes	No
OnDelete	Yes	No
BeforeDelConfirm	Yes	No
AfterDelConfirm	Yes	No
BeforeUpdate	Yes	Yes
AfterUpdate	Yes	Yes
NotInList	No	Yes
Update	No	Yes
OnChange	No	Yes
OnEnter	No	Yes
OnExit	No	Yes
OnClick	No	Yes
OnDblClick	No	Yes

One way to think about macros and events is that macros specify *how* the form should be modified and events determine *when* that change should take place.

Event properties

The list of events in Table 5-2 shows that not all events are related to all objects. This makes sense because not every object is manipulated in the same way. For example, forms can be opened and closed, but individual controls on a form cannot. Access lists all of the possible events that can be triggered by an object on the *event properties* panel of the object's property sheet. Figure 5-1 shows the event properties panel for a form. The data events (OnCurrent, BeforeInsert, and so on) appear at the top of the list, followed by the form events (OnOpen, OnLoad). In addition, this properties list includes mouse, keyboard, focus, and timer events.

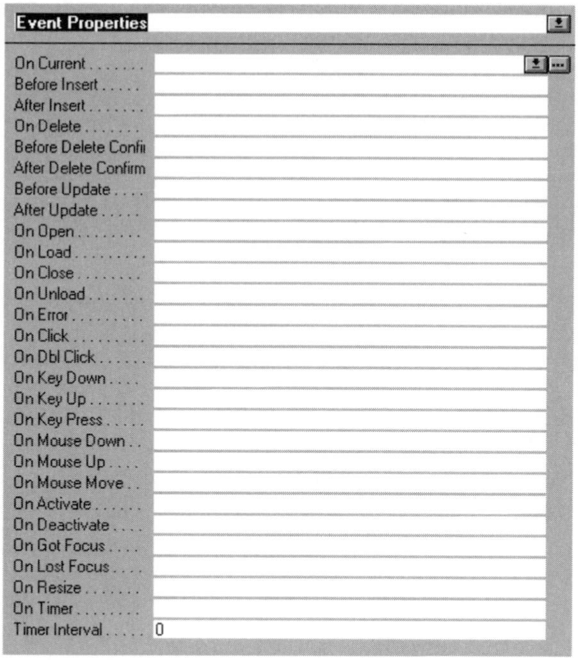

Event Properties	⊕
On Current	⊕ ...
Before Insert	
After Insert	
On Delete	
Before Delete Confir	
After Delete Confirm	
Before Update	
After Update	
On Open	
On Load	
On Close	
On Unload	
On Error	
On Click	
On Dbl Click	
On Key Down	
On Key Up	
On Key Press	
On Mouse Down . .	
On Mouse Up	
On Mouse Move . .	
On Activate	
On Deactivate	
On Got Focus	
On Lost Focus	
On Resize	
On Timer	
Timer Interval	0

Figure 5-1:
The event
properties
sheet for a
form.

Event sequences

To use macros effectively, you need to understand which user actions trigger particular events. Operations that you might think of as a single action may trigger several events. To get a feel for how this works, it's helpful to look at some common operations and the sequence of events that they trigger. One common example is opening a form by selecting the Open button in the Forms panel of the database window. This action generates three events in the following order:

1. **OnOpen.** This event occurs *after* the command to open a form is given but *before* the form appears on the screen.

2. **OnCurrent.** This event occurs each time a new record is selected for display. Because the form must display a record when it is opened, this event automatically follows OnOpen.

3. **OnEnter.** When you open a form, Access automatically moves the focus to the first control on the form. This means that the OnCurrent event is automatically followed by an OnEnter event for that control.

Then suppose you decide to display the next record. This action generates a more complex series of events:

1. **BeforeUpdate**. This event occurs before any changes to the current record are saved.

2. **AfterUpdate**. This event occurs after the changes to the current record are saved, but before any changes are made in the focus. This means that the focus is still on the current control and the current record.

3. **OnExit**. This event is triggered each time the focus moves from one control to another. Even though the insert point may be positioned in the same control in the next record, Access treats the operation as though you are changing the focus to another control.

4. **OnCurrent**. This event is triggered when Access loads the table's next record into the form.

5. **OnEnter.** This event is triggered by moving the focus to the first control in the new record.

Note that the first two events — BeforeUpdate and AfterUpdate — occur only if some change has been made to the current record. If not, the sequence begins with the third event, OnExit.

Any properties that limit entry into a field or control — the Input Mask and Validation Rule properties, for example — will activate before the event properties, such as AfterUpdate. Consider what would happen if a control had both a Validation Rule and an AfterUpdate event. Access would perform the Validation Rule routine before triggering the AfterUpdate event. In other words, the macro associated with AfterUpdate is not executed until the Validation Rule is satisfied. ■

Why are so many events generated by such simple actions as moving from one record to another? Remember that Access automatically performs certain tasks in response to each user interaction. If you are using macros (or Access Basic) to customize the behavior of a form or report, it's useful to be able to perform various actions either before or after Access performs its automatic functions.

When you move from one record to another, Access automatically saves any changes made to the current record and then fills the form's controls with the information stored in the next record in the record source table. However, these changes don't happen all at once. Thanks to events, you can insert your macro action at a specific point in what would otherwise be an automatic operation. For example, in the sequence of five events that take place when you change records in a form, when is the information stored in the next available record? Not until the fourth action, OnCurrent. The three previous events all take place while the previous record is displayed.

When selecting an event that will trigger a macro, you need to carefully consider the status of the form or report at the exact moment when the macro action is to be performed. Suppose you want to automatically insert the system time and date into each record that is changed. This will give you an accurate record of when each record is entered or updated. Which event should you choose as the trigger?

First, the event must come before the OnCurrent event because the change needs to be made before the data in the controls is changed. The most logical point in the sequence is the BeforeUpdate event. This allows the macro to update the record's information, which is then automatically saved as part of the normal procedure executed by Access when displaying a new record.

There are pitfalls, however. For example, suppose you decide to trigger the macro with the AfterUpdate event. This simple change will result in a form that cannot be edited. Why? Because the macro action triggered by the AfterUpdate event would have a head-on collision with Access trying to save the updated record. The diagram in Figure 5-2 illustrates what would happen. Access begins by saving the modified record. This triggers the AfterUpdate event, which executes a macro that changes the contents of the record. Because the record is now changed, it must be saved again before the next record can be displayed. Access backtracks and saves the record again. But this generates another AfterUpdate event.

The cycle repeats endlessly with no resolution because each time Access saves the record, the macro negates that action by changing the record's contents. This type of circular, repeating structure is called an *endless loop*. The only way to break out of this loop is to use the Esc key to discard any changes and thereby avoid triggering the AfterUpdate event.

Most macros won't create an endless loop, but this example emphasizes the need to understand the relationship between a macro action and the status of the form or report when that macro is triggered by an event. The next section explains in detail how, when, and why macros are used to update values on forms.

Figure 5-2: Macro actions might conflict with automatic operations.

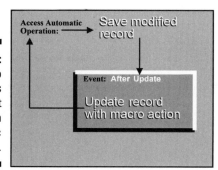

Macro Basics

The single most useful macro action is SetValue. As its name implies, this action lets you set the value of Access database objects, such as fields and controls. It also enables you to set the properties of those objects, which can help you add some surprising features to a form.

Setting values for controls

To display a calculated value on a form, it's common to use an expression as the Control Source property of the control that is the result of the calculation. However, this method has one shortcoming: The controls for which expressions are used are not bound to any of the fields in the underlying table.

For example, look at the form in Figure 5-3. The form uses expressions to calculate the amount of tax and the total value of the invoice. Although these values appear correctly on the form, they are not bound to the *Total Tax* and *Total* fields in the table that is the record source for the form. The data sheet at the bottom of the figure shows that *Total Tax* and *Total* remain empty in the table even though the form displays values for this data. In a sense, the values displayed by the expressions on the form are *temporary* values that disappear when the form is closed.

Whether or not this is a problem depends on how you use the data in the table that is related to the form. For example, suppose you want to create a report based on the invoice information. You will need to manually add calculated controls to the report for the *Total Tax* and *Total* values because those fields are still blank.

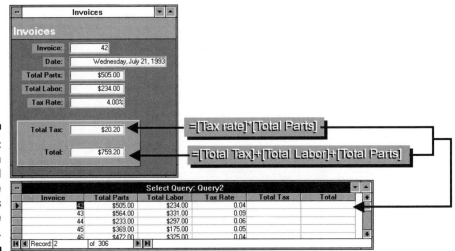

Figure 5-3:
This form
uses Control
Source
expressions
to calculate
values.

In many cases, you can simplify subsequent operations, such as reports, by actually writing the calculated values into fields instead of simply displaying them. When you create a report, you can simply place the field on the report instead of reentering the calculation expression. This is especially important when you want to speed up operations by using the Report Wizard, because the Report Wizard automatically adds fields but not expression columns to a report.

Instead of using a Control Source expression to display a value on a form, you can use a SetValue macro action, which writes the calculated value into a control that is bound to a field in the underlying table.

As shown in the Figure 5-4, the SetValue action requires two arguments:

- ✓ **Item**. This is the identifier name of the object whose value you want to set. Typically, the identifier is a control on a form or report. It can also be an object property.

- ✓ **Expression.** This can be equal any valid Access expression. Because Access assumes that the entry is an expression, you don't need to precede the expression with an = sign. You can display the Expression Builder dialog by clicking the button with the ellipsis (...) icon.

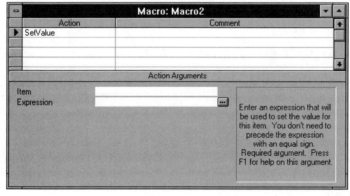

Figure 5-4: A SetValue macro action is used to set the value for a database object.

To set the value of the *Total Tax* control on the form in Figure 5-3, you would use this macro action:

Action	Properties	
SetValue	Item:	[Total Tax]
	Expression:	[Total Parts]*[Tax Rate]

When you define a Control Source property with an expression, you don't need to be concerned with the question of timing. However, when you use a macro to set a value, you need to consider which event or events should trigger the macro. In this example, three events would affect the values of the two calculated fields, *Total Tax* and *Total*:

- ✔ *Total Parts* update. This requires recalculation of both *Total Tax* and *Total* because parts are taxable items.

- ✔ *Total Labor* update. Labor is not taxed, so only the *Total* field requires an update.

- ✔ *Tax Rate* update. A change here requires an update of both *Total Tax* and *Total*.

Thus, a macro to update the *Total Tax* and *Total* fields should be triggered by an AfterUpdate event associated with either *Total Parts*, *Total Labor,* or *Tax Rate*.

In theory, you could create a different macro for the AfterUpdate event for *Total Labor* because a change in *Total Labor* affects *Total* but not *Total Tax*. In practice, it's easier to create a single macro for all three events. Calculating *Total Tax* one more time won't cause problems, so you don't need to create a separate macro just to avoid an unnecessary calculation.

Linking an event to a macro

Now that the solution has been laid out, let's take a closer look at the process of linking a macro to a form event. You start this process in the form's design mode. First you select the control that will trigger the macro. In the example, it is *Total Parts*.

Next you need to display the event properties panel. The property you want to use as the macro trigger is AfterUpdate. When you place the insert point in the AfterUpdate blank, Access displays both a drop-list icon and an ellipsis (...) icon. The drop-list allows you to choose an existing macro. Selecting the ellipsis icon displays the Choose Builder dialog box. The dialog box allows you to invoke the expression, macro, and code (Access Basic) builders. In this case, you would select the Macro Builder.

Access then displays the Save As dialog box so that you can enter a name for the new macro. The name used in this example is Calc Total Tax.

The Macro Builder isn't actually a special dialog box like the Expression Builder. When you select the Macro Builder, Access simply opens a blank macro definition sheet. Table 5-3 shows the toolbar icons that you can use in the macro design mode.

Table 5-3: Macro design toolbar icons

Icon	Name	Function
	Save Macro	Saves the macro (required before running the macro)
	Macro Names	Toggles the display of the Names column on the macro sheet
	Conditions	Toggles the display of the Conditions column on the macro sheet
	Run	Executes the macro
	Step Into	Toggles step-by-step macro execution
	Database Window	Returns to the database window
	Expression Builder	Activates the Expression Builder

The SetValue action

In our example, we need to create a macro consisting of two SetValue actions. The first action sets the value of the *Total Tax* field and the second sets the value of *Total.* In this case, the order in which the macro actions are executed is significant because the value of *Total Tax* is needed to calculate *Total.*

There are three ways to enter the command name into the Action cell:

✔ **Use the drop-list.** You can click on the drop-list icon and select the command from the list.

✔ **Type the command.** If you know the command, you can simply type it in. The case of the characters is not significant.

✔ **Drop and type.** You can combine typing with the drop-list in two ways. You could begin by typing one or more characters of the command and then opening the drop-list. Access will automatically scroll to the first command, if any, that matches the characters you have typed.

If you type *set* and then open the drop-list, Access will highlight SetValue because that is the first item that begins with set. Conversely, you could open the drop-list and type characters to perform a speed search of the list. If you open the list and type *s,* the highlight jumps to the first item that begins with the letter *s,* SendObject. If you type additional characters, the search will narrow.

Once you have selected the action, the Action Arguments panel lists the items that must be filled in for this action.

Pressing F6 switches the focus between the Action list and the Action Arguments panel. To jump directly to the Action Arguments panel from the drop-list, press F6 instead of Enter or Tab. ■

Selecting action arguments

Where possible, Access speeds up macro writing and helps you eliminate errors by providing either a drop-list of identifiers or the ellipsis (...) icon, which opens the Expression Builder dialog box.

With the SetValue action, you can use the Expression builder to specify the argument for either the Item or the Expression. With the Item argument, the Expression Builder is used to select the identifier name of the object whose value will be set.

Figure 5-5 shows how the Expression Builder is used to select an identifier name. This feature is particularly useful because it is difficult to remember the exact name of each identifier in the form window when you are working in the macro window.

As shown in Figure 5-5, the Expression Builder displays the following information:

   ✔ The left-most panel lists all the objects that can serve as the source of the identifier. This panel uses a tree structure to organize objects by type, such as tables, queries, and forms. To select the current form as the identifier source, you double click *Forms*, then *Loaded Forms*, and then the name of the current form, *Example 2*. Forms that are currently open are considered *loaded* forms.

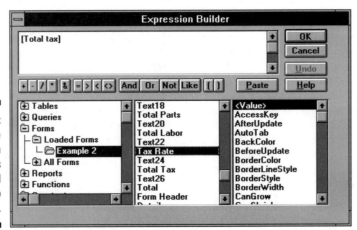

Figure 5-5: The Expression Builder is used to fill out a macro argument.

✔ The center panel lists all the identifier names associated with the selected source object. In Figure 5-5, the center panel lists all the identifiers on the form. Note that this list includes the names of the labels, box, and line objects.

✔ The right-most panel lists the properties for each identifier. The *<Value>* property refers to the current contents of the control.

When you have placed the highlight on the desired identifier, select the **Paste** button to insert the name into the expression box. Note that Access uses the full identifier name rather than the simple name. For example, Access would display

```
Forms![Example 2]![Total Tax]
```

instead of

```
[Total Tax]
```

In this case, either the simple name or the full name will work because the identifier is part of the current form.

If you don't need the full identifier name, you can simplify names and expressions by using the simple name rather than the full name. When you use a simple identifier name — for example, *[Total Tax]* — Access assumes that the name refers to an object that appears on the current form or report. If this isn't the case, you must use the full identifier name — for example, *Forms![Example 2]![Total Tax]* — because the full name explicitly indicates which form or report contains the control.

In cases where the simple name is acceptable, you can always use the full name with no ill effects. There is only one disadvantage of the full name. An expression such as the following:

```
[Tax Rate]*[Total Parts]
```

becomes

```
Forms![Example 2]![Tax Rate]*Forms![Example 2]![Total Parts]
```

As you can see, using the full name increases the complexity of an expresion. ■

In our example, the macro consists of two SetValue actions. The appearance of the macro sheet window is shown in Figure 5-6. The details of each action are as follows:

Action	*Arguments*	
SetValue	Item:	[Total Tax]
	Expression:	[Tax Rate]*[Total Parts]
SetValue	Item:	[Total]
	Expression:	[Total Labor]+[Total Parts]+[Total Tax]

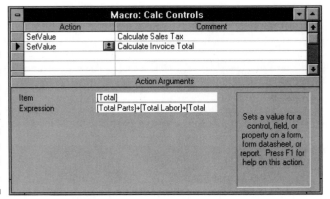

Figure 5-6:
The Calc
Controls
macro sheet
includes
two
SetValue
actions.

When you have entered the desired commands, you can save the macro using the Ctrl-S shortcut. Remember, macros *must be saved* before they can be executed. After saving the macro, you can close the macro window and return to the form design window.

Assigning an existing macro to an event property

Once you have created a macro, you can specify that macro as the action for other controls. In our example, the controls *Total Labor* and *Tax Rate* both need to execute the macro if they are updated. After moving to the Event Properties panel for each of those controls, you can specify the macro — in this case Calc Controls — by entering the macro name directly or by selecting it from the drop-list. Figure 5-7 shows the Event Properties panel with the drop-list displayed.

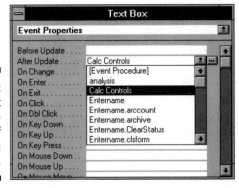

Figure 5-7:
The drop-list
shows the
names of
existing
macros.

In Version 2.0 of Access, the drop-list of macro names includes the names of any macros stored in a macro group. A *macro group* is a single macro sheet that contains a number of individual macros. Macro groups are used to store a group of related macros in a single form. Macro group names appear on the list with the macro sheet name as a prefix. For example, the name Invoice Macros.Calc Sales Tax refers to the Calc Sales Tax macro that is stored on the Invoice Macros sheet. Creation of group macros is discussed in Chapter 6. ◼

The concept of focus

Focus refers to the on-screen item that the user has selected. Depending on the type of element that is selected, that item is usually indicated visually with a highlight, an insert point, an outline, or some other visual cue. When an element has the focus, it generally means that any input made with the keyboard or mouse is directed at the element.

Only one element of each type can have the focus of the system. For example, if you are running Word, Excel, and Access at the same time, only one of the applications can have the focus.

In this book (and most other writing on the subject) the element with focus is referred to as the *active* or *current* application, window, or control. However, it is important to remember that elements without the focus may not be totally inactive. ◼

The drop-list shows all the macros defined in the database. A macro is not linked or restricted to any specific form or report, even though you might have created the macro while designing a particular form. In the preceding example, even though the Calc Controls macro was created while you were designing the Example 2 form, you can associate that macro with any control on any form or report in the database.

As shown in Figure 5-8, when you have completed this example, you have a form that automatically updates *Total Tax* and *Total* whenever there is any change in the values of *Total Parts, Total Lab,* or *Tax Rate.*

Figure 5-8:
The Calc Controls macro can be triggered by an update in any of the three controls.

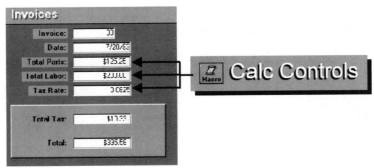

The example used in this chapter highlights two key concepts regarding macros:

- **Values set permanently**. Using a SetValue macro action actually stores a value in a field of the underlying table. If you open the table or create a report based on that table, the values for the *Total Tax* and *Total* fields will be ready for printing.

- **Update triggers**. The macro actions are triggered by the AfterUpdate property of the controls involved in the calculation. Three values (*Total Parts, Total Labor* or *Tax Rate*) can affect the value of the calculated fields. To ensure that the calculated values are accurate, each of these values must be linked to the Calc Controls macro. ■

Chapter 6
Navigating with Macros

• •

In This Chapter

▶ Finding a record

▶ Updating button labels as you navigate

▶ Adding conditions to macros

▶ Entering percentages correctly

▶ Showing and hiding controls

▶ Creating macro groups

• •

*T*he term *navigation* refers to the methods used to move from one item to another in a program. When records are displayed in a form, *navigation* refers to the commands and buttons you use to control which record is currently displayed in the form. Access has several built-in navigation methods. In this chapter, you learn how to use macros to create your own custom methods of navigating through a set of records.

Navigating by Controls

Macros are often used to navigate to specific records or controls. Access automatically provides various means to navigate between records, including the navigation keys, buttons, and menu commands. In many forms, however, a field (or fields) is the most logical way to select a record. For example, in Figure 6-1, the combo box control in the form's header lists all of the company names in the table. To display the record for a given company, you simply choose the company name from the list and a macro action finds and displays the corresponding record.

The *Find Company* control shown in Figure 6-1 requires two elements to operate:

▌ ✔ **A SQL expression.** The list of company names is obtained by using a SQL statement as the Row Source for the combo box. SQL is discussed in Chapter 3.

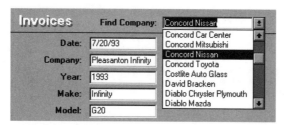

Figure 6-1: A combo box allows users to select a record by company name.

✔ **A macro action.** Once a company name is selected from the list, macro actions are used to search for the selected company name and display the first record that matches that name.

In this example, it's assumed that the field to be searched is a key field or at least a field with unique entries, because the operation finds the first record that matches. Later in this chapter, I'll describe some alternatives for handling multiple matches.

As you'll see in the following sections, the *Find Company* control is a good example of how you can combine several macro actions to produce a result that wouldn't be possible with a single command or action.

Generating combo box lists

The first step in creating a control like the one pictured in Figure 6-1 is to generate a list of the names, numbers, or dates that you want to search for. You can do this either by building a query that selects the names or by writing a SQL statement that selects the same data. As noted in Chapter 3, queries and SQL statements are really two sides of the same coin. They are simply different forms of the same instructions for retrieving a data set.

In Version 2.0 of Access, the Control Wizard executes automatically when you place a combo or list box control on a form. You don't need the Control Wizard for the example in Figure 6-1 because you can enter a SQL statement directly into the Row Source property. Before you create the control, be sure to turn off the Wizard icon in the toolbox palette. ■

You begin the process of creating the example control by placing an unbound combo box control in the header of the form. The control is placed in the header to suggest visually that it isn't part of the table information displayed on the form. Locating the control in the header doesn't affect how it functions. It could be placed in any section of the form. In this example, the name of the control is *FindIt*.

When it comes to Row Sources for combo or list box controls, it's probably easier to write out the SQL statement instead of creating and saving a query. In this example, you want to get a list of the *Company* field from the Invoices table. The following SQL statement will obtain that list (note that the SQL keywords appear in **bold**):

```
Select Company From Invoices;
```

This statement can be entered exactly as it appears into the Row Source property of the control's Data Properties panel. Remember to end the statement with a semicolon.

Note that the SQL statement is directed at the information stored in a specific field in a specific table. In this example, the table — Invoices — is the same as the Record Source for the form. This doesn't have to be the case. The SQL statement operates independently from the rest of the form, so it is possible to draw information for lists from any table in the database. (Chapter 15 describes how this allows you to create several list controls that interact with one another.)

Although the preceding SQL statement will correctly return the list of company names, you may want to consider two modifications to the statement. First, assume that the *Company* field is not a key field. In other words, it may contain duplicate names. You can eliminate the duplicates by adding the SQL keyword *Distinct* to the statement:

```
Select Distinct Company From Invoices;
```

A second consideration is blank records that can occur in non-key fields. If one or more records have no entry in the field, the list will begin with a blank. You can use the *Where* clause to eliminate that blank:

```
Select Distinct Company From Invoices Where Company Is Not Null;
```

The Goto and Find actions

Simply choosing a name from a list doesn't affect the displayed record. So far, you've only stored the name in the *FindIt* control. Now you need to create a macro that uses that name to find the corresponding record. This requires the use of two macro actions:

- ✔ **FindRecord.** This macro action is equivalent to the **Edit** | **Find** menu command. In the example, FindRecord is used to locate the record that corresponds to the item selected in the list.

- ✔ **GotoControl.** This macro action allows you to move from one control to another on the form as part of a macro action.

Which event should trigger this macro action? Once again, it should be an AfterUpdate event generated by the combo list. In plain English, you want the macro to run each time a new name is chosen from the list of company names. To create the macro, you start by placing the insert point in the AfterUpdate property of the *FindIt* control and clicking the ellipsis (...) icon. Then, you select the Macro Builder. The name of this macro will be Find Company. As shown in Figure 6-2, three actions are needed in this macro.

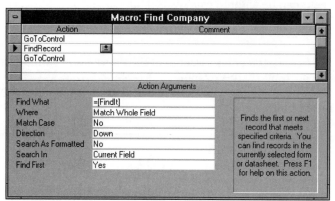

Figure 6-2:
The Find Company macro uses three actions to display the selected company.

The first action is a GotoControl action that moves the focus from *FindIt* to *Company*. Why? The change in focus is intended to limit the scope of the search to the *Company* field. If you've ever used the **Edit | Find** menu command, you will recall that you can choose to search all fields or the *current* field. When the macro begins, the current field is *FindIt*, not *Company*. You need to place the focus on the correct field before you start the search:

Action	*Argument*
GotoControl	ControlName: Company

The next action is the FindRecord action. In this action, the Find What property uses the value *FindIt*. You don't need to worry about the Where or Match Case properties because the search criteria are taken directly from your previous entry and therefore are certain to be entered correctly. This also means you don't need to worry about not finding a match. If the name appears on the list, there is a record that matches the name.

Note that the Direction property is set to Down, and the Find First property is Yes. These settings combine to force the search to begin at the first record in the table, regardless of the currently displayed record.

Action	*Arguments*
FindRecord	Find What: =[FindIt]
	Where: Match Whole Field
	Match Case: No
	Direction: Down
	Search As Formatted: No
	Search In: Current Field
	Find First: Yes

The final action is another GotoControl action. This action isn't absolutely necessary because the desired record is already located and displayed when the FindRecord action is completed. However, the focus has been moved to the *Company* control. Users might find it confusing that the focus has jumped to a different control, so you should make the operation feel more natural by returning the focus to the *FindIt* control:

Action	*Argument*
GotoControl	ControlName: FindIt

Returning the focus to the original control also allows the user to perform a second or third search by making another selection from the list. (If you left the focus on *Company*, the user might not realize that the focus had moved and might accidentally make an incorrect entry into *Company*.

My reason for allowing the focus to return to *FindIt* at the end of the macro is subjective. In creating this macro, I'm guessing how the person using the application will react. Although you might not agree that returning the focus improves the feel of the macro, I want to emphasize that writing good programs is partly a matter of anticipating how users will perceive your macros and programs. The Find Company macro doesn't do anything that users couldn't do on their own with the **Edit** |**Find** command. However, it performs the task in a manner that gives users the impression that something else a bit more powerful is taking place. In designing an operation, it helps to put yourself in the shoes of the person who will be using your application.

Handling multiple matching records

With the Find Company macro, I assumed that only one record matches the selected company name. This may not always be the case. In the example of an invoice form, it would not be unusual to have several invoices in the same table for the same company. As currently constructed, however, the Find Compnay macro will always find the first record. There are several solutions to this problem. This section describes two of the simpler ones.

One solution is to change the Find First property from Yes to No. With this change, the search will start from the current record:

Action	*Arguments*
FindRecord	Find What: =[Findlt]
	Where: Match Whole Field
	Match Case: No
	Direction: Down
	Search As Formatted: No
	Search In: Current Field
	Find First: No

However, this solution doesn't ensure that each search starts with the first match. If you're at the last record in the table, any search you perform will fail to find a record because the search always moves toward the end of the table.

A better approach is to leave the *Findlt* control as is — finding the first match — and add a second control. In this example, you want to add a command button that searches for the next match, if any. Figure 6-3 shows a command button labeled *Next*. This button will advance to the next record in the table that matches the selected name.

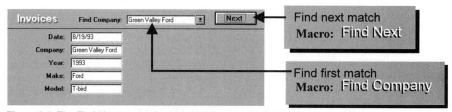

Figure 6-3: The Find Next macro is executed by a command button.

So add this capability to the form, you need to add a command button. You should turn off the Control Wizard so that you can manually define the following properties of the control:

Name:	Find Next
Caption:	Next
Click On:	Find Next

The Click On event property means the macro is triggered by clicking the button.

You can use the Macro Builder — the ellipsis (...) icon — to create a macro called Find Next. This macro is identical to the Find Company macro, with the exception of the items shown in **bold**:

Action	*Arguments*
GotoControl	**ControlName: Find Next**
FindRecord	Find What: =[FindIt]
	Where: Match Whole Field
	Match Case: No
	Direction: Down
	Search As Formatted: No
	Search In: Current Field
	Find First: No
GotoControl	**ControlName: Find Next**

After saving this macro, you can locate the first record by selecting the name from the list. Then click the Next button to move to the next matching record. If the search reaches the end of the table, nothing changes when the Next button is clicked.

It might be useful to display a message when the end of the table is reached. To do this, you need to use a conditional macro. Conditional macros are covered later in this chapter.

Matching any company

The Find Next macro uses the selection from the FindIt combo box control as the criterion for locating the next record. However, the *FindIt* control might show a different name than the *Company* control. This can happen because the name in the *FindIt* control doesn't change when you use the built-in navigation buttons or keys to change records. As a result, the FindIt box might show *Concord Auto Glass* while the actual company displayed is *Hilltop Jeep*. If you clicked the Next command button, the search would look for *Concord Auto Glass*, not *Hilltop Jeep*.

It might be better to look for the next record containing the company name that appears in the *Company* field. You can make this change by modifying the FindRecord action in the Find Next macro as follows (changes are shown in **bold**):

Action	*Arguments*
FindRecord	**Find What: =[Company]**
	Where: Match Whole Field
	Match Case: No
	Direction: Down
	Search As Formatted: No
	Search In: Current Field
	Find First: No

This change allows the Next button to find the next record for the same company even if the first record wasn't located using the *FindIt* control.

Setting Properties

Objects in Access — such as tables, forms, and controls — have properties. Property settings control the appearance or behavior of the object. When you work manually with Access, you set property values in the various design modes. For example, the caption for the Find Next command button was set to *Next* when you entered that text into the Caption property of the control.

However, you can use SetValue macro actions to change most of the properties of such objects as controls on a form. This means that you can use macro actions to alter the appearance of a control while the form is being displayed and edited.

You can apply this concept to the Next command button. Using the label *Next* for the command button is a bit ambiguous. Unless someone explains the operation of this button, the user could reasonably conclude that its function is identical to the Next button that appears on the bottom bar of the form, which simply moves to the next record. You need to indicate that your command button searches for the next record with the same company name, not just the next record.

An effective solution involves using a SetValue macro action to alter the button's caption. As shown in Figure 6-4, the selected company name is integrated into the button caption, which is updated each time a new record is displayed. This display clearly indicates that the button finds the next record for the same company.

How can you do this? The simplest way would seem to involve using an expression as the Caption property. With the following expression, I want Access to treat the caption of the button like a calculated control and update the caption to match the *Company* control value:

Name:	Find Next
Caption:	**= [Company]**
Click On:	Find Next

Unfortunately, this won't work. If you try this, you will end up with a button labeled *=[Company]*. Why? Because Access assumes anything typed into the Caption box on the property sheet is a *literal*.

Figure 6-4:
The button caption reflects the current company name.

But don't give up. Using macros to alter the appearance of controls is a useful technique and you can get Access to do it, but there's a trick to making it work. The method uses the SetValue macro action. However, unlike the previous examples in which SetValue was used to alter the value of a control, this time you want to change a property of the control.

The key lies in the concept of a property identifier. When you use a control name, Access assumes you are referring to the current value of that control. If you want to refer to a property of that control, you must add a property name as a suffix. The following identifier refers to the Caption of the Find Next control:

```
[Find Next].Caption
```

You would use this identifier in the Item argument of a SetValue action to indicate that you want to change the appearance of the control. The following SetValue action is designed to set the Caption of the Find Next button to the name that appears in the *Company* control. Note that the expression is not preceded by an equal sign.

Action	*Arguments*
SetValue	Item: [Find Next].Caption
	Expression: [Company]

You can expand the text of the message by adding the word *Next* as a text literal so that the button caption will read *Next Hilltop Jeep*. The following macro is called Set Button Caption:

Action	**Arguments**
SetValue	Item: [Find Next].Caption
	Expression: "Next " & [Company]

In either case, the macro must be executed each time a new record is displayed. This means it should be triggered by the OnCurrent event property of the form. To set this property, select the form and enter the macro name, Set Button Caption, in the OnCurrent property.

To modify the form's property sheet, you must select the form. You can do this by using the **Edit** | **Select Form** menu command or by clicking the gray area in the form window. ■

With this change, the button's caption is updated to reflect the current company name.

Macros with Conditions

Up to this point, all the macros we've created have consisted of one or more macro actions that are all executed when the macro is triggered by an event. These macros have the following characteristics:

- ✔ All of the actions entered into these macros are executed. These macros end after the last instruction is carried out.
- ✔ The instructions are executed in the order in which they were entered.

In many cases, however, you might want to control or limit macro actions on the basis of a condition or the status of a particular object on a form or report. For example, the sample invoice form in Figure 6-5 contains information about the location of the sale and the sales tax rate. Although Access has no way of knowing it, the tax rate is directly related to the address. For example, if the state is CA, the tax rate ought to be 8.25%.

In some states, the sales tax rate varies within the state due to additional taxes levied by local entities. For simplicity, this example ignores this fact.

Because the tax rate depends on the state, it would be useful to create a macro action that updates *Tax Rate* whenever there is a change in *State*. The following action will do the trick:

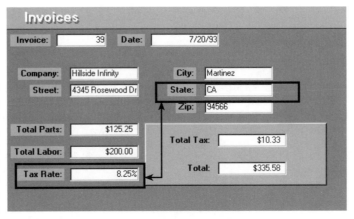

Figure 6-5:
The value of
the State
and Tax
Rate
controls are
related.

Action	*Arguments*
SetValue	Item: [Tax Rate]
	Expression: .0825

But there is something missing from this macro. If entered as shown, the macro
will set the tax rate to 8.25% each time the AfterUpdate event for the *State* control is triggered. What you really want to do is execute the action only if the
State entry is CA. Recall from Chapter 2 that you can express this idea with a
comparison expression:

```
[State]="CA"
```

But how can this comparison expression be used to limit the operation of a
macro action? The answer involves the use of the Condition column in the
macro sheet. Figure 6-6 shows a macro sheet that contains an additional column on the left with the heading *Condition*. This column is used to enter a comparison expression that limits the scope of the action entered in the next
column. You display the Condition column by clicking on the Conditions button
on the toolbar.

The operation of the Condition column is simple. If the comparison expression
is true, the macro action on the same row is executed. If the expression is false,
the action is not executed. Access then moves to the next row of the macro
sheet to execute the action, if any, that follows.

The macro in Figure 6-6, Set Tax Rate, is assigned to the AfterUpdate property
of the *State* control. When used on the form, this macro inserts .0825 in the *Tax
Rate* control only when CA is entered in *State*. If anything else is entered in *State*,
Tax Rate is the default value 0.

Name:	State
Control Source:	State
AfterUpdate:	Set Tax Rate

This macro functions as a sort of *delayed default value*. Recall that a default value is automatically entered into a field or control when a new record is added. However, because each new record is blank in both the *State* and *Tax Rate* fields, the automatic setting of *Tax Rate* must wait until the user makes an entry into *State*.

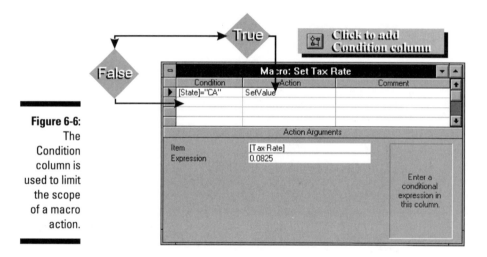

Figure 6-6: The Condition column is used to limit the scope of a macro action.

Alternative Actions

The macro shown in Figure 6-6 works correctly for the initial entry in a new record. Assuming that the default value for the *Tax Rate* control is 0, that rate will be changed to .0825 only if the user specifically enters CA in the *State* field.

But the macro isn't sophisticated enough to handle subsequent editing changes. For example, suppose that after initially entering the state as CA, the user corrects the record to show a different state. What happens to the tax rate?

Unfortunately, it remains at .0825. The Set Tax Rate macro in Figure 6-6 sets the value only when the state is CA. Nothing in the macro accounts for the need to change *Tax Rate* back to 0 if *State* is changed from CA to something else.

You can solve this problem by using the Condition column to set up an alternative action that sets the tax rate to 0 if the expression *[State]="CA"* is false. The key concept is that the two actions — SetValue to .0825 and SetValue to 0 — are *mutually exclusive*. In other words, either one action or the other — but not both — takes place each time a change in the *State* field triggers an AfterUpdate event.

In programming languages such as Access Basic, statements such as If…Then…Else, are used to create this type of structure. In Access macros, these structures are created in a more round about fashion, involving a set of four rules:

✔ Macro conditions and actions are evaluated in the order in which they are entered, starting with the first row in the macro sheet.

✔ Once started, a macro terminates when Access encounters a blank row (no conditions or actions) or when the StopMacro action is executed.

✔ If a condition is false, the macro skips the action on that line and moves to the next line of the macro sheet.

✔ You can link a series of actions to a single condition by placing an ellipsis (…) in the Condition column.

The logical structures available for macros are all based on these rules. You need to use all of them to solve the problem. As shown in Figure 6-7, the macro consists of three actions:

1. **SetValue**. This sets the tax rate to 8.25%

2. **StopMacro**. This terminates the macro. When this action is encountered, no further actions are performed.

3. **SetValue**. This sets the tax rate to 0%.

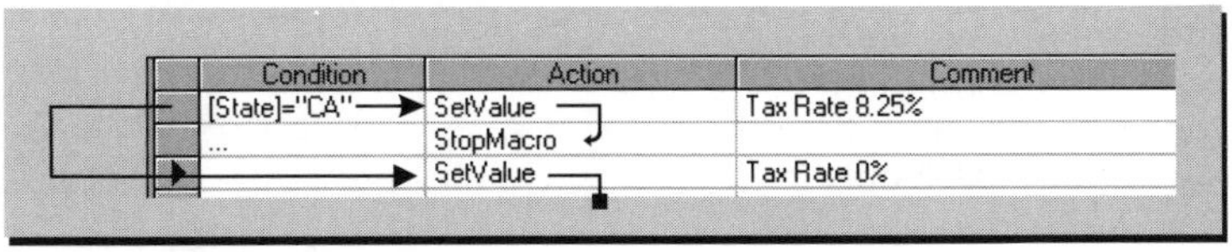

Condition	Action	Comment
[State]="CA"	SetValue	Tax Rate 8.25%
…	StopMacro	
	SetValue	Tax Rate 0%

Figure 6-7: The Condition column sets up alternative actions.

In addition to StopMacro, Access also has an action called StopAllMacros. StopAllMacros is used when you have macros that execute other macros using the RunMacro action. In this example, both actions would have the same result because only one macro is executing at a time.

The trick is to get Access to perform either action 1 or action 3, but not both. The key is the use of the ellipsis (…) in the Condition column of the StopMacro action. The ellipsis indicates to Access that this action is part of a group of actions controlled by the condition *[State]="CA"*. This is important because if Access finds *[State]="CA"* to be false, it skips any actions that are part of the group controlled by that condition. In other words, Access will skip actions 1 and 2 and execute action 3 if *[State]="CA"* is false.

With the exception of the macro name, which is discussed later in this chapter, there isn't much else to say about logical structures in macro sheets. The macro listed in Table 6-1 establishes two mutually exclusive paths by which one action or another will be performed, based on a condition.

Table 6-1: The Set Tax Rate macro

Condition	Action	Properties
[State]="CA"	SetValue	Item: [Tax Rate] Expression: .0825
...	StopMacro SetValue	Item: [Tax Rate] Expression: 0

By applying the four basic rules for executing macro actions, you can use conditions to build macros that perform many tasks. Figure 6-8 shows an expanded version of the macro with a series of conditions, such as *[State]="CA"* and *[State="NV"]*. This macro sets specific values for several states (CA, NV, and OR). If none of these conditions are true, the last SetValue action sets the tax rate to 0.

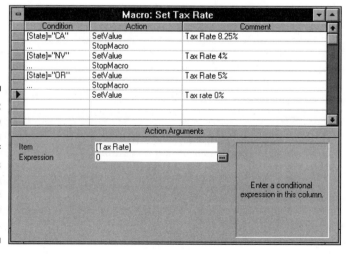

Figure 6-8: A macro uses a series of conditions to create a multiple choice structure.

The macro shown in Figure 6-8 is simply an extension of the pattern established in the simpler macro in Figure 6-7. Note that each condition — for example *[State]=“CA”* — is grouped with a StopMacro action. The StopMacro action makes each condition a separate branch. If you remove the StopMacro actions, the *Tax Rate* value always ends up as 0 because there is nothing to stop Access from reaching the last action in the list.

Recall that in Chapter 4, the *Switch( )* function was used to perform a similar calculation using an expression. You can achieve the same result by using a single SetValue action with a *Switch( )* function in the expression.

The advantage of the method shown here is that you can easily read, revise, add, or delete conditions and actions. Writing one large expression to do the same task is more tedious and error prone. Although the macro sheet looks like more work than writing a single expression, it is probably faster and easier to create the macro than it is to type a long expression with all the correct identifiers and syntax.

You may have noticed that many of the rows in a macro are duplicates, or at least very similar. You can speed up macro writing by using **Copy** and **Paste** to duplicate rows and then edit the items that need to be changed. To copy an entire row or group of rows, use the row selector buttons on the left side of the macro window. You can move a row to another location by dragging the row selector up or down. ▪

The Percentage Problem

When a field or control on a form requires the user to manually enter a percentage value — for example, a tax rate, a markup, or an interest rate — there is potential for a common misunderstanding. The user might enter the percentage in one of three ways: with a percent sign, without a percent sign, or as a decimal. Access treats .06 and 6%, for example, as the same value. The number 6 without the percent sign is treated as 600%.

You can place text on the form reminding users of the proper form for the percentage, but you can’t be sure that they will read this note. A better solution is to create a macro that ensures that the value entered into the control is a percentage — that is, a decimal number less than 1.

You can do this with a SetValue macro action that uses the condition *[Tax Rate]>=1*. This condition means that the SetValue action will execute only when the value entered as a percentage is greater than 1. If the user enters a value greater than 1, the SetValue action replaces the current value of *[Tax Rate]* with *[Tax Rate]/100*. For example, if the user enters a value of 6, the macro changes it to 6/100, or .06.

Condition	*Action*	*Properties*
[Tax Rate]>=1	SetValue	Item: [Tax Rate]
		Expression: [Tax Rate]/100

Which event should trigger this macro? The macro should be executed each time the *[Tax Rate]* control is updated. This is specified by entering the name of the macro, *Percent*, in the AfterUpdate property:

```
After Update: Percent
```

This macro ensures that the value in the *Tax Rate* control is always a decimal value, regardless of whether the user enters a percentage, a decimal, or a whole number.

Macros that Refer to Themselves

The Percent macro is specifically designed to work with a control named *[Tax Rate]*. However, the Percent macro could be used in any number of forms where a percent entry is required. In its present state, you would need to edit the macro in each case to match the name of the control it was designed to change. For example, to apply the macro to a control named *Interest Rate*, you would need to make the following changes to the macro (changes are in **bold**):

Condition	*Action*	*Properties*
[**Interest Rate**]>=1	SetValue	Item: [**Interest Rate**]
		Expression: [**Interest Rate**]/100

You can see that the structure of the macro is unchanged. To apply the macro to a different field or control, you need to change only the name of the identifier. To make matters easier, the identifier name will always be the control that is currently being edited, because an update to that control triggers the macro.

Is there some way the macro could be written so that it automatically picks up the name of the current control and uses it as the identifier name? This would allow you to create a Percent macro that you could use in any number of different forms to ensure the proper entry of a percentage, regardless of the name of the control being edited.

The solution comes in the form of the Screen object. The Screen object can refer to the form or report with which the user is currently interacting, or to the currently selected control on that form or report. You identify the specific object by using one of the following object identifier names:

```
Screen.ActiveForm
Screen.ActiveReport
Screen.ActiveControl
```

For example, you can substitute the Screen object *Screen.ActiveControl* for the specific name of the identifier in the Percent macro:

Condition	*Action*	*Arguments*
Screen.ActiveControl >=1	SetValue	Item: Screen.ActiveControl
		Expression: Screen.ActiveControl /100

You can apply this version of the Percent macro to any control without modification. Thus, a single macro can be used to control the entry of percentages on any number of forms.

The Percent macro is an example of a *generalized solution* to a problem. The initial solution was designed for a specific control on a specific form. Upon further analysis, we determined that the macro could be applied to any percentage type control.We then found a method for automatically inserting the specific control name into the condition and arguments of the macro. (In this case, the Screen object automatically supplied the needed identifier name.) A generalized macro or program is more valuable than a specific macro because it can be used repeatedly without modification in different forms, reports, and databases.

Hide and Seek (Setting Property Values)

As discussed earlier in this chapter, a macro action such as SetValue can be used to alter both the properties and the values of controls. By combining the setting of properties with macro conditions you can create some interesting visual effects.

Figure 6-9 is an invoice form that is used to record sales information. The problem in this example is that the form can be used to record either wholesale or retail transactions. These two types of invoices share some fields, for example, invoice number, date, and total. However, some fields are used only for wholesale, and others are only for retail. For example, a wholesale invoice uses *Company*, but a retail invoice needs *First Name* and *Last Name*. Similarly, wholesale doesn't need *Tax Rate* or *Total Tax*, but retail sales does.

Figure 6-9:
Not all
controls
need to be
filled out for
every
record.

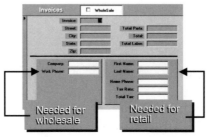

To emphasize a point in this example, the various controls in Figure 6-9 are separated into groups: common, wholesale, and retail. In practice, these controls would probably be mixed together. But the technique used here would still apply.

You can eliminate unwanted controls by using SetValue to turn the Visible property of selected controls on or off, depending on whether the sale is wholesale or retail. The type of sale can be determined by a Yes/No type field displayed as a check box control. This Wholesale control appears in the header of the form in Figure 6-9. Each time the AfterUpdate property of this control is triggered, a macro with a series of SetValue actions is performed. The following shows what such a SetValue action would look like:

Condition	*Action*	*Arguements*
[Wholesale]	SetValue	Item: [Company].Visible
		Expression: True

A few points about the action are worth noting:

- ✔ The condition is simply the name of the Yes/No field *Wholesale*. Because the value of *Wholesale* is either True or False, no comparison operator is needed. One of the benefits of using a Yes/No field is that you can use this simplified form as a condition.

- ✔ The Item uses the *object.property* form to specify the Visible property of the *Company* control.

- ✔ Because the Visible property can be either Yes or No, you can use True, Yes, or 1 to turn on the Visible property, and False, No, or 0 to turn it off.

Figure 6-10 shows the entire macro needed to toggle the two sets of controls between visible and invisible. The macro consists of two sections that contain nearly identical sets of SetValue actions. The group at the top, controlled by the condition *[Wholesale],* turns on the Visible property for the controls *Company* and *Work Phone*. It turns off the Visible property for *First Name*, *Last Name*, *Home Phone*, *Tax Rate*, and *Total Tax*. The second group of

SetValue actions, following StopMacro, is identical except the True and False values are reversed.

Figure 6-10: The Show Controls macro toggles the Visible property of various controls.

Condition	Action	Comment
[WholeSale]	SetValue	Company On
...	SetValue	Work Phone On
...	SetValue	Last Name Off
...	SetValue	First Name Off
...	SetValue	Home Phone Off
...	SetValue	Tax Rate Off
...	SetValue	Total Tax Off
...	StopMacro	
	SetValue	Company Off
	SetValue	Work Phone Off
	SetValue	Last Name On
	SetValue	First Name On
	SetValue	Home Phone On
	SetValue	Tax Rate On
	SetValue	Total Tax On

The result of this macro is the form shown in Figure 6-11. The appearance of this form is altered dynamically while the form is in use. When the check box for *Wholesale* is checked, the controls related to retail are removed from the form. Conversely, when *Wholesale* is unchecked, the wholesale controls are removed and the retail controls become visible.

The ability to use macros (or Access Basic) to alter the properties of objects such as controls, forms, and reports while they are in use is a very powerful tool.

Macro Names and Groups

So far, each macro has been stored in its own macro sheet with a unique name that appears in the Macros panel of the main database window. Access provides another means of storing macros so that a single macro sheet can contain any number of distinct macros, yet add only a single name to the list of macros in the database window. This is accomplished by displaying the Macro Name column in the macro sheet. To do so, use **View** |**Macro Names** menu command or click the Names icon on the toolbar.

Figure 6-12 shows a single macro sheet, *Macros For Invoice Form,* that contains four macros. The names of the macros are entered in the Macro Name column on the same line as the first action in the macro.

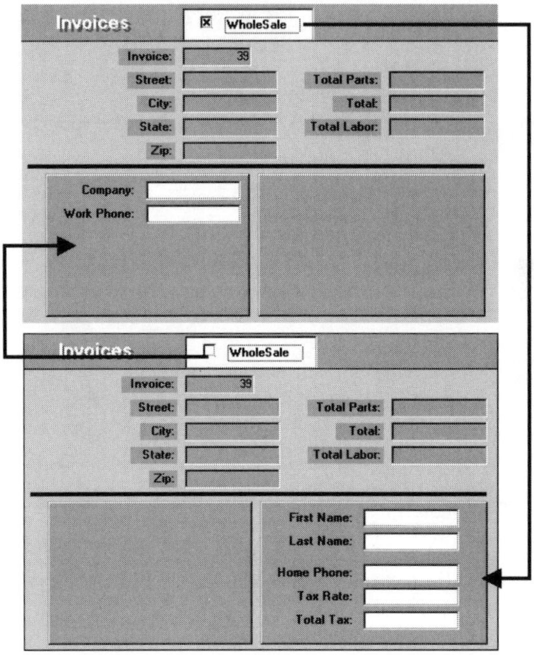

Figure 6-11:
The Show
Controls
macro
changes the
appearance
of the form
in response
to a change
in the
value of
Wholesale.

Access recognizes each macro name as a fixed partition that marks the end of the macro, and terminates execution without continuing to the actions of the next macro. This enables you to consolidate several macros into a single sheet. In this example, a single macro sheet is used to store all the macros for a specific form — *Invoices*. This simplifies the task of finding macros because it reduces the number of macro sheets stored in the database and allows you to store related macros together in the same sheet.

You can refer to a named macro in a macro sheet using the following identifier syntax:

```
Macrosheet.MacroName
```

Macro Name	Condition	Action	Comment
Calc Controls		SetValue	Calculate Sales Tax
		SetValue	Calculate Invoice Total
Find Company		GoToControl	
		FindRecord	
		GoToControl	
Set Tax Rate	[State]="CA"	SetValue	Tax Rate 8.25%
	...	StopMacro	
	[State]="NV"	SetValue	Tax Rate 4%
	...	StopMacro	
	[State]="OR"	SetValue	Tax Rate 5%
	...	StopMacro	
		SetValue	Tax rate 0%
Show Controls	[WholeSale]	SetValue	Company On
	...	SetValue	Work Phone On
	...	SetValue	Last Name Off
	...	SetValue	First Name Off
	...	SetValue	Home Phone Off
	...	SetValue	Tax Rate Off
	...	SetValue	Total Tax Off
	...	StopMacro	
		SetValue	Company Off
		SetValue	Work Phone Off
		SetValue	Last Name On
		SetValue	First Name On
		SetValue	Home Phone On
		SetValue	Tax Rate On
		SetValue	Total Tax On

Macro: Macros For Invoice Form

Figure 6-12:
This macro
sheet
contains
four named
macros.

To assign an event property to the named macro Set Tax Rate, which is stored
in the *Macros For Invoice Form* macro sheet, you would enter

```
Macros For Invoice Form.Set Tax Rate
```

In Version 2.0 of Access, all the named macros in each macro sheet are listed
when you open the drop-list for an event property. Figure 6-13 shows an
example of such a listing.

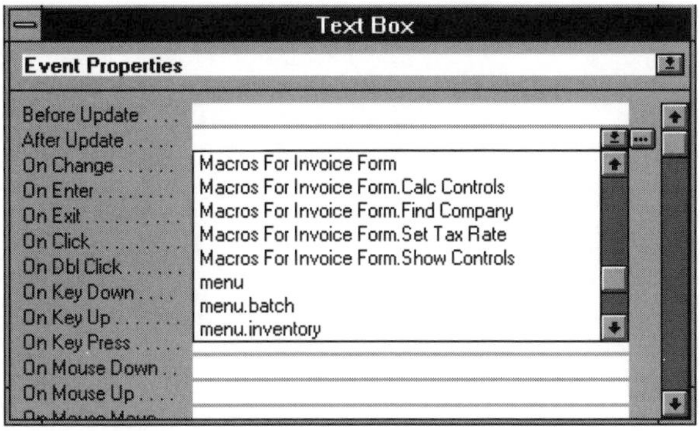

Figure 6-13:
Named
macros
appear in
the drop-list
for event
properties.

Text Box

Event Properties

Before Update . . . .
After Update . . . . .
On Change . . . . . .
On Enter . . . .
On Exit . . . .
On Click . . . .
On Dbl Click . . . . .
On Key Down . . . .
On Key Up . . . . . .
On Key Press . . . . .
On Mouse Down . .
On Mouse Up . . . .
On Mouse Move

Macros For Invoice Form
Macros For Invoice Form.Calc Controls
Macros For Invoice Form.Find Company
Macros For Invoice Form.Set Tax Rate
Macros For Invoice Form.Show Controls
menu
menu.batch
menu.inventory

Named macros are also used to create user-defined menus that can be attached
to individual forms.

Chapter 7
Testing and Debugging Macros

● ●

In This Chapter

▶ Stepping through macros action by action

▶ Monitoring macros with message boxes

▶ Printing macro sheets

▶ Executing macros with shortcut keys

● ●

*N*o matter how hard you try, most macros don't work correctly the first time you try them. The final macro is often a product of a process in which you write a macro, try it, and then revise it several times to eliminate all of the problems. This process is called *debugging*. This chapter shows you how to use Access to test and debug your macros.

Types of Macro Errors

Three basic types of problems can occur when you are creating a macro:

✔ **Syntax errors.** These errors involve entering macro actions incorrectly. Access eliminates almost all potential syntax errors by checking the actions and conditions as you enter them. For example, if you enter *setvalues* as a macro action, Access rejects the entry because it isn't a valid macro action.

✔ **Parameter errors**. These errors are similar to syntax errors in that they are caused by the incorrect entry of an identifier as an action argument. Although Access can automatically check the syntax of an identifier — for example, to ensure that the name is correctly enclosed in brackets — it doesn't know before execution whether the identifier actually exists. Similarly, Access can't tell in advance whether the value of the identifier fits its use in the macro — for example, that the value is a date when a date is required.

> ✔ **Logical errors.** These errors are the most difficult to understand and correct because they occur even when all the macro actions and conditions are correct. A macro with a logical error runs but fails to achieve the result you had in mind. Perhaps the actions are arranged in the wrong sequence, or maybe the actions simply cannot achieve the result you want.

Access has features that eliminate almost all syntax errors and, if you use the Expression Builder, most identifier problems. That leaves logical errors as the primary problem. In a sense, this book is about logical errors. Programming is about choosing the right action or command to get the result you want. There is no magic formula for correcting logical errors. However, the techniques in this chapter can help you get additional information about what is happening during a macro so you have a better opportunity of finding your errors.

Stepping Through a Macro

Access normally executes the actions in a macro as quickly as possible. When you are trying to debug a macro, however, you may find it useful to slow down the execution of actions so that you can inspect the results of each part of the macro. To meet this need, Access provides the *step* mode, in which a special dialog box appears *before* each action in a macro is executed.

Step mode is activated by selecting the Step icon, from the macro toolbar. The Step icon is shown in Figure 7-1.

Figure 7-1:
The Step
icon.

When you select Step mode, the macro executes one action at a time whenever it is triggered by an event. Before each action, Access displays the dialog box shown in Figure 7-2.

This dialog box displays the following information about the macro action that is about to be executed:

▌ ✔ **Macro Name.** This is the name of the macro that is being executed.

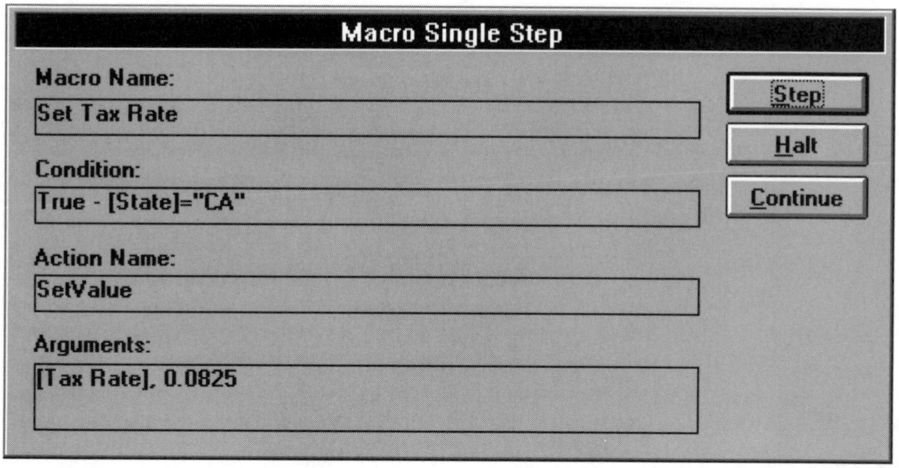

Macro Single Step	
Macro Name:	Step
Set Tax Rate	Halt
Condition:	Continue
True - [State]="CA"	
Action Name:	
SetValue	
Arguments:	
[Tax Rate], 0.0825	

Figure 7-2:
The Step dialog box shows details of each macro action right before it is executed.

✔ **Condition.** If you have entered a condition for the macro action, this box shows the status of the condition as well as the expression that defines the condition. The status is always either True or False. The expression is the comparison expression entered into the Condition column of the macro action. If you haven't entered a condition for the action, its value is automatically True and the expression is left blank.

✔ **Action Name.** This box shows the action that is about to executed, for example, SetValue or StopMacro.

✔ **Arguments.** This box lists all the arguments used by the action. For example, if the action is SetValue, this box lists the item and expression arguments. The arguments are separated by commas. Note that Access simply lists the arguments without labeling them. This means that you must remember the argument names in order to know what each value stands for.

The display of the arguments in the Step dialog box is affected by the way you enter the expression into the macro sheet. If you enter the expression without an equal sign — for example, *[Tax Rate]*[Total Parts]* — the Step dialog box shows the expression text. If the expression is preceded by an equal sign — for example, *=[Tax Rate]*[Total Parts]* — the Step dialog box shows the value of the expression (such as 41.25), in the argument box. The equal sign has no effect on the operation of a SetValue action, only on the value displayed in the Step dialog box. ■

The Step dialog box has three buttons that are used to determine how the macro should proceed:

✔ **Step.** This command executes the action described in the dialog box and displays another dialog box before executing the next action.

> ✔ **Halt.** This command terminates the macro before the next action can take place. It is the equivalent of a StopMacro action.
>
> ✔ **Continue.** This button performs two actions. First, it turns off the Step mode for the current macro, and then it executes the remainder of the actions in the macro. In other words, the macro proceeds to the end without stopping. The next time the macro is executed, it will run in normal mode, not step mode.

The Step mode is a valuable tool for examining the effect of the actions executed in a macro. When you save a macro, remember that the step status is saved along with it. If you turn on the Step mode and then save a macro, it will execute in the Step mode the next time it is triggered.

You can halt the execution of any macro by pressing Ctrl-Break. Access pauses the macro at that point and automatically activates the Step mode. The Step dialog box is displayed with information about the next action. You can then use the Step, Halt, or Continue buttons to handle the rest of the actions. ■

Monitoring Messages

Although the Step mode is a valuable tool for working out the bugs in a macro, it isn't always the best way to determine what's happening during the execution of a macro. After all, stopping before every action may get a bit tedious. In many cases, you may want to stop the macro only at certain critical points. Access provides two macro actions that can be used to display information during the execution of a macro:

> ✔ **Echo.** This action allows you to write information on the status line of the Access application window.
>
> ✔ **MsgBox.** This action displays the results of an expression in a dialog box. The box remains on the screen until you click OK or press Enter.

The dialog box displayed by the MsgBox action is called a modal dialog box. A *modal* dialog box or window does not relinquish the focus until you specifically close the box. In other words, once a modal dialog box is displayed, you cannot select anything outside the box. If you attempt to click on another window, a beep sounds. ■

The Echo action is hard to use with most macros because Access automatically overwrites any text on the status line as soon as the macro is done with its standard messages, such as *Form View*. Unless the macro takes more than a few seconds to run, any messages generated during the macro probably will be overwritten before you can read them.

The MsgBox action is more useful for debugging simple macros because it pauses the execution of the macro until you close the dialog box. You can use the MsgBox action to stop the macro at specific points and display a message. If you are using MsgBox as a debugging tool, the message you display probably will be the result of an expression that tells you something about what's going on during the macro.

For example, suppose you want to determine the values that are being used for the identifiers *[Tax Rate]* and *[Total Parts]* before they are used by a SetValue action. You could insert a MsgBox action into the macro just before the SetValue action, as shown in the following **bold** entries:

Action	*Arguments*
MsgBox	Message: **="Rate= " & [Tax Rate] & " Parts = " & [Total Parts]**
	Beep: Yes
	Type: None
	Title:
SetValue	Item: [Total Tax] Expression: [Tax Rate]*[Total Parts]
SetValue	Item: [Total] Expression: [Total Labor]+[Total Parts]+[Total Tax]

Figure 7-3 shows the message box that appears when this macro is executed.

Figure 7-3: The MsgBox action displays information during the execution of a macro.

The expression used with the MsgBox action combines text and numbers into one long message in which each of the numeric values has a text label to identify its meaning. The message box stays on the screen until you close it by clicking OK or pressing Enter. You can terminate the macro at this point by pressing Ctrl-Break, which activates the Step mode. When the Step dialog box appears, select the Halt button.

If you want to display several different values, you can use the *Chr( )* function to insert new lines within the message. Access recognizes *Chr(10)* and *Chr(13)* as line feed and carriage return characters, respectively. The following expression displays a three-line message in a message box:

```
="Rate= " & [Tax Rate] & Chr(10) & Chr(13) & " Parts = "
& [TotalParts] & Chr(10) & Chr(13) & "Tax = " & [Tax
Rate]*[Total Parts]
```

Figure 7-4: Line feed and carriage return characters are used to create a multiline message box display.

Depending on the type of expression you use with the MsgBox, you can get all sorts of information about what's happening during the macro. For example, the following expression lets you display the name of the control that was selected when the macro was triggered:

```
="Active Control = " &Screen.ActiveControl
```

You can also use the MsgBox to display information about control properties. For example, the following expression lets you determine the number of characters selected in the current control by displaying the SelLength property of the active control:

```
="Selection = " & Screen.ActiveControl.SelLength & " chars"
```

If SelLength is zero, the insert point is displayed in the current control.

Suppressing the Message Boxes

One problem with using MsgBox actions to monitor macro execution is that you can't turn off the message boxes except by editing the macro and deleting the MsgBox actions. In some cases, it would be useful to turn the message boxes on or off without deleting actions from the macro.

One way you can do this is by using the Condition column to control whether or not a message box action — or for that matter, any action — is executed. Figure 7-5 shows a macro sheet that has two MsgBox actions and two SetValue actions. Placing *False* in the Condition column of the first action causes Access to skip that action when the macro is executed. Entering *True* or simply leaving the condition blank allows Access to execute the action.

Figure 7-5:
The Condition column can be used to suppress specific actions.

This is a valuable general-purpose debugging technique. For example, suppose you aren't sure which of several actions or variations on an action (such as different expressions) works best with a form. Instead of editing the same action, you can enter several actions and use the Condition column to select which one is executed. By changing the True and False conditions, you can try out alternative operations without deleting actions. This makes it much easier to figure out which action works best.

Printing Macros

In Version 2.0 of Access, the **File | Print | Definition** command enables you to create and print a report that contains the detailed information entered into a macro.

To print a report, select the macro from the macro panel of the database window, and select **File | Print | Definition**. As shown in Figure 7-6, Access displays a dialog box with three optional categories of information that your report can include or exclude:

✔ **Properties**. The properties of the macro sheet, such as the date the macro was created.

✔ **Actions.** A list of the names, conditions, actions, and arguments contained in the macro.

✔ **Permissions**. Information about the security access settings, if any, associated with the macro.

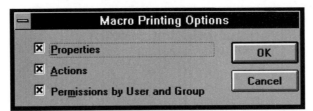

Figure 7-6: Access offers three options for generating a macro report.

Access then generates a special report that contains the selected information about the macro. The report is displayed in the preview mode. In addition to printing the report, Version 2.0 of Access gives you the option of outputting reports to an Excel spreadsheet, a standard text file, or a RTF (Rich Text Format) document, which can be read by such applications as Word for Windows or WordPerfect for Windows.

Executing Macros Manually

Most of the macros you create probably will be linked to database objects — in particular, forms and controls on forms — by means of event properties. Some times, however, you may find it useful or necessary to execute a macro manually. This can be done in two ways:

✔ **The Run button**. You can execute any macro by selecting its name in the Macro panel of the database window and then selecting the Run button. The macro actions are executed exactly as they were entered, so they may not work as intended when run from a database window instead of from the form or report for which they were designed.

✔ **AutoKeys.** Macros can be assigned to shortcut key combinations by creating a special macro sheet with the name AutoKeys.

Creating an AutoKeys macro

In some cases, it is useful to create a macro that executes whenever you enter a special key combination. For example, you might want to create a key combination to display information about the current form or control without having to enter the design mode.

You can do this by creating a new macro sheet with the name *AutoKeys.* You associate a key combination with a macro by entering the key symbol as the name in the Macro Name column.

You assign a Ctrl-key combination by using ^*key.* For example, ^p is the symbol for Ctrl-p[. The plus sign (+) is the symbol for the Shift key. The symbol +^p stands for Ctrl-Shift-p. Special key names are enclosed in {}. For example, {F3} represents the F3 function key and {End} means the End key. You can also combine special keys with Ctrl and Shift. For example, +^{F3} stands for Ctrl-Shift-F3.

The following macro action is assigned to ^{F1}, that is, Ctrl-F1:

Macro Name	*Action*	*Properties*	
^{F1}	MsgBox	Message:	=Screen.ActiveForm.RecordSource & Chr(10) & Chr(13)& Screen.ActiveControl.ControlSource
		Beep:	Yes
		Type:	None
		Title:	

This macro displays a message box that contains the name of the Record Source of the form and the Control Source of the current control. Because the argument makes use of the Screen object rather than the name of a specific form, it can be applied to any form in the database.

The expression used as the message argument is too long to fit on a single line in this book. The shading indicates that these lines should be combined into a single line when you enter them into your macro sheet.

After saving the AutoKeys macro, you can execute the macro from anyplace in the database by pressing the correct key combination. Figure 7-7 shows the message box defined in the preceding Ctrl-F1 macro, displayed on top of a form. The box lists the table and field to which the current control is bound, without changing to the design mode.

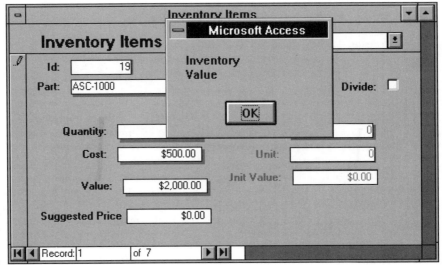

Figure 7-7:
This
Message
box macro
executed by
Ctrl+F1 key
combination.

Keep in mind that Access has several built-in functions that are assigned by default to special key combinations. For example, Ctrl-S is **Save** and Ctrl-P is **Print**. If you assign one of these keys to an AutoKeys macro, the macro takes precedence over the built-in key assignment.

Also remember that AutoKeys macros are not restricted to any part of the database. Even though an AutoKeys macro requires that a certain form is open in order to work, that key combination might still be used accidentally when the wrong form (or no form at all) is open, resulting in an error message.

Chapter 8
Using Access Basic

● ●

In This Chapter

▶ Why should you use Access Basic?

▶ Creating a procedure

▶ Compiling procedures

▶ Debugging a procedure

▶ Using the Immediate window

▶ Adding notes and comments to procedures

● ●

*A*s mentioned in the Introduction, databases are peculiar among software applications in that they are often created by one person so that other people with less computer knowledge can use the program for a specific task, for example, processing invoices.

In other types of software such as word processing and spreadsheets, macros alone are usually sufficient for automating repetitive tasks. However, because database software is often used to create unique software applications, you may find that macros alone don't provide the level of control and customization needed for your application.

Access Basic provides the necessary power, control, and customization to create applications that go beyond macro actions,. This chapter describes how Access Basic operates in Access and shows you how to construct Access Basic programs.

Access Basic versus Macros

Access Basic is a programming language that is built into Access. You use Access Basic for the same basic reason that you use macros — to automate routine, repetitive tasks involving Access database objects. However, Access Basic provides greater power and more detailed control than Access macro actions.

Essentially, Access macro actions duplicate the operations you can perform manually using the Access menus and shortcut keys. Access Basic goes beyond simply automating sequences of actions. Access Basic provides a set of tools that allows you to create custom-designed applications based on the elements of Access and the objects in Access databases.

The advantages of Access Basic

If you've used macros, you already know the advantages of automating tasks that would otherwise involve manually entering one command at a time. Access Basic extends your ability to create custom operations in the following ways:

- **Accessing record sets.** With macro actions, you are typically limited to operating with the record or set of records currently displayed on the screen. Access Basic lets you work with any set of records in the current database or in other databases.

- **Manipulating objects.** Access Basic provides methods for creating and modifying Access objects. For example, you could use Access Basic to create a new form or table as part of a program. Many of the operations carried out in the table, form, and report design modes also can be carried out through Access Basic. The Wizards that help you design new tables, forms, reports, and controls are all Access Basic programs.

- **Creating user-defined functions.** You can use Access Basic to build user-defined functions. These functions can then be included in Access expressions, just like the built-in functions.

- **Defining conditions.** Access Basic offers more powerful ways to evaluate conditions and use those results to control how an operation is carried out.

- **Easy debugging.** Access Basic allows you to step through a program one command at a time or to set breakpoints in a program. A *breakpoint* is a place in a program where you want Access to pause so that you can check on how the program is proceeding. You can also check values, display values, perform calculations, or even enter additional commands through the Immediate window, which is described later in this chapter.

Working with Windows Applications

Access Basic is a variant of Microsoft's Visual Basic language. Microsoft is promoting Visual Basic as a standard language for all Windows applications. It is currently supported with Access, Word for Windows, and Excel. Each of these applications uses the same fundamental language — Visual Basic — to provide programming capabilities. The primary difference is that each application uses a different set of objects. In Word for Windows, objects are documents and bookmarks within documents. In Excel, objects are spreadsheets and cells within the spreadsheets. In Access, there are tables, fields, queries, forms, reports, and so on.

With this standard programming language, once you learn how to write programs in any of the applications, you can directly transfer your skills to all of the other applications. All you need to learn about a new application is how its unique objects operate.

Access Basic also supports a set of statements that perform Dynamic Data Exchange (DDE) and Object Linking and Embedding (OLE) operations. DDE and OLE allow Windows applications to interact by exchanging data items or entire objects.

In addition to DDE and OLE, Access Basic supports Microsoft's Data Access engine. Data Access allows different applications to access, update, and modify information stored in MDB database files. Visual Basic, Access Basic, and Excel Visual Basic currently can use the same code to perform operations involving tables and queries stored in an Access MDB file. This means you can write the same program using the same commands in both Access and Excel.

Which should you use?

The purpose of Access macros and Access Basic overlap in some areas. You can achieve a high degree of customization with macro actions alone. However, almost all macro actions have Access Basic equivalents or can be executed as part of an Access Basic program. In other words, Access Basic is a *superset* of Access macros. Access Basic commands include all the macro actions as well as additional features that can be performed only in Access Basic.

User-defined menus, keyboard shortcut keys, and toolbar icons can be implemented only with macro actions. However, the Access Basic DoCmd statement allows you to execute macro actions from within an Access Basic program. ∎

Which should you use? While Access 1.0 was being tested, I heard heated arguments about macros versus Basic. I tend to prefer Access Basic. In practice, I find it is easier to monitor, revise, and debug an Access Basic function than a similar macro. This might not seem to make sense at first because writing program lines is subject to more initial mistakes than simply selecting macro actions and filling in property sheets. However, once you get comfortable with the Access Basic language, you will find that editing a program is often quicker than changing the structure of a macro sheet.

One critical difference between Access Basic and Access macros is that macros are limited to *actions*, whereas Access Basic consists of *commands* and *statements*.

All macro actions change or manipulate some part of the database. For example, you might create macros for printing a report, setting a control's value, or closing a form.

Access Basic uses commands to carry out actions. However, statements add another dimension to Access Basic. Statements allow Access Basic to create powerful structures, such as programming loops, which can process large amounts of data. Access Basic also has powerful tools for manipulating database objects, such as record sets, tables, forms, and controls.

The commands and statements you write as part of an Access Basic module are called *code*. The term refers to the fact that programming languages have their own vocabulary and grammar that dictate how the lines should be written. Because the vocabulary and grammar differ from plain English, reading a program is like reading a secret code. Only those people who know the key words can understand what the code means.

Event Procedures and Modules

In Version 2.0, Access Basic can be used to program in twotypes of things:

- **Event procedures.** Forms and reports, and the controls that appear on them, have event properties that can be used to trigger macro actions. Access allows you to define an Access Basic procedure instead of a macro for any of the event properties possessed by a form, a report, or any of the controls that appear on either. These procedures are stored as part of the form.

- **Module functions.** If you want to create Access Basic procedures that are not linked to a specific event on a form or a report, you can create your own Access Basic functions stored in modules. A *module* is an Access object whose only purpose is to store Access Basic code and procedures. Once a function is defined and stored in a module, you can use it in any expression, just like the functions that are built into Access.

Event procedures are the easiest way to begin using Access Basic because the code is stored as part of a form, report, or control. On the other hand, code entered as an event procedure cannot be used in other circumstances. Functions defined in modules are available anywhere in Access. Keep in mind that they both use the same set of Access Basic commands and statements. Access Basic functions are discussed in Chapter 10.

Creating an Event Procedure

Event procedures are similar to macros in that they are automatically triggered when user interaction with a form or report generates a specific event. Instead of using macro actions, event procedures use Access Basic commands and statements. There are a few reasons for using an event procedure instead of a macro:

✔ **Style.** After you become acquainted with Access Basic code, you may find that you prefer it to creating macros. Because writing code is like editing text, you can often speed up the process with such features as copy and paste, and search and replace.

✔ **Features.** You can duplicate almost all macro actions with Access Basic commands. In addition, Access Basic provides commands, statements, and operations that are beyond the scope of Access macros.

To understand how to create Access Basic event procedures, you can revisit some of the examples used in Chapter 5 to illustrate how macros operate. The first example is the form pictured in Figure 8-1. In Chapter 5, SetValue macro actions were used to calculate the *Total Tax* and *Total* values. A macro called Calc Controls was created and linked to the AfterUpdate event property of the three controls — *Total Parts, Total Labor, Tax Rate* — that are used to calculate the value of *Total Tax* and *Total*.

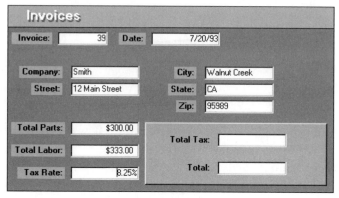

Figure 8-1:
This invoice
form needs
a procedure
to calculate
Total Tax
and Total.

How can you accomplish the same calculation with Access Basic event procedures? You start exactly as you would if you were creating a macro:

1. Place the form in the design mode and select the control whose update will trigger the calculation. In this case, *Total Parts* is one of the controls that triggers the update of *Total Tax* and *Total*.

2. Display the Event Properties sheet for this control and select the event that will trigger the Access Basic procedure.

In this example, the AfterUpdate event will trigger the calculation because any change in the value of *Total Parts* must then be reflected in *Total Tax* and *Total*.

3. Click on the ellipsis (...) icon to display the Choose Builder dialog box. Up to this point, the process has been identical to that used to create a macro. The change comes when you select the Access builder.

4. Select the Code Builder.

As shown in Figure 8-2, Access displays the event procedure window. You use this window to enter the code that Access will run when the AfterUpdate event is triggered.

Figure 8-2:
The Code
Builder
displays the
event
procedure
window.

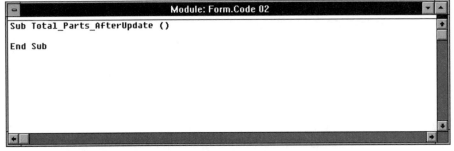

```
Module: Form.Code 02

Sub Total_Parts_AfterUpdate ()

End Sub
```

The window already contains two statements:

✔ **Sub**. This statement indicates the beginning of a subroutine. The Sub statement is followed by the name of the procedure. Because this is an event procedure, Access creates a name composed of the control name and the event name: Total_Parts_AfterUpdate. The name of the procedure is always followed by parentheses ( ). Later you will see how the parentheses are used to pass values from one procedure to another.

✔ **End Sub**. This statement indicates the end of the current procedure. Recall that a macro ends when the last action is executed or a Sto Macro action is entered. Every procedure must have a statement that marks its end.

All the commands and statements to be included in the procedure must be entered between the Sub and End Sub statements.

The toolbar icons for the Access Basic event procedure window (the module design mode) are shown in Table 8-1.

Table 8-1: Module design toolbar icons

Icon	Name	Icon	Name
	Previous Procedure		Step Over
	Next Procedure		Reset
	New Procedure		Toggle Breakpoint
	Run		Expression Builder
	Compile Modules		Immediate Window
	Step Into		Calls

Entering Access Basic code

The term *code* refers to the text entered into a procedure. Access Basic is composed of statements and commands that must conform to a set of established rules. Access automatically checks each line you enter for any obvious errors. This syntax checking process is discussed later in this chapter.

Aside from the structure of the individual commands and statements, a few general rules apply to all Access Basic code:

- Each command or statement must be written on a single line. You cannot break up a long command into consecutive lines.

- If you want to, you can place more than one command on a single line by inserting a colon between commands.

- White space — spaces, tabs, or blank lines — is ignored and has no effect on the code. You can take advantage of this by using tabs to indent lines of code to indicate relationships. Indenting related lines of code can make the code easier to read. It has no effect on how Access executes the code.

- Access Basic is not case sensitive. In this book and in the Access documentation, commands are entered in various combinations of upper- and lower- case letters. This can make the code easier to read. It has no effect on the procedure.

In this book, all the Access Basic commands and statements between Sub and End Sub are indented at least one tab from the left to indicate that they are contained within the subroutine. Other statements may be further indented to highlight logical structures within the procedure. More about this later. The next step is to start entering the code into the procedure.

Setting Values

The purpose of this procedure is to set the value of two controls by performing some simple arithmetic. We need to multiply *Total Parts* by *Tax Rate* to get the *Total Tax*. In Chapter 5, this was accomplished with a SetValue action. In Access Basic, it is accomplished with the *Let* statement. Let evaluates an expression and assigns the calculated value to the specified item. The Let statement has the following general form:

```
Let item = expression
```

Using the current example, the following statement assigns the result of the expression *[Total Parts]*[Tax Rate]* to *[Total Tax]*:

```
Let [Total Tax]=[Total Parts]*[Tax Rate]
```

If you have some programming experience, the preceding statement may look unusual. The keyword *Let* is optional and has been so in many forms of the Basic programming language for more than a dozen years. Many programmers never use Let. Instead, they simply write the statement as *item=expression:*

```
[Total Tax]=[Total Parts]*[Tax Rate]
```

Access Basic recognizes this as a *Let* statement — the equivalent of a SetValue macro action.

Throughout this book, I will follow the convention and omit the word *Let* in these statements. However, when you see a line of code like the preceding statement, you need to remember that it is a statement, *not* an expression. The equal sign in a statement has a different meaning than it has in an expression. I can illustrate this with the following statement, which is commonly referred to as a *counter* :

```
x = x+1
```

What does this mean? If you treat it as an expression, it makes no sense. How can a value *x* be equal to itself plus 1? Such an expression would always evaluate to a False value. But it is not an expression — it is the commonly used form of the Let statement. As such, it should be read as *Let x be assigned the value of x plus 1*. This form of the Let statement is called a counter because it increases some value each time it is executed. This is how a counter field works when a new record is added to a table.

To understand Access Basic code, you may find it helpful to mentally insert the word *let* when you read these statements. This will remind you that the meaning of these statements differs from comparison expressions that also contain equal signs.

To enter the first statement into the procedure, do the following:

1. Press **Tab** to indent the line.

2. Type **[Total Tax]=[Total Parts]*[Tax Rate]**

3. Press **Enter.**

Checking syntax

When you pressed **Enter** after the preceding line of code, you probably noticed that Access rewrote the line and inserted spaces between the identifiers and the operators:

```
Your Entry:      [Total Tax]=[Total Parts]*[Tax Rate]

Changed To:      [Total Tax] = [Total Parts] * [Tax Rate]
```

How and why? The Access code syntax checking feature automatically examines each line of code for obvious syntax errors and omissions. As part of this process, the syntax checker must parse the command or statement. The term *parse* refers to breaking up the sentence into its individual parts. It's similar to the way you used to analyze sentences in English class.

The syntax checker analyzes the parts to see if they form a correctly entered command or statement. This process actually rewrites the command, often changing the capitalization and inserting spaces to make the lines more readable.

Access also supports an auto-indent feature. Notice that the insert point is positioned at the same tab as the preceding line, not the left edge of the window. Auto-indent assumes that you want to continue entering lines at the same indent unless you specifically add or delete a tab.

The extra spaces added to the previous entry have no effect on the meaning of the code; they are purely cosmetic. What would happen if you made a mistake? Find out by making another entry:

1. Type **[Total Amount]=Total Parts+[Total Labor]+[Tax Rate]**

2. Press **Enter**.

As soon as you press Enter, Access analyzes the command and displays the dialog box shown in Figure 8-3. The message indicates that Access encountered an error in the newly entered line of code. In addition, the syntax checker highlights the part of the line that appears to be in error.

The error message reads *Expected: end-of-statement*. The error message is displayed, because the identifier *Total Parts* is not enclosed in brackets — [ ]. Without the brackets, the line appears to use two identifier names — *Total* and *Parts* — with no operator between them. Select **OK** to close the error message box and return to the procedure window. Correct the line to read:

```
[Total Amount]=[Total Parts]+[Total Labor]+[Tax Rate]
```

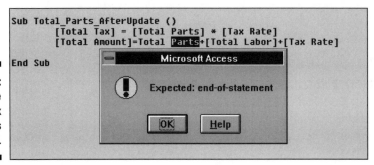

```
Sub Total_Parts_AfterUpdate ()
        [Total Tax] = [Total Parts] * [Tax Rate]
        [Total Amount]=Total Parts+[Total Labor]+[Tax Rate]

End Sub              ┌───── Microsoft Access ──────┐
                     │                             │
                     │ (!)   Expected: end-of-statement │
                     │                             │
                     │      ┌──OK──┐   ┌──Help──┐  │
                     │      └──────┘   └────────┘  │
                     └─────────────────────────────┘
```

Figure 8-3:
A code
syntax
error is
encountered.

Complete the entry by pressing **End** and then **Enter**. This time, Access analyzes the line, inserts spaces, but does not display an error message. This means the code is entered correctly. Or does it?

Compiling Code

Before you can run an Access Basic program, it must be compiled. *Compiling* is a process that converts your code into a form that can be executed by Access. As part of the compiling process, Access also performs a series of checks to help ensure that the statements you have entered are correct.

In Access, you don't need to specifically compile your procedures. If you haven't manually compiled your code before you try to run it, Access automatically initiates the compiling process for you.

Why does Access check your code if each line has already been checked when you entered it? A statement may be grammatically correct — that is, it may have the right number of brackets and operators — but still be logically incorrect.

For example, consider the statement you just entered. The identifier you need to set is actually named *Total,* not *Total Amount.* When you run the program, Access won't be able to carry out the instruction because it won't be able to find a control named *Total Amount* on the current form.

To catch logical errors such as using the wrong identifier name, Access has a second level of checking that is part of the compiling process. Access automatically compiles all of the code before it is executed. You can also manually initiate a compile at any time by using the **Run | Compile Loaded Modules** command or the Compile icon on the toolbar.

When you select the Compile icon, Access locates the logical error in the second statement. As shown in Figure 8-4, Access highlights the identifier *[Total Amount]* and displays a message box with the error message *Invalid object reference.*

Figure 8-4:
Compiling
seeks
logical
errors such
as incorrect
identifier
names.

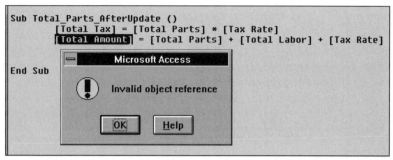

```
Sub Total_Parts_AfterUpdate ()
        [Total Tax] = [Total Parts] * [Tax Rate]
        [Total Amount] = [Total Parts] + [Total Labor] + [Tax Rate]

End Sub
```

Of course, there is no magic involved. When compiling, Access checks the controls on the form to determine whether the identifier name exists. In this case, Access can't find a control with the name *Total Amount,* so an error message is produced. Select **OK** and make the correction; change the name to *Total.* You can then compile the code again. Because there are no more errors in the code, the compiling process will proceed to completion, confirming that no errors were found. See figure 8-5.

```
Module: Form.Code 02
Sub Total_Parts_AfterUpdate ()
        [Total Tax] = [Total Parts] * [Tax Rate]
        [Total] = [Total Parts] + [Total Labor] + [Tax Rate]
End Sub
```

Figure 8-5: The completed Access Basic event procedure sets control values.

Note the difference in the two types of checking performed by Access. The line-by-line syntax check finds errors in each line of code. Compiling checks the items in the lines against the objects defined in the procedures or in the objects directly addressed by the procedure. In this example, the object is the form in which the code will be stored.

In some instances, you may find line-by-line syntax check annoying. This is particularly true when you are entering code in partial or incomplete lines. For example, while you are entering a command, you often need to jump to another line or another window to check some information. The syntax checker will stop you each time you leave a line that is incomplete. The **View** | **Options** command lets you turn off line-by-line syntax checking. Select **Module Design** and set the Syntax Checking property to No. ■

Debugging a Procedure

Access provides several tools to help you test your code and identify needed changes. Although the code in Figure 8-5 is a very simple procedure, it is still useful for understanding how to use these features.

Setting breakpoints

One of the most effective methods for testing and debugging a procedure is to set one or more breakpoints. You can designate any line in your procedure as a breakpoint. When Access executes the procedure, it halts execution of the code before the breakpoint line is executed.

To set a breakpoint, place the insert point on the line you want to designate as the breakpoint, and then selecting **Run** | **Toggle Breakpoint** or press **F9**. Breakpoints are similar to the Step mode used with macros. However, you can set breakpoints at any location in the procedure.

To execute the example procedure in a manner similar to Step mode, you need to place a breakpoint on the Sub statement at the beginning of the procedure. To do this, place the insert point on the Sub line and press **F9**. See Figure 8-6.

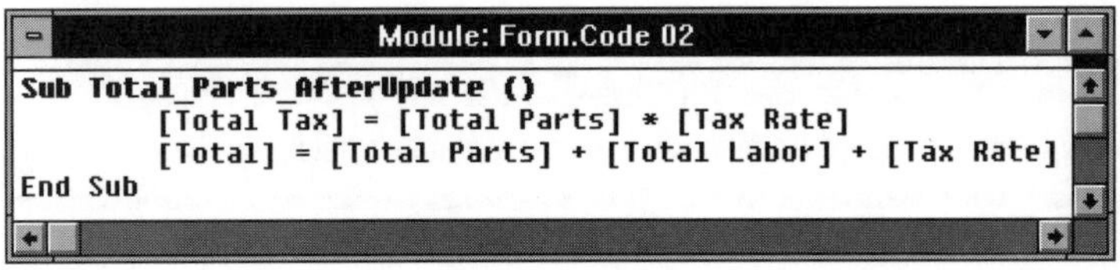

```
┌─────────────────────────────────────────────────────────┐
│ ⊟              Module: Form.Code 02                ▼ ▲  │
├─────────────────────────────────────────────────────────┤
│ Sub Total_Parts_AfterUpdate ()                       ↑  │
│        [Total Tax] = [Total Parts] * [Tax Rate]         │
│        [Total] = [Total Parts] + [Total Labor] + [Tax Rate] │
│ End Sub                                              ↓  │
├─────────────────────────────────────────────────────────┤
│ ◄ ▮                                                  ► │
└─────────────────────────────────────────────────────────┘
```

Figure 8-6: A breakpoint is placed at the start of the procedure.

To run the procedure, you must return to the form design window. However, you don't want to close the code window, because doing so automatically turns off all the breakpoints. Instead, you can switch back to the form design window by clicking on that window (if it is visible), by selecting it from the **Window** menu, or by using the shortcut key **Ctrl-F6**.

As shown in Figure 8-7, the Event Properties sheet for the *Total Parts* control lists [Event Procedure] as the AfterUpdate property. Access shows [Event Procedure] for every event property for which an Access Basic procedure has been created.

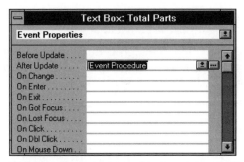

Figure 8-7: [Event Procedure] indicates that an Access Basic procedure has been defined for this property.

At this point, you are ready to test the procedure by placing the form in the design mode and editing the control that triggers the procedure:

1. Click on the Form View icon.

2. Move the insert point to the *Total Parts* control and enter a new value.

3. Press **Tab** to update the control.

This action triggers the procedure created for the AfterUpdate event. Because you set a breakpoint, Access halts execution of the procedure *before* the first command or statement. As shown in Figure 8-8, the breakpoint causes Access to display the code window and place an outline around the line of code that will be executed next if you continue the procedure.

Figure 8-8: The breakpoint halts execution of the procedure and outlines the next command.

When you halt the procedure with a breakpoint, you have four options:

✔ **Step Into (execute next).** The **Run** | **Step Into** command executes the currently highlighted line and then halts execution again. This is equivalent to stepping through the procedure one command at a time. The shortcut key is **F8**. You can step through the procedure by pressing **F8** once for each command.

> ✔ **Step Over. <u>R</u>un | Step Over** skips the outlined command and moves to the next command in the procedure. The shortcut key is **Shift-F8**.
>
> ✔ **Continue.** This restarts execution of the procedure beginning with the next command and continuing until the procedure is complete or another breakpoint is encountered. The shortcut key is **F5**.
>
> ✔ **Reset.** The **<u>R</u>un | <u>R</u>eset** command terminates execution of the procedure before the next command is executed.

Using the Immediate window

One of the reasons for using a breakpoint is to examine the objects as the procedure is executed. You can also do this with the Immediate window. The *Immediate window* is a special window that can be viewed only when you are working in an Access Basic code window.

Open the Immediate window by selecting the menu command **<u>V</u>iew | <u>I</u>mmediate Window**. Access displays a blank window. The window title shows the name of the form and the name of the currently executing procedure. The Immediate window can be used to perform a variety of tasks that are related to, but not a permanent part of, the current procedure.

The most common task performed in the Immediate window is the display of various values indicating exactly what's going on during the execution of the procedure. This is done through the use of the **Print** command. Print displays the value of a field, a control, a property, or any valid Access expression.

For example, one of the purposes of the example procedure is to change the value of the *Total Tax* control. To see if this happens, you can use the Immediate window to display the value of the control at different points in the procedure. You do this by entering a Print command into the Immediate window:

1. Type **print [Total Tax]**.

2. Press Enter.

   Access responds by displaying the current value of the control. Figure 8-9 shows that the current value of the control in the example is 0.

3. Press **F8** to execute the next command in the procedure.

The command that is executed should change the value of *Total Tax*. You can confirm this by returning to the Immediate window and displaying the value of *Total Tax*. To return to the Immediate window, simply click on it.

You can save some time by using the shortcut name for the Print command, which is **?**. The use of **?** for Print is common to most versions of Basic. In this example, you should type the following:

? [total tax]

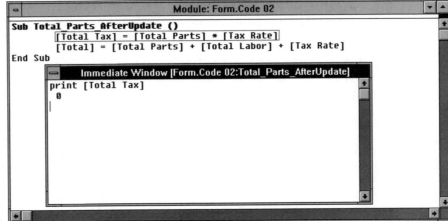

Figure 8-9:
The Immediate window displays values during execution of a procedure.

As shown in Figure 8-10, Access displays the newly calculated value of *Total Tax*. This confirms that the Access Basic statement just executed had the desired effect of changing the value of the *Total Tax*.

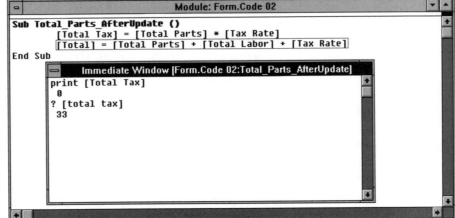

Figure 8-10:
The Immediate window shows the change in the value of Total Tax.

You can avoid reentering the same command in the Immediate window by reexecuting the command. Place the insert point on any command line in the Immediate window and press **Enter**. Access executes the command again. The new result replaces the previous result. ▪

Keep in mind that you can display any type of value in the Immediate window, not just values related to the current procedure. Complete the procedure by pressing **F5**, the Continue command.

When the procedure is completed, Access does not return the focus to the form. The focus remains in the Access Basic window until you specifically switch back to the form — for example, by pressing Ctrl-F6.

The Immediate window retains the displayed information for the duration of the current session. This means that you can close and open windows — including the Immediate window, the Access Basic code window, or even the form window — without losing the items in the Immediate window. You can execute one or more procedures several times and compare various values that occur during different runs to determine how accurately your code is processing the data. In many cases, the information in the Immediate window is the only way you can tell exactly what's going on during the execution of Access Basic code.

You can manually erase commands and output from the Immediate window by highlighting the items and pressing **Del**. A shortcut method of clearing the entire window when the insert point is at the bottom of the window is to press **Ctrl-Shift-Home** to highlight all the items to the top of the window, and then to press **Del** to delete the text.

Clearing breakpoints

To run the procedure without breakpoints, you must clear any breakpoints in the procedure using one of the following methods:

- ✔ **Close the code window.** When you close the procedure's code window, Access automatically clears all breakpoints from the code.
- ✔ **Toggle with F9.** You can turn off breakpoints one at a time by placing the insert point on a breakpoint line and pressing **F9**. This removes the line as a breakpoint. The text is no longer displayed in bold.
- ✔ **Clear All.** The **Run** | **Clear All Breakpoints** command clears all breakpoints in the current module.

The last two methods can be used when you want to leave the Access Basic window open but don't want to halt the procedures as they execute. This is useful when you want to use the *debug* object, which is discussed in the next section.

The Clear All Breakpoints command affects all procedures in the current module, not just the displayed procedure. Access stores all of the event procedures defined for one form in a single module stored as part of the form. This module is called the Form module.

The debug object

In the preceding section, you learned how to use the Immediate window to display values when you manually enter print commands. Another approach to using the Immediate window is through the debug object. In effect, the Immediate window is the debug object — that is, you can direct Access Basic to display information in the Immediate window by referring to *debug* as a database object. The following command prints the value of the *Total Tax* control in the Immediate window.

```
debug.print [total tax]
```

In this command, **print** is called a *method*. Methods are actions that can be performed on specific database objects. You will learn more about methods as you get deeper into Access Basic. In this case, the print method is used to indicate which action should be performed on the object (the Immediate window).

In the current version of Access, the debug object has only one method, print. In other words, debug.print is the only form available at this time.

By using debug.print to place information in the Immediate window, you can test a procedure through normal interaction with the form, without jumping back and forth between the form and the Access Basic code window. At the same time, you still produce a detailed picture of what's going on during execution of the procedure.

In the following example, a series of debug.print statements have been added to the procedure. The group of statements at the beginning of the procedure writes the current value of *Total Tax* and *Total* when the procedure begins. The second group of statements, positioned after the calculation section of the procedure, writes the ending values into the Immediate window.

```
Sub Total_Parts_AfterUpdate ()
    Debug.Print "Start Procedure Total Parts AfterUpdate"
    Debug.Print "Total Tax = ", [Total Tax]
    Debug.Print "Total = ", [Total]
    [Total Tax] = [Total Parts] * [Tax Rate]
    [Total] = [Total Parts] + [Total Labor] + [Tax Rate]
    Debug.Print "End Procedure Total Parts AfterUpdate"
    Debug.Print "Total Tax = ", [Total Tax]
    Debug.Print "Total = ", [Total]
End Sub
```

It is important to remember that debug.print writes information to the Immediate window regardless of whether the Access Basic procedure window or the Immediate window is open. For example, suppose you closed the procedure window by pressing Ctrl-F4.

Access doesn't prompt you to save the procedure code, because the code is stored in the form's Access Basic module. Access saves all of the procedures in one form as a single unit when the form is saved. Conversely, if you discard changes that you've made to a form, Access discards all the changes you've made to any of the procedures attached to that form. ■

You can now change to the form view mode and interact with the form as much as you like. In this example, each time you update the *Total Parts* control, Access executes the procedure that inserts new values into *Total Tax* and *Total*. The debug.print statements have no visible effects. However, you shouldn't conclude that they aren't working. Even though you can't see the information, it is written into the Immediate window each time the procedure executes.

To check the operation of the procedure, place the form in the design mode and open the Access Basic code window. Because there is only one Immediate window, it doesn't matter which procedure is displayed when you inspect the Immediate window. For this example, however, it makes sense to open the Total_Parts_Update procedure:

1. Select the *Total Parts* control.

2. Select the ellipsis (...) icon button in the AfterUpdate property.

As shown in Figure 8-11, this reveals the information written into the Immediate window. For each time the procedure was executed, the Immediate window shows the starting and ending values.

```
Module: Form.Code 02
Sub Total_Parts_AfterUpdate ()
        Debug.Print "Start Procedure Total Parts AfterUpdate"
        Debug.Print "Total Tax = ", [Total Tax]
        Debug.Print "Total = ", [Total]
        [Total Tax] = [Total Parts] * [Tax Rate]
        [Total] = [Total Parts] + [Total Labor] + [Tax Rate]
        Debug.Print "End Procedure Total Parts AfterUpdate"
        Debug.Print "Total Tax = ", [Total Tax]
        Debug.Print "Total = ", [Total]
        Debug.Print
End Sub
        Immediate Window [Form.Code 02]
        Start Procedure Total Parts AfterUpdate
        Total Tax =        33
        Total =            400.0825
        End Procedure Total Parts AfterUpdate
        Total Tax =        82.5
        Total =            1000.0825
```

Figure 8-11: Debug.print writes information to the Immediate window.

Adding Notes

Because debug.print statements don't affect the normal Access display, you can leave these statements in your procedures as long as you like. However, you might want to remove these statements after you are sure that the procedure performs as desired.

Instead of deleting statements, you can turn them into notes. A *note* is a line in an Access Basic procedure that is ignored when the procedure is executed. A note is designated by placing a single quote (") as the first visible character in the line. Notes have two purposes:

- ✔ You can *turn off* statements by placing a single quote at the beginning of the statement. This allows you to run the procedure without the effect of the statement, but without deleting it. If you change your mind and want to reactivate the command, just delete the single quote.

- ✔ You can insert informational notes about the purpose and function of the procedure. The purpose of a procedure may be clear when you are working on it, but a few weeks later you may not be able to recall what you were trying to accomplish. Notes can also help other people understand your procedures.

The following block of code uses single quotes to turn off all the debug.print statements without deleting them:

```
Sub Total_Parts_AfterUpdate ()
        'Debug.Print "Start Procedure Total Parts AfterUpdate"
        'Debug.Print "Total Tax = ", [Total Tax]
        'Debug.Print "Total = ", [Total]
        [Total Tax] = [Total Parts] * [Tax Rate]
        [Total] = [Total Parts] + [Total Labor] + [Tax Rate]
        'Debug.Print "End Procedure Total Parts AfterUpdate"
        'Debug.Print "Total Tax = ", [Total Tax]
        'Debug.Print "Total = ", [Total]
End Sub
```

Changing a command or statement to a note can be used in a variety of ways when you are testing a procedure. For example, suppose you want to test several variations of the same command. You can enter all the versions into the procedure and place single quotes in front of all the lines except one. Then you can test each variation by running the procedure with a different command left "un-noted" each time. ∎

Notes can be entire lines or they can be attached to the end of an existing statement. In the following example, informational notes are added to the end of calculation statements:

```
[Total Tax] = [Total Parts] * [Tax Rate] 'Calc sales tax
[Total] = [Total Parts] + [Total Labor] + [Tax Rate] 'calc invoice total
```

Access ignores any portion of a line that follows a single quote.

Chapter 9
Access Basic Form Modules

●●

In This Chapter

▶ Writing procedures in a form module

▶ Linking one procedure to several events

▶ Selecting procedures in the code window

▶ Altering object properties with Access Basic

▶ Using If...Then...Else

●●

*A*ll Access Basic procedures are stored in *modules.* Each module can contain one or more procedures. Access supports two types of modules:

✔ **Form or report modules.** The procedures in this type of module are created during the design of a form or report, and they are stored as part of the form or report. The procedures you store in a form or report module are available only when you are using that specific form or report.

✔ **Database modules.** These modules are not attached to a specific form or report, and they are saved independently from all other database objects. Access displays the names of these modules on the Module list in the database window. Procedures stored in these modules are accessible from any object in the database.

This chapter shows you how to use a form module to manage event procedures for the objects in a form or a report. Database level modules and procedures are covered in chapter 10. Report modules are identical to form modules except there are fewer ways in which the user can interact with a form than a report. Specific report operations are discussed in Part IV.

Form Procedures

Forms contain three types of objects that can generate events:

✔ **The form.** The *form* refers to properties and actions that affect the form as a whole, such as opening and closing the form or updating an entire record.

✓ **Sections.** All forms have at least one section called the *detail section*. You also have the option of adding header and footer sections to the form. Access supports separate print and display header and footer sections, giving you a total of five possible sections on each form.

✓ **Controls.** Controls are the most important elements in a form, particularly when it comes to such user actions as data entry and editing.

You can display the form's module code window at any time with the **View** | **Code** command. ▪

The form's Access Basic module can hold a separate procedure for *each* of the possible events for all of these controls. Access keeps track of all these event procedures with two list boxes that appear on the left side of the Access Basic design toolbar. The list on the left in Figure 9-1 is called the *object* list. The object list includes the name of every control on the form that can have an event procedure defined for it, as well as the name *Form* for the overall form, and the names of any sections currently in use, such as *Detail0* or *FormHeader1*.

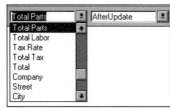

Figure 9-1: The object list shows all objects in the form for which event procedures can be defined.

The second list, which is shown in Figure 9-2, is called the *procedures* list. For the selected objects, the procedures list identifies all of the possible events for which separate procedures can be defined.

Figure 9-2: The procedures list shows events that can be defined for the current object.

A check mark is displayed next to the names of events for which a procedure is defined. Those without check marks are *possible* event procedures for this object; in other words, no code has been entered for the events.

You can use these two lists to navigate among all of the actual and possible event procedures for a single form, without returning to the form design window. As you'll see in the next section, this is handy when you want to define interactions among procedures in the same form.

 A text control that functions as a label for a data control doesn't have its own event properties. However, label controls that are individually placed on the form using the Label tool have mouse event properties. This means you can define macro or Access Basic procedures that are triggered by a mouse click or movement onto these controls. ■

Linking Event Procedures to Other Event Properties

It's often necessary to trigger the same set of calculations each time a specific event affects the value of one or more controls. For example, the macros you created in Chapter 5 calculate new values for *Total Tax* and *Total* each time an AfterUpdate event is triggered by the editing of any one of three controls — *Total Parts, Total Labor,* or *Tax Rate.*

In Chapter 5, the problem was solved by executing the same macro, Calc Control, from each control's AfterUpdate event property. This is possible because all macros are stored in a macro sheet that is independent of any one form. A macro defined in one form can be used in any other form in the database, assuming that its action fits that form.

Access Basic event procedures are stored as part of the form and cannot be accessed from other forms. But what about using an event procedure for another control in the *same* form?

You can do this, but the method is different for event procedures than it is for macros. Procedures stored in a form's Access Basic module can interact with each other by calling one procedure from another procedure. A call is made with the Call statement followed by the name of the procedure you want to execute. The following example calls the procedure Total_Parts_AfterUpdate:

```
Call Total_Parts_AfterUpdate
```

The term *call* has a specific meaning in Access Basic. When one procedure calls another, control is transferred from the calling procedure to the procedure that is being called. Access then executes the entire called procedure.

When that procedure is finished, Access returns to the calling procedure and executes the next statement, if any, in the calling procedure.

A simple Call operation is diagrammed in Figure 9-3. A procedure named *A( )* contains a statement *Call B*. When Access executes this statement, control is passed to the procedure named *B( )*. Access executes all of the statements in *B( )* until *End Sub* is reached. When *B( )* is finished, that is, when Access reaches the *End Sub* statement in *B( )* , Access returns to *A( )* and continues by executing the next statement in *A( )*, if any.

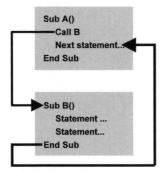

Figure 9-3: A Call statement executes a subroutine procedure and then returns to the calling procedure.

As with the Let statement, the Call keyword is not required in most versions of Basic. You can simply enter the name of the procedure you want to call as a complete statement:

```
Total_Parts_AfterUpdate
```

This statement calls Total_Parts_AfterUpdate.

If you are new to Basic, you may want to consider using the Call keyword to make it absolutely clear which lines in your code call other procedures. However, most programmers never use Call, and I follow convention and use the simplified form throughout the rest of this book.

In the current example, you want to call the procedure defined for the AfterUpdate property of the *Total Parts* control. The call should come from the AfterUpdate event property of either the *Total Labor* or the *Tax Rate* control.

The technique you use is the same as the one for writing a new procedure. You begin by selecting the control and an event property for which you want to define a procedure:

1. Select the *Total Labor* control.

2. Select the AfterUpdate event property.

3. Select the ellipsis (...) icon to open the Builder dialog box.

4. Select Code Builder.

You have opened the form's Access Basic code window. This is the same window you used to create the previous procedure. However, it's opened to a different object and event — Total_Labor_AfterUpdate — because all the event procedures for one form are stored in the same module.

You can now enter the *call* to the Total_Parts_AfterUpdate procedure:

1. Press **Tab**.

2. Type **Total_Parts_AfterUpdate**

Selecting Procedures in the Code Window

You also want to execute the Total_Parts_AfterUpdate procedure when the AfterUpdate event property of the *Tax Rate* control is triggered. When the code window is displayed, you can display any event procedure related to the current form without leaving this window. Access provides several methods for selecting the procedure you want to display:

✔ **Next Procedure and Previous Procedure.** You can scroll through the procedures contained in the current form's Access Basic module using the **View** | **Next Procedure** and **View** | **Pre̲vious Procedure** commands. You can also use the Ctrl-Down arrow and Ctrl-Up arrow keys, or click the Next Procedure and Previous Procedure toolbar icons.

Note that these commands will display only procedure events for which you have entered Access Basic code.

✔ **The object and procedures lists.** The module design toolbar contains two boxes (Figure 9-1 and Figure 9-2) that allow you to display any event procedure for any object on the form. This method allows you to access event procedures for which no Access Basic code is entered.

✔ **The Procedures dialog box.** When any module window is active, you can display the Procedures dialog box shown in Figure 9-4 by pressing **F2**. This box lists all of the procedures stored in any of the modules (form, report, or standalone) in the current database. The module names appear in the Modules list. The names of the procedures in the highlighted module appear in the Procedures list. The names of form modules are preceded by *Form_*.

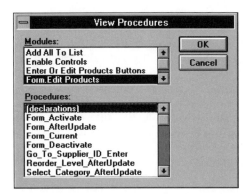

Figure 9-4: In the Procedures dialog box, all of the procedures stored in all of the modules of the current database are displayed.

In this case, you want to display the procedure for the AfterUpdate event of the *Tax Rate* control:

Select **Tax Rate** from the Object list box.

Access changes the procedure display to the BeforeUpdate procedure for *Tax Rate*. BeforeUpdate is displayed because it is the first event property available for the *Tax Rate* control. Next, change the event to AfterUpdate:

Select **AfterUpdate** from the property list box.

Because this event should trigger the same code used for the object event Total_Parts_AfterUpdate, enter a Call statement to execute that procedure:

Press **Tab**.
Enter **Total_Parts_AfterUpdate**

You have now set up the form so that any change in *Total Parts*, *Total Labor*, or *Tax Rate* will execute the code stored in the Total_Parts_AfterUpdate procedure.

Changing Properties with Access Basic

As mentioned, almost all the operations you can perform with macros can be accomplished with Access Basic. In Chapter 6, macros were used in creating a single invoice form that displays different controls depending on whether the user specifies a retail invoice or a wholesale invoice.

As shown in Figure 9-5, the form is divided into three sections. The top section contains controls that are used by all invoices. The bottom is divided into a wholesale section and a retail section . In Chapter 6, a macro was used to change the Visible property of the wholesale and retail controls. The idea was to hide wholesale controls (such as *Company*) on a retail invoice and retail hide controls (such as *Tax Rate*) on a wholesale invoice.

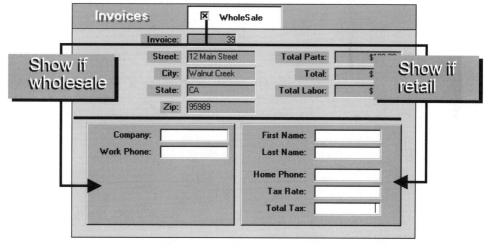

Figure 9-5:
This form displays different controls for retail and wholesale invoices.

How would you implement this concept using event procedures instead of macro actions? Are there advantages to using Access Basic?

First, you need to determine which event procedure you should use. In Chapter 6, you used the AfterUpdate event property of the *Wholesale* control (a check box control). This corresponds to the Wholesale_AfterUpdate procedure. How do I know this? Access generates procedure names by combining the name of the control with the name of the property. It's a simple matter to anticipate the procedure name for a given event.

Having decided in advance which procedure is needed, you can open that code window using a method I haven't discussed yet. Begin by opening the form in the design mode. Instead of selecting a control and using its property sheet, go directly to the Access Basic module of the form by using the **View** | **Code** command.

This time the code window is opened to the *general* section. The command **Option Compare Database** is automatically entered into this section. For now, don't be concerned about the general section and the meaning of the **Option Compare** statement. (The general section and Option Compare are discussed in greater detail in Part III.)

You can use the object and procedures lists on the toolbar to display the code window for any possible event on the form:

Select **wholesale** from the object list on the toolbar.

The *general* section and Option Compare

Each Access Basic module has a *general* section or procedure. This section is used for entering statements that affect all of the procedures in the module. The most common statement is one that defines a non-table identifier name (more commonly called a *variable*) so that it can be used in multiple procedures. You can also declare constants.

The Option Compare statement sets the method used for evaluating comparison expressions with operators such as =, >, or <. The Database option (inserted by default) causes case insensitive matches, such as *"rob"="Rob"*, to be true. It also causes inexact matches, for example *"Rob"="Robert"*, to be true. Greater-than and less-than comparisons use the sort order specified when the database was created. This is meaningful if you select a foreign language sort order. If you delete the Option Compare state-

ment, the previous examples would be treated as false. Only *"Rob"="Rob"* would be true.

Immediately following the Option Compare Statement is a single quotation mark. This signifies that what follows is a descriptive note. Access Basic ignores all characters following a single quotation mark on a line. If you place a single quotation mark at the beginning of a line, Access Basic ignores the entire line.

The **Option Compare Database** statement appears in the *declarations* section of the module. The declarations section is used to enter any statements that are designed to affect the operation of all the procedures in the module. Declarations become important when you have several functions in a module that interact with each other. (The use of the declarations section is discussed in Chapter 11.)

The code window changes to show the procedure for WholeSale_Click. In this case, use the AfterUpdate event to trigger the code:

Select **AfterUpdate** from the procedure list on the toolbar.

To set a property in Access Basic, you use a Let statement. (Remember that a Let statement is the equivalent of a SetValue macro action.) The following statement sets the Visible property of the *Company* control to True — that is, On:

```
Let [Company].Visible = True
```

Recall that the keyword Let is optional in Access Basic. This allows you to enter the statement as follows:

```
[Company].Visible = True
```

You need to enter one statement for each control property that you want to change:

```
[Company].Visible = True
[Work Phone].Visible = True
```

To make a control invisible, simply change the assigned value from True to False:

```
[First Name].Visible=False
[Last Name].Visible=False
```

The constants True and False could be replaced with numeric values — that is, 0 for False and any non-zero number, such as 1, for True. Typing 1 or 0 is simpler than typing the words True or False, but the meaning of the statements is more obscure. Remember that code is not only executed by the computer (which is indifferent to style), but also read by humans (who are influenced by appearances). ▪

The If...Then...Else Structure

The statements in the preceding section toggle the Visible property of the controls on and off. By themselves, however, they don't accomplish the desired goal. What's needed is a method by which certain statements are executed when *Wholesale* is checked (true) and other statements are executed when *Wholesale* is unchecked (false).

In macro actions, you use the Conditions column to create this type of structure. In Access Basic, this structure is created by the use of three statements:

✔ **If *expression* Then**. This statement is placed at the beginning of the structure. It contains a comparison expression that is evaluated as either true or false. If the expression is true, Access executes the next statement in the code. If false, Access skips to the next **Else** or **Endif** statement it encounters.

✔ **Else**. This statement is used by itself as a *marker* within the code. It indicates the point in the structure at which the *If true* statements end and the *If false* statements begin.

✔ **Endif**. This statement marks the end of the structure. Any statements that follow *Endif* are not affected by the *If* expression.

The *Else* statement is similar to the StopMacro action discussed in Chapter 6. There are differences, however. StopMacro can be used anywhere in a macro to halt execution. The *Else* statement can exist only inside an *If...Endif* structure. *Else* doesn't stop execution. Rather, it functions as a sign-post that indicates which block of statements should be skipped based on the value of the *If* expression. ▪

Figure 9-6 shows a diagram of how the *If* structure works. When Access encounters an *If...Then* statement, it evaluates the expression contained on that line as either true or false.

If the expression is true, Access moves to the next statement following the *If...Then* statement. Access continues to execute statements until either an *Else* statement or an *Endif* statement is encountered.

On the other hand, if the expression is false, Access ignores all statements until it encounters either an *Else* statement or an *Endif* statement. If an *Endif* statement is encountered, Access executes all commands between the *Else* and the *Endif* statements.

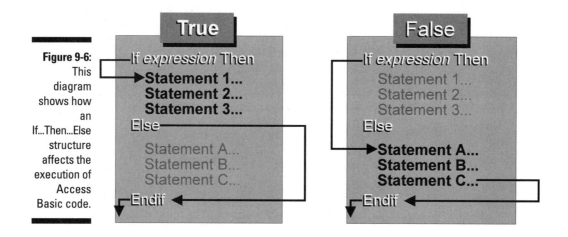

Figure 9-6: This diagram shows how an If...Then...Else structure affects the execution of Access Basic code.

In either case, *Endif* marks the end of the *If* structure. Any statements following *Endif* are not affected by the structure and are executed regardless of the value of the *If* expression.

An *If* structure allows you to have two blocks of statements that are mutually exclusive. Either one block or the other is executed — but never both.

Remember that the *Else* statement is optional. In cases where you don't need an alternative, you can simply use *If...Then* and *Endif.* Figure 9-7 shows this simpler form of *If...Then*, in which a single block of statements is either executed or ignored, based on the value of the condition in the *If* statement.

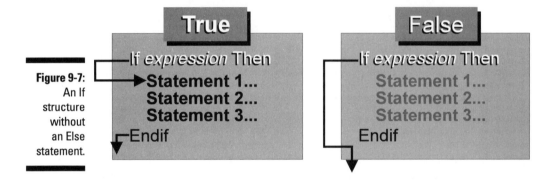

Figure 9-7: An If structure without an Else statement.

The *If* structure is an example of a decision structure. It's called a *decision* structure because Access decides which of the statements included in the procedure should be executed. Decision structures such as *If...Then* allow a single procedure or program to react to different conditions that may occur when the code is executed.

Decision structures work by creating branches within a procedure. A *branch* represents one possible sequence of statements that can be executed. The goal of all programming is to create a procedure or a set of procedures that provides a code branch for each of the possible actions that a user might take.

Of course, such a goal can never be fully achieved. People are just too unpredictable. The key to creating good, if not perfect, applications is the ability to anticipate the most likely user actions and creates branches that accommodate those actions.

A good program will have a *trap* that can handle any unexpected data or actions by having the procedure ignore the input or action. The worst thing a programmer can do is leave a hole in a branch structure. A *hole* occurs when a user action or entry falls through all the branches and traps, and freezes up the computer. Fortunately, Access handles most problems.

Digital versus fuzzy logic

Decision structures, such as those created with *If...Then* statements, are critically important to any programming environment or language. Without the capability to evaluate conditions, it would be impossible to create all but the simplest procedures or macros.

However, if you are new to programming, you need to be keenly aware of the limited nature of the decision branches that can be implemented with computer languages. In today's computers, all expressions, no matter how complicated or elaborate, must be either true or false. Computer logic is strictly a yes - or - no world. An invoice is either wholesale or retail. A city is either New York or not New York. This is called *digital logic* because computers represent all information in off/on notation, usually represented by the numeric values 0 and 1.

Conversely, the real world (in which people conduct business, live their lives, participate in organizations, and so on), is filled with concepts that are not as distinct. In other words, they have many shades of meaning. For example, you may refer to a location such as Englewood Cliffs, N.J. as part of the New York area, while judging that Trenton, N.J. is not in the New York area. But how would you get a computer to make such a judgment? The only way would be to create a list of cities and assign them a distinct value for territory. In other words, you would have to create a concrete list of items from which the computer could make a match — once again, a distinct yes - or -no choice.

Computer researchers have been working on an alternative type of decision structure that would allow computers to use fuzzy logic. *Fuzzy logic* is concerned not with discrete decisions but with rules (most of which overlap to some degree) for making decisions. Each rule would have a statistical weight that would be used to resolve conflicts and overlaps. Fuzzy logic holds out the promise of making computer programming much more similar to human reasoning than it is today. For now, good programming on any level requires the programmer to boil down the fuzzy logic of the world into a form that can fit into structures like *If...Then.*

You can apply an *If* structure to the problem of turning on and off the Visible property of a series of controls. The solution is the following block of Access Basic code:

```
If wholesale Then
        [Company].Visible = True
        [Work Phone].Visible = True
        [First Name].Visible = False
        [Last Name].Visible = False
        [Home Phone].Visible = False
        [Tax Rate].Visible = False
        [Total Tax].Visible = False
```

```
Else
        [Company].Visible = False
        [Work Phone].Visible = False
        [First Name].Visible = True
        [Last Name].Visible = True
        [Home Phone].Visible = True
        [Tax Rate].Visible = True
        [Total Tax].Visible = True
End If
```

This might seem like a lot of typing for changing a few controls. This would be true if you simply entered the text line - for - line as it appears. However, if you look closely at the code, you'll see that many of the lines follow a pattern that lends itself to some editing shortcuts. For example, you can use **Copy** and **Paste** to duplicate text without entering it manually. Here are some tips for entering the procedure with a minimum of typing:

✔ Many of the lines have identical characters, for example:
   ].Visible=
   Once you type the first line, [Company].Visible = True, you can copy].Visible and then paste it on each succeeding line.

✔ The *If* and *Else* statements are mirror images. The statements are identical except that the True and False values are reversed. Once you finish the statements between *If* and *Else*, you can copy and paste the entire block to fill in the *Else...Endif* statements. You need to change only True and False to complete the statements.

✔ You can use **Edit** | **Replace** to swap True and False in various statements.

When writing code, it's important to always look for editing shortcuts. You can often cut down significantly on the amount of typing that is required.

You can use **Copy** and **Paste** to insert the examples of Access Basic statements that appear in the Access help files. Most Access Basic help topics show an example of how the statement is used, or you can open a special window that shows a full code example of the statement. In either window, you can use the **Edit** | **Copy** command or the **Copy** button to open a window in which the text of the topic or example can be selected in part or in whole. You can then paste that command or example into the code window.

You can also paste a generic example of any Access function into a procedure by selecting the Builder icon on the toolbar and opening the Built-In Functions list. A generic version of a function shows phrases in place of each argument — for example, DLookUp(«expr», «domain», «criteria»). You must replace these phrases with valid values or identifiers. ■

Once the code has been entered into the WholeSale_AfterUpdate procedure, you need to consider whether any other events are needed to execute this code. In fact, there are. In addition to reacting to a change in the value of *Wholesale*, the

Figure 9-8:
Access
Basic code
used to
determine
which
controls are
displayed on
a form.

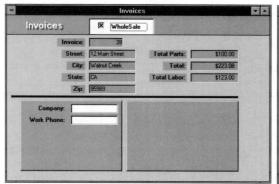

controls must be evaluated each time a different record is displayed on the form, since this may also change the current value of *Wholesale*. See Figure 9-8.

You need to enter a Call statement in the form's OnCurrent event property procedure. Display the Form_Current procedure using the Object and Property lists on the module design toolbar:

1. Select **Form** from the object list on the toolbar.
2. Select **Current** from the procedure list on the toolbar. (Hint: Current is at the top of the property list.) You can call a procedure from another procedure by entering the name of the procedure with or without the Call keyword.
3. Press **Tab**.
4. Type **Wholesale_AfterUpdate**

You have now linked two events — Wholesale_AfterUpdate and Form_OnCurrent — to the same Access Basic code. Figure 9-8 shows the form and the Access Basic procedure that determines which of the controls is visible for any given record.

Chapter 10

Access Basic Functions

- -

- -

*E*vent procedures such as those described in the preceding chapter are only one side of Access Basic. Event procedures that are stored as part of a form affect only that form.

A broader application of Access Basic procedures involves the creation of user-defined functions that are available for use in any expression in the current database. You create your own function by writing an Access Basic procedure that performs the desired task. Once created, you can use the function just like any of the built-in functions supplied with Access.

User-defined functions are powerful tools because they aren't tied to a specific form or report, but can be used in any part of Access, including macros and other Access Basic procedures. This chapter shows you how to create user-defined functions and use them in expressions.

Creating Your Own Functions

The alternative to a form-based module is a standalone Access Basic module. Procedures stored in a standalone module aren't associated with any specific object (form or report) and can be accessed from an expression entered in any part of the database. Standalone modules are listed in the *Modules* section of the database window, which is shown in Figure 10-1.

The primary advantage of using a standalone Access Basic module is that the procedures stored in these modules can be used anywhere in the database.

These modules are used primarily to create user-defined functions. Access has several hundred built-in functions. As you know, these functions are used in expressions to perform special calculations or to return special values. For example, *PMT( )* calculates the monthly payment for a loan, and *Date( )* returns the current system date. A *user-defined function* is an Access Basic procedure that is used to carry out a text, numeric, or chronological calculation of your own design. Once you create a user-defined function, you can use it in any expression in any part of the database, just like the built-in functions supplied with Access.

Figure 10-1:
Stand-alone
modules are
listed in the
Modules
section of
the
database
window.

You may get the impression that functions can be created only in the modules you define on the database level and not on the form level. In fact, you can create both subroutines (Sub...End Sub) and functions in any Access Basic module, including form modules. Subroutine procedures are typically used with form modules because form modules are closely linked to specific event properties. Conversely, database level modules are common for user-defined functions that can be used in many different places. However, you are free to use either type of procedure in either type of module. ■

Identifying Workdays

Suppose you want to determine whether a given date is a *Workday( )*. A workday in this case is defined as any date that falls on a Monday, Tuesday, Wednesday, Thursday, or Friday. Access contains several built-in functions related to dates, but none specifically distinguish a workday from a weekend day. Figure 10-2 shows a simple form with two controls. The first control, Invoice Date, contains a date. The second control is supposed to contain information that indicates whether the invoice date is a weekday.

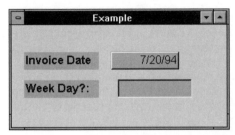

Figure 10-2: A user-defined function is needed for the Week Day control.

The first step in creating a function is to open a new or existing Access Basic code module. In this case, start by opening a new module:

1. Select the Module icon in the database window.

2. Click the **New** button.

Access opens a blank code window showing the general section of the module. For now, ignore the general section and the Option Compare Database statement that appears automatically.

You can create a new function procedure in two ways:

✔ **Select the Edit | New Procedure command**. This command displays the dialog box shown in Figure 10-3. This dialog box allows you to enter the name of the new procedure and select either a Subroutine or Function type procedure. You can also display the dialog box by clicking the New Procedure icon on the toolbar.

✔ **Type in the function.** Access automatically creates a new procedure if you enter a function or sub statement into a code window.

Figure 10-3: You can use the New Procedure dialog box to create a subroutine or function procedure.

If you want to type in the function, the insert point must be on a blank line in any open Access Basic module window. The window can display the general section or a procedure. For example, to create a function procedure named *WorkDay()*, you would type **Function Workday( )** and press **Enter**.

When Access checks the syntax of the statement you have entered (syntax checking is triggered when you press Enter), it finds the Function statement and automatically creates a new procedure with the specified name.

At this point, the window changes and an empty function code window is displayed. In this example, the window begins with a Function statement and ends with an End Function statement. As in a subroutine procedure, the first statement, Function, assigns the name to the function:

```
Function Workday()

End Function
```

The Weekday ( ) function

The key to the user-defined function you are trying to create is a built-in function called *Weekday()*. As shown in Table 10-1, this function returns a numeric value for the day of the week.

Table 10-1: *Weekday ()* values

Day	Value
Sunday	1
Monday	2
Tuesday	3
Wednesday	4
Thursday	5
Friday	6
Saturday	7

This means that if the *Weekday( )* function returns 1 or 7, the date is a weekend. Any other value, (2-6) is a workday. You can express this concept with an *If* structure. The following *If* structure is written in pseudocode that shows how a date is classified as either a weekend or workday:

```
If Weekday(Invoice Date) = 1
```

```
Or Weekday(Invoice Date) = 7
The date is a weekend

Else
The date is a working day

Endif
```

Pseudocode is a block of text that is written partly in computer language and partly in English. In the previous example, the portions in **bold** are Access Basic code. The portions in *italic* are English phrases that hold the place of a statement, an expression, or an identifier that you need to fill in before the code is ready to run.

Pseudocode is used in the Expression Builder when a function is pasted into the window. Pseudocode is useful because it allows you to set up the basic structure of a program and then fill in the details. In this case, two details must be added before the code is ready for use.

Passing a value to a function

In the If structure that I've outlined in pseudocode, the *If* statement uses the phrase *Invoice Date* to represent the date value that the function will analyze. Exactly which identifier should be used in place of this phrase?

One possibility would be to use the name of the control on the form that currently displays the date, for example, *Forms![Example]![Invoice Date]*. This would change the *If* statement to read:

```
If Weekday(Forms![Example]![Invoice Date]) = 1
Or Weekday(Forms![Example]![Invoice Date]) = 7
```

Although this approach will work, it isn't the best method because it links the function to a specific control on a specific form. A better approach would allow you to insert any date, value, or identifier name that represents a date value into the function. This would allow you to use the function in any expression in any part of the database, not just in a specific form and control.

The method for doing this with functions is called *argument passing*. Recall from Chapter 2 that an argument is a value or an identifier that is inserted into a function. The following examples show how a date, a value, or a reference to a date control can be used with a user-defined function such as *WorkDay( )*:

```
WorkDay(#7/24/94#) or WorkDay([Invoice date])
```

The user-defined function works like a built-in function. The argument (or arguments) is inserted between the parentheses that follow the function name. But how does that value get inserted into the function's code?

The solution is to create an argument variable in the Function statement. A *variable* is a special identifier that is created during an Access Basic procedure for use while the procedure is executing. A variable is similar to a control that is not bound to a field in a table. The variable is assigned a value that can be used in expressions or modified with a Let statement. Unlike a control, a variable isn't an object and it doesn't appear on the screen. The only way to manipulate a variable is by using the variable name in statements and expressions.

Variables operate like a scratch pad where values can be temporarily stored for use while a procedure is executing. When the procedure is over, the variables are erased from memory and have no further meaning in the database.

The following Function command uses the name *Idate* — Initial Date Value — as an argument:

```
Function WorkDay(IDate)
```

The diagram in Figure 10-4 shows how a value can be passed to a procedure from a function that is used in an expression.

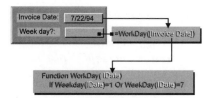

Figure 10-4: The Function argument is passed to the procedure as an argument.

In this case, the expression *=WorkDay([Invoice Date])* is entered into the Control Source property of a control on a form. The identifier *[Invoice Date]* is used as the argument for the *WorkDay()* function:

```
Control Source:  =WorkDay([Invoice Date])
```

When the expression is evaluated, the value of the identifier entered as the function argument is passed to the variable name that appears as the argument in the Function statement. In this case, the value of *Invoice Date* is assigned to the variable *IDate*. Once the date value is assigned to *IDate,* that variable name can be used in expressions or other statements. In this example, *IDate* is used in the *If* statement that determines whether the date is a workday or a weekend.

I used *IDate* rather than *Date* because *Date* frequently appears as a field name and can also be confused with the *Date( )* function.

Variable names can be any combination of characters, numbers, and under-scores (_) up to a length of 40 characters. You cannot use spaces in variable names.

By passing a value as a function argument, you create a function that isn't tied to any particular form or control. You can use the function in any expression in any part of the database. The only requirement is that this function must contain an argument that is a date value. The following examples show the *WorkDay( )* function used with a literal argument, #8/7/94#, and a date function, *Date( )*, as an argument:

```
WorkDay(#8/7/94#)

WorkDay(Date())
```

Returning a value

Another technique is needed to complete the structure of the user-defined function. You need to pass another value. This time the value is passed from the function's Access Basic code to the expression in which the function is used. In other words, when an expression such as =*WorkDay([Invoice Date])* is evaluated, what value should be returned?

In Access Basic, the value returned by the function is determined by the value assigned to a variable with the same name as the function. For example, if you have a function named *WorkDay( )*, you also need a variable named *Workday that* is assigned a value somewhere in the function.

The variable name must match the function name, character for character. The case of the characters is not important. ■

When the End Function statement is encountered, the current value of the func-tion name variable is returned as the value of the function. If the variable is modified more than once in the function, the *last* assigned value is the one that is returned.

What type of values should *WorkDay( )* return? You might return a simple True or False value, as shown in the following example:

```
WorkDay = False or Workday = True
```

Note that the constants True and False are actually the numeric values -1 and 0. Depending on the format property of the control, the value might appear as a number or a Yes/No format.

> In Access and other Microsoft Basics, any non-zero value is considered a True value. This means that 1 or -1 would both be treated as True. Only 0 is False. The built-in constant True used in Access is -1. ■

You might also choose to return a text phrase:

```
WorkDay = "Workday" or WorkDay="Weekend"
```

Passing values back and forth

You are now ready to convert the pseudocode used a few sections back into Access Basic code. The completed function follows:

```
Function WorkDay(IDate)
    If Weekday(IDate) = 1 Or Weekday(IDate) = 7   Then
        WorkDay="Weekend"
    Else
        WorkDay = "Workday"
    Endif
End Function
```

This simple procedure illustrates two techniques that require the use of variables within the procedure:

- ✔ **Passing values as arguments.** The variable shown in bold, *IDate*, is used to receive a value from the expression in which the user-defined function appears. Once assigned to **IDate**, the value can be accessed by all of the statements in the procedure. The variable is erased from memory when the procedure is finished.

- ✔ **Returning a value.** The variable shown in bold italic, *WorkDay*, is used to return a value from the function to the expression in which it is used. The name of this variable *must* match the name of the function. The function name follows the keyword **Function** in the first line of the procedure.

Figure 10-5 shows the code for the *WorkDay( )* function and a simple form on which the function is used as the Control Source property of a control.

Although the *WorkDay( )* function is rather simple in its structure, it includes all of the basic elements you need for creating a wide variety of user-defined functions. It demonstrates how values are passed to function procedures and how the procedures can return values to expressions in which the functions appear. It also shows how you can create a user-defined function that you can use in a variety of locations within a database, in contrast to form-level procedures, which are closely tied to the event properties of a specific form.

In Chapters 20 and 21, you will apply these concepts to create functions that solve various problems related to calendars and schedules.

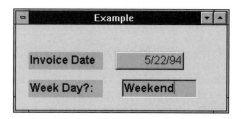

Figure 10-5:
The
WorkDay()
function is
used to
determine
the status of
an invoice
date.

```
Module: Module1
Function WorkDay (idate)
    If Weekday(idate) = 1 Or Weekday(idate) = 7 Then
        WorkDay = "Weekend"
    Else
        WorkDay = "Workday"
    End If
End Function
```

Using Macros in Access Basic

You can use Access Basic to perform almost any task that can be performed with macro actions. This is accomplished in two ways:

 ✔ **Equivalent statements.** Access Basic contains statements that duplicate the functions of certain macro actions. For example, the SetValue macro action is equivalent to the Access Basic Let statement.

 ✔ **DoCmd.** The DoCmd statement is used in Access Basic to execute a macro action. Most macro actions can be expressed as Access Basic statements that begin with DoCmd.

User-defined menu bars are an exception to this rule. The AddMenu action has no equivalent in Access Basic. You must use macros to implement this feature.

Why would you want to insert macro actions into an Access Basic procedure? There are a few reasons why this may be useful:

 ✔ If you already know how to perform a certain task using a macro action, you can use that same technique as part of a procedure.

 ✔ You may find that you prefer writing and editing Access Basic code to using the more highly structured macro sheets. For example, you can use **Copy** and **Paste** more effectively in a code window than in a macro sheet.

The DoCmd statement

The DoCmd statement allows you to execute macro actions within an Access Basic procedure. For example, in Chapter 6, you created a macro called Find Next that moved to the next record with the same company name as the current record. This section shows you how those macro actions can be entered in an Access Basic procedure. In addition, the Find Next macro is used to solve a problem that was left unresolved in Chapter 6.

The key to performing macro actions in Access Basic procedures lies in the DoCmd statement. DoCmd is followed by the name of the macro action to perform and any arguments for that action as follows:

```
DoCmd Action Argument1, Argument2, ...
```

For example, the GoToControl action is used in the Find Next macro. How would you write that action as an Access Basic statement? For a GotoControl action, the action name is *GotoControl* and the argument is the name of the control — in this case, *Company*. If you are entering a literal name as the argument, the control name must be enclosed in quotation marks:

```
DoCmd GotoControl, "Company"
```

The Find Next macro is triggered when the user clicks on a button on the form, shown in Figure 10-6. The macro consists of three actions: GotoControl, FindRecord, and another GotoControl .

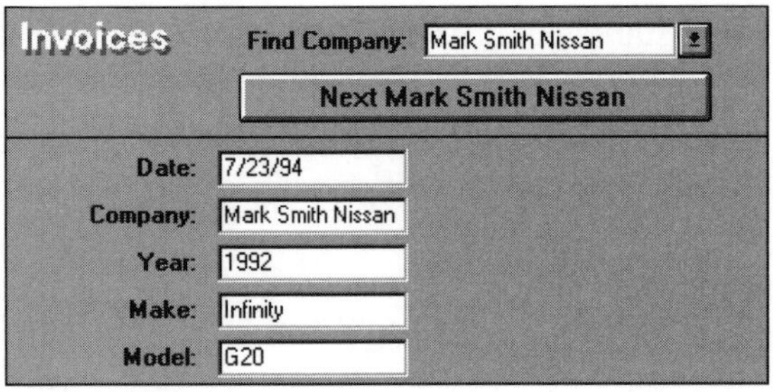

Figure 10-6:
Pressing a
button
triggers a
series of
macro
actions.

To create an Access Basic event procedure that performs the same task follow these steps:

1. Open the correct procedure window. Select the OnClick event property of the command button control called *Find Next*. Select the builder icon to open the builder dialog box, and select **Code Builder.** This opens the *Find_Next_Click* procedure window. The first action is a GotoControl action that moves the focus to the control that needs to be searched — *Company*.

2. Press **Tab** (to indent). Type **DoCmd GotoControl "Company"**

3. Press **Enter**.

The next action is FindRecord. The Access Basic statement begins with **DoCmd FindRecord**. (That's the easy part.) The FindRecord action can accept seven arguments. The FindRecord action has the following general form:

```
FindRecord find , where , matchcase , direction , search formatted ,
            searching , findfirst
```

The argument in bold italic is required. The arguments in *italic* are optional. Many of the arguments can be filled in with intrinsic constants. For example, Access recognizes *A_ANYWHERE, A_ENTIRE,* or *A_START* for the *where* argument. The intrinsic constants used for various arguments are listed in the help screen for each action and in the Access Basic reference guide.

In this case, you need to specify only two of the arguments:

- ✔ **Find.** This argument is required. It specifies which value the search is looking for. In this example, it is the value in the *Company* control, which is *[Company]*.

- ✔ **FindFirst.** This argument determines whether the search begins with the current record or the next record. In this operation, the search must not begin with the current record because you are using the company name that appears on the current record as the search criteria. If you allow Access to begin with the current record, it will immediately find a match and stop. For this search to work, Access must skip the current record and start the search with the next record. You specify this by setting the *findfirst* argument to False.

You can use the default values for the other arguments because they will not affect this search. Because only two arguments are needed, you might think it's acceptable to enter a statement like this:

```
DoCmd FindRecord [Company], False
```

This statement is not correct because Access assumes the argument following *find* is *where*, not *findfirst*.

To avoid this problem, insert a comma for each argument that you are not specifically entering a value for. You are skipping five arguments, so you must insert five additional commas (a total of six) between the current arguments.

```
DoCmd FindRecord [Company], , , , , , False
```

The Access syntax checking feature won't catch the mistake in the following statement because the statement is not entirely incorrect:

```
DoCmd, FindRecord [Company], False
```

The second argument in the statement is the *where* argument, which identifies the part of the field (entire, any part, or start) that should be used to determine a match. False is a constant that is equal 0, and 0 is a valid entry for the *where* argument, which can accept 0, 1, or 2. ▪

The final action is another GotoControl that returns the focus to the *Find Next* button. The entire procedure follows:

```
Sub Find_Next_Click ()
    DoCmd GoToControl "Company"
    DoCmd FindRecord [Company], , , , , , False
    DoCmd GoToControl "Find Next"
End Sub
```

When there's nothing more to find

The problem with the current procedure, as with its macro equivalent, is that the procedure doesn't indicate when you have reached the last match. The only way you can tell that there are no more matching records is to keep clicking the button until you notice that the displayed information doesn't change. It would be better to display a message informing users that they have reached the last record.

Intrinsic constants

The developers of Access recognized that entering macro action arguments as numeric values would make DoCmd statements difficult to create and almost impossible to understand. To simplify the process, they created a set of *intrinsic constants* that could substitute for numeric values in macro action arguments. An *intrinsic constant* is simply a variable name that is assigned a numeric value such as 0, 1, or 2. What's special about these constants is that they are automatically available to any Access Basic procedure. They can't be erased or modified, so they are always valid. The constants are assigned names that are supposed to indicate the option

they represent, for example, A_Form or A_Current. This makes them easier to remember and much easier to read.

Remember that these constants are simply identifiers for values. You can verify this by entering a command such as ? A_Form in the Immediate window. Access responds by displaying the value 2. This means that anywhere you would use the constant A_form, the number 2 will do just as well, and vice versa. For example, the expression *Amount=A_Form+A_Form* would assign the value 4 to *Amount* because that's the numeric value of the constants.

How can you get Access to recognize that it is displaying the last record for the current company? The answer can be found by thinking about how you know when you've reached the end of the search — that is, when the data in the record doesn't change after the FindRecord action is performed.

To solve the problem, you need to select a key value that ought to change after each search. In Access, the ideal value is a counter field or control, since by definition each record must have a unique value in that field. The invoice number is a likely candidate for this example, because it should be unique for each invoice.

You now have a *conceptual* answer to the problem. The next step is to translate that concept into statements and actions that Access understands. The solution is found by using a variable to temporarily store the invoice number of the record that is current *before* the FindRecord action. The following statement assigns the current value of *Invoice* to the variable *CurrentRecord*:

```
CurrentRecord = [Invoice]
```

Remember that the variable *CurrentRecord* maintains its value until the end of the procedure. After the FindRecord action, you can use an *If* statement to determine whether a new record has been located or the same record is still being displayed. The following statement evaluates as True if the value of the *Invoice* control doesn't change after the FindRecord action:

```
If [Invoice]=CurrentRecord Then
```

If this statement is True, a message box should be displayed to inform users that they have reached the last record for this company. You can use the MsgBox statement (which is functionally equivalent to the MsgBox macro action) to display a message:

```
MsgBox " No More Matches", 48
```

The value 48 is used to select the message box style. The style determines which icon is displayed in the box and the number and types of buttons displayed.

The completed procedure is as follows:

```
Sub Find_Next_Click ()
    CurrentRecord = [Invoice]
    DoCmd GoToControl "Company"
    DoCmd FindRecord [Company], , , , , , False
    DoCmd GoToControl "Find Next"
    If [Invoice] = CurrentRecord Then
        MsgBox "No More Matches", 48
    End If
End Sub
```

Figure 10-7 shows the message box that appears when there are no more records for the current company.

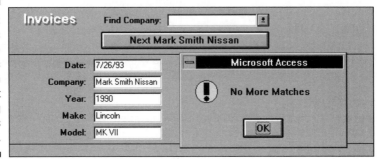

Most of the actions taken in this procedure are generated through DoCmd statements that simply execute macro actions. However, Access Basic can easily solve some problems that would be much more difficult with macros. With Access Basic, you can define variables for use during the execution of a procedure. These variables provide a means for saving values that can be used later in the procedure.

This capability is very important when the procedure involves changing the active record. Once you change from one record to another, the data in that record is no longer available. In many cases, you may want to perform an operation that uses data from more than one record. In this example, the invoice numbers from two records are needed to evaluate the effect of a search.

Storing the original invoice number at the beginning of the procedure allows the procedure to look backward in the table to the last record displayed. This allows the procedure to operate much as you would in determining that the data in the record hasn't changed. In other words, the technical solution to the problem became apparent by thinking about how a human would determine whether there were any more records left to display. This is often the key to designing a procedure.

Modifying a control property

The message box displayed by the procedure is a modal window. A *modal* window limits the focus to the contents of that window. You can't change windows or select anything outside the modal window until it is closed and removed from the screen. Modal windows are used when you want to display a message that cannot be ignored and that requires user acknowledgment through some action, such as selecting the OK button.

The *No More Matches* message probably isn't that critical. Some users may find it annoying if they have to close the message box before continuing. In general, you shouldn't display too many message boxes because they tend to interfere with the user's interaction with the form.

It might suffice to simply display the message in a noticeable place on the form without forcing users to perform additional actions such as closing the message box.

Instead of displaying a message box, suppose you alter the caption of the *Find Next* button to read *No More Matches*. You do this by setting the Caption property of the command button control. In Chapter 6, a SetValue macro action was used to set the Caption of this button to reflect the name of the company:

Action	*Arguements*	
Set Value	Item:	[Find Next].Caption
	Expression:	"Next"&[Company]

Because this macro is triggered by the OnCurrent form event property, the caption is automatically updated each time a new record is displayed. However, an exception occurs when the FindRecord action fails to find any more records. Because the record doesn't change, the OnCurrent property isn't triggered. In such a case, you can use a Let statement in the Access Basic procedure to change the caption of the button to *No More Matches*. The new command is shown in **bold** in the revised version of the procedure:

```
Sub Find_Next_Click ()
    CurrentRecord = [Invoice]
    DoCmd GoToControl "Company"
    DoCmd FindRecord [Company], , , , , False
    DoCmd GoToControl "Find Next"
    If [Invoice] = CurrentRecord Then
        [Find Next].Caption = "No More Matches",
    End If
End Sub
```

Changing the caption is a less obtrusive method of giving the user a message. If you try both methods, I believe you'll find that the caption method has a more comfortable feel. Message boxes generally should be reserved for situations in which you specifically want the user to acknowledge the message by selecting a button in the message box.

Part III
Making Access Smarter

The 5th Wave — By Rich Tennant

CARTOON GRAPHICS SOFTWARE SUPPORT PHONE: 911

"YES, I THINK IT'S AN ERROR MESSAGE."

In This Part...

In many ways, programs such as Access start out being pretty dumb. They don't really do much of anything. However, if you add a touch of imagination and a modest amount of Access Basic code, you can make Access a lot smarter.

In the chapters following, you improve the way Access works by building smart forms, buttons, and lists. The examples show you how to put Access Basic to work to make your screen forms do all sorts of useful tricks. At the end of Part III, you'll have a whole repertoire of programming techniques to make Access smarter and smarter as you get smarter and smarter about programming.

Chapter 11

Smart Navigation

● ●

In This Chapter

▶ Finding the last edited record

▶ Setting the focus

▶ Using the declarations section

▶ Adding pictures to command buttons

▶ Setting and finding bookmarks

● ●

*I*n Part II, you looked at the three basic tools available in Access: expressions, macros, and Access Basic procedures. Here in Part III, you learn how to use these tools to enhance the basic elements in Access, particularly forms. You can use these techniques in almost any application that you develop with Access. This chapter explains how to move from record to record in a form, one of the most basic tasks involved in using any form.

Logical Navigation

Navigation refers to operations that allow you to control which record is displayed in a form. All Access forms have built-in physical navigation tools for moving to the first, last, next, or previous record. I call them *physical* navigation tools because every table with five or more records must have a first, last, next, and previous record. Buttons allowing movement to these records appear by default on the bottom bar of each form window. The same commands are available from the Goto submenu on the Records menu.

Logical navigation controls are in contrast to physical navigation buttons and commands. Logical navigation refers to locating records based on the content of the records or a particular user interaction. For example, the FindRecord macro action in Chapter 6 uses a combo box control to list all of the company names in a table. When the user selects a name, the macro searches for and displays the first record for that company name.

This is an example of logical navigation because the movement through the table is based on a specific value rather than the physical sequence of the records. When selecting records by company name, the user isn't concerned with the order in which the records are arranged.

This chapter revisits the search for company names, this time using Access Basic techniques. The following sections show how Access Basic allows you to expand the concept of logical navigation to include methods for returning to the previously selected company and locating the last edited record in a table. Along the way, you'll also learn some important Access Basic techniques, including the use of table bookmarks.

Searching for a Record

In most cases, the basic navigation tools for going to the first, last, next, and previous record need to be enhanced with other methods of selecting records for display. In Chapter 6, macro actions are used to locate a record based on a selection from a combo box list. Figure 11-1 shows a form with a combo box control that lists all of the company names in the table. This is accomplished by creating a combo box control that uses a SQL statement to create the items for the list.

Figure 11-1: This form includes a combo box list for navigating to the selected company.

The properties of this control, which are discussed in detail in Chapter 6, are as follows:

Name:	Find
Control Source:	
Row Source Type:	Table/Query
Row Source:	Select Distinct Company From Invoices
	Where Company Is Not Null;

The *Distinct* keyword eliminates duplicate names and the *Where* clause is added to eliminate blanks from the list.

The SetFocus method

After defining the Row Source for the *Find* combo box control, you need to create an AfterUpdate procedure that locates the selected record. To do this, select the AfterUpdate event property and use the builder icon to open the *Find_AfterUpdate* procedure.

As mentioned in Chapter 6, before using the FindRecord action, you must move the focus to the control that's bound to the field you want to search. If you want to search by company, you need to move the focus to the *Company* control. This is accomplished with a GotoControl action. The DoCmd statement allows you to execute this macro action in an Access Basic procedure:

```
DoCmd GotoControl "Company"
```

An alternative available in Access Basic is the SetFocus method. SetFocus changes the focus to the specified object — for example, a form or a control.

A *method* is an action that can be performed on a specific object. The syntax of a method is generally simpler than the syntax of a DoCmd statement. The SetFocus method has the following general form:

```
objectname.SetFocus
```

For example, the following statement changes the focus to a control named *Company*:

```
Company.SetFocus
```

Note that this statement is a much simpler, more direct way of telling Access Basic what to do. You could write the procedure as follows, using two SetFocus methods (shown in **bold**) in place of GotoControl actions:

```
Company.SetFocus
DoCmd FindRecord [Find]
Find.SetFocus
```

This simple Access Basic procedure enables the combo box control to locate the *first* record that matches the selected company name. Remember that there may be many records with the same company name.

There is an Access Basic method that can take the place of the FindRecord action, but it requires using an additional concept (database object variables) that will make more sense a little later. For now, the FindRecord action will do. ■

Going back

After using the *Find* control to locate a specific company, suppose you want to undo the search and go back to the previously displayed record. This isn't easy because the *Find* control allows random movement through the table. The command **Records** | **Goto** | **Previous** won't work because it doesn't consider how you arrived at the current record — that is, by searching for a specific company.

One way to go back to the previous record is to remember the company name and search again for that company. However, this may not work if there are multiple records with the same company name. The only sure way to go back is to recall a value that uniquely identifies the record and use that value to return to the record. The current example involves invoice records, and it's safe to assume that each invoice number is unique.

This poses an interesting problem. How can you get Access to remember a value that appeared on the previous record, not the current record?

One convenient solution is related to the use of the declarations section of the form's Access Basic module. You may recall that every Access Basic module automatically has a declarations section, in addition to any procedures or functions you add to that module. The declarations section is used for statements that affect all of the procedures and functions in the module.

In this case, the issue involves the scope and lifetime of any variable defined by Access Basic procedures. *Scope* specifies which modules can use a variable; *lifetime* refers to how long Access retains the variable in memory.

One of the characteristics of a variable is that it is a temporary value. It can be defined and used in a procedure, but it is discarded once that procedure concludes. In other words, the scope of the variable is limited to a single procedure, and its lifetime is limited to the time it takes to execute the procedure.

Access allows you to expand the scope and lifetime of a variable through the declarations section of the Access Basic module. This is accomplished by entering the Dim (dimension) statement in the declarations section of the form's Access Basic module:

> ✔ **Scope**. The variable is available to any procedure in the current module. For example, you might set the value of a variable named *LastInvoiceNumber* in one event procedure and then use that value in other procedures to search for that invoice number.

> ✔ **Lifetime**. The variable is retained as long as the form is open or until you use the **Run** | **Reset** command on the module design menu. While a form is open, the same or different procedures can use or modify the last value stored for that variable.

The following statement *declares* a variable named *LastInvoiceNumber:*

```
Dim LastInvoiceNumber
```

Unique numbers and counter fields

You can make sure that items such as invoice numbers are unique by putting them in a counter type field. When you do so, you give up the ability to control the invoice numbers, because Access automatically generates the numbers, starting with 1.

However, you can trick Access into starting a counter field at a particular value. Suppose that you have a table called Invoices with a counter field called Invoice Number that you want to start numbering at 100000 rather than 1. After you have created the table, but before you add any records, create a second table with a single field. This is a dummy table that you can discard after you have used it to set the counter value in Invoices.

For simplicity, call the dummy table Dummy. The structure of the dummy table should have one number type field that has the same name as the counter field in the table you want to modify.

In this example, you need to create a field called *Invoice Number*. Remember that this field should be a *number* type field, not a counter.

You can set the field size to Long Integer because this is the field size used for all counter fields.

Open the Dummy table and enter 100000 into the *Invoice Number* field. This is the starting value you want to use for the *Invoice Number* field in the Invoices table.

The next step involves creating an Update query that will force the value from Dummy into Invoices. Select the Dummy table. Click on the New Query icon to create a new query form. When the Wizard dialog box appears, select **New Query**. Drag the *Invoice Number* field from the Dummy field list into the first column.

Select the **Query** | **Append** command. Enter or select the name of the table you want to modify, — Invoices — in the Table Name box. Click on OK. Then process the query by clicking on the Run icon in the query design toolbar. Confirm that you want to append one record onto the Invoices table.

You can discard the query form and open the Invoices table. The first record in the table now has the specified value, 100000, in the counter field.

Remember that this chapter describes the function of the declarations section in a form-level module. The lifetime of variables used in database-level modules (the ones that appear in the modules list of the database window) are different. Those variables remain in memory until the database is closed.

The solution to the problem of remembering the previous record lies in storing the invoice number in a memory variable that is defined in the declarations section, because the value remains in memory even after a procedure ends.

The trick is to use the same variable in procedures triggered by different events:

1. As part of the Find_Update procedure, the invoice number of the current record is assigned to the variable *before* the FindRecord action takes place. This means the invoice number is preserved in memory when the next record is displayed.

2. Then you can define a procedure that uses the stored invoice number to backtrack to the corresponding record.

Statements in the declarations section

To create a module-level variable, you must enter a Dim statement in the declarations section of the form's Access Basic module. If the module window is not open, you can open the declarations section by using the **View** | **Code** command on the form design menu bar. If the module window is already open, you can use the toolbar lists. Select General from the object drop list on the toolbar. General is always at the top of the list. Selecting General automatically displays the declarations section, because this is the only section available under the General object name.

By default, the declarations section contains the Option Compare Database statement. In this example, the Option Compare Database statement has no effect on the procedure. As shown in Figure 11-2, you should place the insert point on the line below the Option statement and enter the following Dim statement:

```
Dim LastInvoiceNumber
```

It's important to understand that the Dim statement is different than the Let statement. Dim doesn't assign a value to the variable. Its purpose is to indicate to Access the scope and lifetime of any values assigned to this variable. The actual assignment of a value is performed in various procedures by statements such as *LastInvoiceNumber=[Invoice]*.

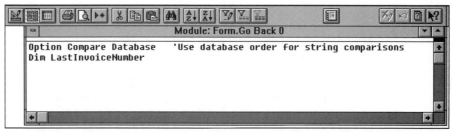

Figure 11-2: A variable is declared in the declarations section of a form's Access Basic module.

In this example, the operation should take place each time the procedure Find_AfterUpdate is triggered. You want to store the current record's invoice number before the FindRecord action changes the active record. The following procedure shows one additional statement, in **bold**, that assigns the value in the [Invoice] control to the variable that was defined in the declarations section, *LastInvoiceNumber:*

```
Sub Find_AfterUpdate
    LastInvoiceNumber=[Invoice]
    Company.SetFocus
    DoCmd FindRecord [Find]
    Find.SetFocus
End Sub
```

After the Find_AfterUpdate procedure concludes, the invoice number stays in memory. The last step is to create another procedure that uses this value to go back to the previous record.

Creating buttons with pictures

A command button is the best type of control for an operation like Go Back, because it is consistent with the general approach used in the Access interface. Recall that Access already provides buttons on the form border to move to the first, last, next, and previous records.

By default, command buttons are assigned caption text, such as *Button12.* You can edit this default text to create your own caption for the button. The Picture property of command buttons provides an alternative to editing the button caption. The Picture property allows you to display an image instead of text inside the command button.

To add a button with a picture, select the command button icon in the form design toolbox and place a button on the form. Because the button in this example is meant for navigation between records, it should be placed in the form header or footer section, as shown in Figure 11-3.

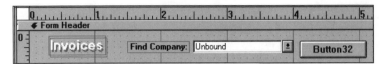

Figure 11-3: A command button placed in a form header section.

There is no functional reason for placing the button in the header; the button performs the same function no matter where it appears on the form. However, placing the button in the header or footer helps indicate that the button is not part of a particular record's data, but is part of the overall form's structure.

Change the name of the control to *GoBack*. Access automatically sets the button's caption, height, and width. In this example, you want to change the appearance of the button from a text caption to a picture. To do this, select the **Picture** layout property and click on the builder icon. Access displays the Picture Builder dialog box, which is shown in Figure 11-4.

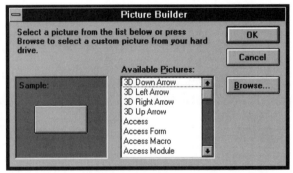

Figure 11-4: Use Picture Builder dialog box to select a button image.

This dialog box provides two methods of selecting an image for the button:

- **Available Pictures list.** Access supplies a set of 60 images that you can select from this list. You can preview an image by clicking on its name in the list. The corresponding image appears in the Sample box.

- **Browse button.** The Browse button opens a file selector dialog box that allows you to select an image stored in the Windows Bitmap format. These files have a BMP extension. BMP format images can be created and modified with graphics applications such as the Paintbrush program supplied with Windows.

When you select an image for a button, remember that you can't scale the image. Access displays the image at full size — the size of the image when it was created. All the images included with Access are about 0.4" square. You can crop the image by setting the button height and width to a size smaller than the image size.

For this example, select the Left Point image, which is shown in Figure 11-5.

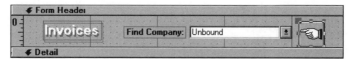

Figure 11-5: The Picture property is used to display the left-pointing image.

The Picture property of a command button is limited in two ways. First, you can use only images stored in the Windows BMP format. Second, you can't reduce or enlarge the image to fit a certain button size. You can get around this limitation by using two different controls in combination. First, place an OLE Object frame control on the form. Then, create or load a graphic image from a file using any of the OLE server applications available on your system. For example, you can insert clip art images supplied with such programs as CorelDraw and Micrografx Designer. Once the image is inserted, you can use the Size Mode property to scale the image to fit the designed OLE frame width and height.

The hard part comes next. The OLE frame can't be used like a command button. Instead, place a command button control directly over the OLE frame. Change the **Transparent** layout property to Yes. This allows the image of the OLE frame to show right through the command button. When the form is active, you see the OLE frame image, but any actions such as clicking are controlled by the event procedures of the transparent command button. ■

The GoBack procedure

The final step is to create a procedure for the *GoBack* control that will return to the previous record. Select the OnClick event property and open the GoBack_Click procedure window.

This procedure uses the same basic structure as the Find procedure. The only difference is that the search is conducted in the *Invoice* field rather than the *Company* field. The procedure uses the value stored in the *LastInvoiceNumber* variable to return to the previous record. This technique works only when LastInvoiceNumber has been defined as a module-level variable in the declarations section. The GoBack procedure is as follows:

```
Sub GoBack_Click()
    Invoice.SetFocus
    DoCmd FindRecord LastInvoiceNumber
    Goback.SetFocus
End Sub
```

In this example, a value set in one procedure is then used at some later point by a different procedure in the same module.

Using Bookmarks

The preceding example depends on the existence of a field with unique values (in this case, a counter field) that can be used to identify each record displayed by the form. But suppose there is no such field? How would you implement the GoBack button?

Access provides a solution in the form of bookmarks. Each record in a set — for example, the set of records displayed by a form — is assigned a unique value called a bookmark. It is important to understand that the value of a record bookmark is not the same as the record number that appears on the bottom bar of the form window. In fact, you can't display the bookmark value as you would the value of a field or a control.

But how can you work with a value that you can't display? You can use variable names to store and retrieve specific bookmark values. In the preceding example, the invoice number is used to keep track of the previous record displayed. However, it isn't really necessary to know the invoice number. Even if the *Invoice* control was invisible, the procedures would work just as well. What's important is knowing that each record has some unique value — invoice number or bookmark — that identifies it within the current set of records. This is exactly what a bookmark does, so you should be able to rewrite the procedures using record bookmarks instead of the invoice number.

Why bother? Not every table will have a convenient field like *Invoice Number*. By changing the procedures to work with bookmarks, you create procedures that can be applied to almost any form or table. In other words, you create a more generalized solution to the problem of navigating through a record set.

The Bookmark Property

How can you change the procedures to use bookmarks rather than field values? It's useful to think of the bookmark as an invisible field or control. In the previous example, this statement was used to assign the value of the *Invoice* field to the variable *LastInvoiceNumber*.

```
LastInvoiceNumber = [Invoice]
```

Notice that this statement uses the short form of the control identifier. As shown in **bold** in the following statement, the full identifier name would include the name of the form on which the control appears:

```
LastInvoiceNumber = Forms.[Show Invoices].[Invoice]
```

From this point of view, the bookmark of the currently displayed record can be substituted for the control name *Invoice*. The result is the following statement in which *Bookmark* appears as a property of the current form:

```
LastInvoiceNumber = Forms.[Show Invoices].Bookmark
```

You can take this process one step further and get a statement that works in just about any form. The following statement is directed at the records in the active form, because the Screen object *Screen.Active* is substituted for the specific form name:

```
LastInvoiceNumber =Screen.ActiveForm.Bookmark
```

This statement will store a value that you can use to identify the current record. Because it doesn't depend on specific form or control names, you can use it with any form. The following procedure shows how the bookmark technique can be applied to the Find_AfterUpdate procedure:

```
Sub Find_AfterUpdate
    LastInvoiceNumber=Screen.ActiveForm.Bookmark
    Company.SetFocus
    DoCmd FindRecord [Find]
    Find.SetFocus
End Sub
```

The bookmark property can be used also to change the active record. You do this by reversing the order of the items in the Let statement. Instead of setting a variable equal to a bookmark, you set the form's bookmark property equal to a specific value stored in a memory variable. The following statement sets the form's bookmark to the value stored in *LastInvoiceNumber*:

```
Forms.[Show Invoices].Bookmark = LastInvoiceNumber
```

Setting the bookmark property of a form to a specific bookmark has the effect of making the corresponding record the current record. In other words, this statement tells Access to "go to" the record that has a bookmark matching *LastInvoiceNumber*.

You can generalize this statement in the same way as the previous example by substituting the Screen object for the specific form name:

```
Screen.ActiveForm.Bookmark = LastInvoiceNumber
```

This technique greatly simplifies the code needed for the GoBack_Click procedure. In fact, it boils down to a single statement:

```
Sub GoBack_Click()
    Screen.ActiveForm.Bookmark = LastInvoiceNumber
End Sub
```

The result of these procedures is the form shown in Figure 11-6. This form has a button that lets users return to the previously displayed record.

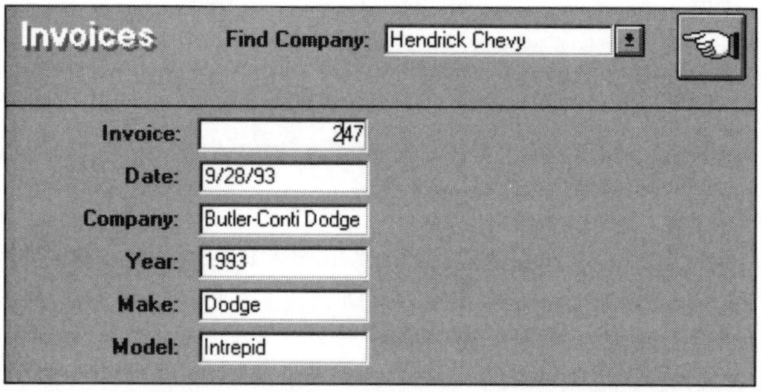

Figure 11-6: This form uses bookmarks to return to the previously viewed record.

This technique is possible because module-level variables — that is, variables defined with Dim statements in the declarations section of the module — retain their value after the procedure is finished. The module-level variables function as a sort of scratchpad where values can be stored by one procedure and picked up for use by other procedures that are triggered later. In other words, module-level variables give forms a memory so that they can recall items defined earlier in the session.

Using multiple bookmarks

The bookmark technique can be used to track several items in the same set of records. For example, you might need to locate the last record that was modified or edited, as well as the last item that was searched for.

You can define as many variables as necessary in the declarations section of the form's module. For example, you could use two variables: one to keep track of the last record displayed before a search, and another to keep track of the last updated record. By entering the following statement in the declarations section, you establish two module-level variables that can be used to store bookmark values:

```
Dim LastInvoiceNumber,LastInvoiceChanged
```

To keep track of the last record changed, you use the form's AfterUpdate property — that is, the Form_AfterUpdate procedure. The form's AfterUpdate event takes place each time an edited record is saved. While the form is open, the most common trigger for this event is moving to a different record. Remember that AfterUpdate always occurs before the focus changes to a different record.

To display the property sheet for the form, make sure the property sheet box is open and then use the **Edit** | **Select Form** command or click on an unused portion of the form design window. All you need to do is insert a statement into this procedure that assigns the bookmark for the modified record to the variable *LastInvoiceChanged* in the Form_AfterUpdate procedure:

```
Sub Form_AfterUpdate ()
    LastInvoiceChanged=Screen.ActiveForm.BookMark
End Sub
```

As shown in Figure 11-7, the second change to the form is to add another button that goes back to the last edited record by using the bookmark value stored in *LastInvoiceChanged*.

Figure 11-7:
A second
button is
added to go
back to the
last edited
record.

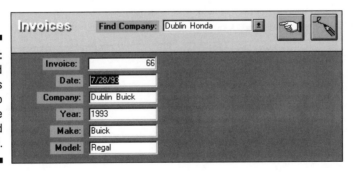

The command button control is called *Last Change*. The image used in the button is the *Pencil in Action* image supplied in the Picture Builder. The following procedure is executed when this button is clicked:

```
Sub Last_Change_Click ()
    Screen.ActiveForm.BookMark=LastInvoiceChanged
End Sub
```

Chapter 12

Working with Multiple Page Forms

· ·

· ·

*W*hen you are working with all but the simplest tables, you will probably have trouble fitting all of the fields on a single screen. Of course, Access allows the user to scroll up and down through a long form. However, this is a risky approach to designing a database because users might not realize that the data they want is on a part of the form that isn't currently visible. As described in this chapter, multiple page forms offer a simple but effective solution to this problem.

Using Form Pages

When you are creating a form with many controls, it's difficult to design a single form that displays all the fields. In many cases, it's better to organize the fields into related groups and display each group in a separate section. For example, a mailing list form could be divided into sections for name, address, phone, and personal information.

There are two methods for presenting the various sections:

> ✔ **Multiple forms.** You can design a separate form for each of the sections. This approach is covered in Chapter 17 as part of a general discussion of multiple form and subform operations.
>
> ✔ **Multiple pages.** You can create separate pages on a single form.

The multiple page method is by far the simpler approach. You can divide a form into pages by inserting a page break control at any location. These page breaks usually do not affect the appearance of the form on the screen when users are scrolling through a long form with the vertical scroll bar. The effect of the page breaks becomes obvious only when the form is printed.

If a form is used only for screen display and data entry (which is the case with many forms), you can use the page break controls to divide a single form into multiple sections that can be displayed one at a time.

The diagram in Figure 12-1 shows the basic approach for creating a multiple page screen form.

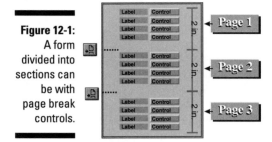

Figure 12-1:
A form divided into sections can be with page break controls.

The controls that should appear in each section are grouped together, and a page break control is placed between each of the sections. Each section should be roughly the same height — in this case, 2 inches — so that when the form changes from one page to another, the page fills the form window. Of course, this is merely a cosmetic consideration. The goal is to create the illusion that the pages in the form are distinct sections. What often counts is not the underlying structure of a form, but how it looks and feels to the user. In other words, users can benefit from optical illusions you create by manipulating the form's elements in particular ways.

As detailed in the next few paragraphs, the GotoPage method is used for navigating between the pages of this form. It's important to remember that the GotoPage method simply positions the upper-left corner of the selected page in the upper-left corner of the form window. If the window is longer than the size selected for each page, you will see more than one page at a time. To create the illusion that you are looking at one page at a time, you need to adjust the height of the form to match the height of each page.

Once the pages of the form have been laid out, you can think about the tools you will provide for navigating between the pages. The key to this technique is either the GotoPage action (if you are using macros) or the GotoPage method (if you are writing Access Basic procedures). Access Basic is the preferred method in this book, though macros would work just as well for this simple example. The GotoPage method has the following general form:

```
FormName.GotoPage PageNumber
```

To go to page 2 of the Mail List form, you would use this statement:

```
Forms![Mail List].GotoPage 2
```

Assuming that you are changing pages on the current form, you can use the Screen object in place of a specific form name:

```
Screen.ActiveForm.GotoPage 2
```

It can be quite simple to create a control for selecting pages if you use an option group to enclose either option buttons or toggle buttons. An *option group* is a box that contains two or more buttons that represent a list of choices for a single item. Option groups can contain option buttons, check boxes, or toggle buttons. Figure 12-2 shows an option group called *Sections* that contains four toggle buttons. Each button has a picture that indicates (more or less) the purpose of each section.

Figure 12-2: An option group with four toggle buttons.

Most options groups display all of the choices using the same type of control. However, it is possible to insert in a single group any combination of option buttons, check boxes, and toggle buttons. ■

Because of the way option group controls work, the Sections_AfterUpdate procedure requires only a single statement. Each of the buttons in an option group returns a number, starting with 1. The second button is 2, the third is 3, and so on. If each button corresponds to a page, all you need to do is use the control's value as the page number argument, which is exactly what the following procedure does:

```
Sub Sections_AfterUpdate ()
    Screen.ActiveForm.GotoPage [Sections]
End Sub
```

You may want to enhance the procedure by displaying text on the form to indicate the name of the displayed section. To do this, place a text label control on the form to display the name of the first section, for example, *Name Information*.

In this example, the control is named *Text101*. This is typical of the generic control names generated by Access during form design. Although you can give every control a descriptive name, it's unlikely that you would want to take the time and trouble to do so. I use the generic name in the example because you'll have to deal with this type of name when you are creating procedures.

You can change the label dynamically each time a different page is selected by using an Access Basic statement to redefine the Caption property of the control. The following statement is used to change the label on the form:

```
[Text101].Caption = "Telecom Information"
```

The effect of this statement is illustrated is Figure 12-3.

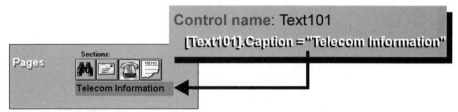

Figure 12-3: Access Basic can be used to change the contents of a label control.

You can coordinate the text label with the page selection buttons by adding a Select Case structure to the Sections_AfterUpdate procedure:

```
Sub Sections_AfterUpdate ()
    Screen.ActiveForm.GotoPage [Sections]
    Select Case [Sections]
        Case 1
            [Text101].Caption = "Name Information"
        Case 2
            [Text101].Caption = "Address Information"
        Case 3
            [Text101].Caption = "Telecom Information"
```

```
        Case 4
            [Text101].Caption = "Notes"
      End Select
End Sub
```

In this example, the Case structure uses the value of the *Sections* control, which is determined by which button is clicked. The Case structure then executes one of four statements that redefine the text label's caption. The result, which is shown in Figure 12-3, is seen each time the user changes the displayed page.

Setting the default page

The viewed portion of a form usually remains the same when the displayed record is changed. For example, if a form is longer than the current form window and you are viewing the bottom of the form, the bottom section will still be displayed when you change records.

With a multiple page form, it may make more sense to display the first page each time the user changes records rather than maintaining the page that was last displayed on the previous record.

One solution to this problem is to use the form's OnCurrent event procedure to reset the form to page 1 each time a new record is displayed. The following procedure uses three statements to set page 1 as the default page for each record:

```
Sub Form_Current ()
   [Sections] = 1
   Screen.ActiveForm.GotoPage 1
   [Text101].Caption="Name Information"
End Sub
```

The first statement changes the value of the *Sections* control to 1. This has the effect of selecting the first button in the option group. Remember that this is done merely for cosmetic purposes. The toggle button is synchronized with the page that is being displayed because it might seem odd to the user if the toggle button was left on page 3 when page 1 was being displayed.

The next statement, *Screen.Active.Form.GotoPage 1*, changes the displayed page to page 1.

The last statement in the procedure updates the text label to match the first page. Note that this is also a matter of appearance. If you don't update the label, the text won't match the page that is displayed.

You might notice that the Form_Current procedure repeats some of the operations that are performed by the Sections_AfterUpdate procedure. Instead of duplicating those statements, you could simply call the procedure. This changes the Form_Current procedure to only two statements:

```
Sub Form_Current ()
    [Sections] = 1
    Call Sections_AfterUpdate
End Sub
```

The first statement in this example selects the page from within the procedure rather than waiting for the user to make a selection. The procedure then calls the Sections_AfterUpdate procedure. It's important to note that this Sections_AfterUpdate procedure is unaffected by the method used to set the value of *Sections*. It doesn't matter if the value is set by a user selection or an Access Basic statement. The example shows, once again, how a single procedure can be invoked by other events on the same form.

Correcting an error in the procedure

The method shown in the preceding section has a flaw. The flaw won't become obvious until you close the form and then try to open it again. When you try to open the form, Access displays the error message: *No form is active*. As shown in Figure 12-4, Access displays the procedure that caused the error, Sections_AfterUpdate, and highlights the *Screen.ActiveForm.GotoPage [Sections]* statement.

What causes this error? The procedure appeared to run correctly when it was first designed. Why does Access execute the Sections_AfterUpdate procedure when you try to open the form?

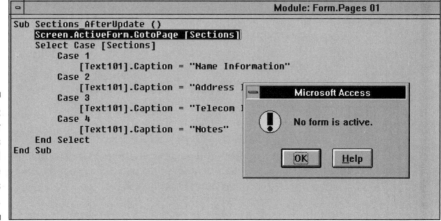

Figure 12-4:
An error message is generated when the form is opened.

Beginning with the last question first, the AfterUpdate event property of the *Sections* control didn't trigger execution of the Sections_AfterUpdate procedure. Rather, the procedure was called by the form's OnCurrent event procedure. You can check this by opening the Calls dialog box:

1. Select **OK** to close the error dialog box.

2. Select **View** I **Calls**.

As shown in Figure 12-5, Access displays a dialog box that lists all of the procedures that are currently executing.

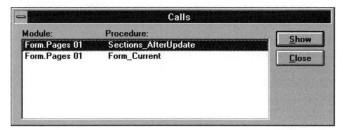

Figure 12-5: The Calls dialog box shows which procedures have been called.

Here, it shows that the Form_Current procedure was executing when the Sections_AfterUpdate procedure was called. You can use the **Show** button in the dialog box to display the code for any of the listed procedures. Close the dialog box by selecting **Close**.

You still need to uncover the source of the error. A clue can be found by relating what you see on the screen to what the error message says. The message indicates that there is no active form. The screen has not yet displayed the form even though the Open button was used to open it. Why this apparent anomaly?

The answer lies in the details of the event sequence that is triggered by the opening of a form. The following six events are triggered when a typical form is opened (forms with subforms have a longer sequence):

1. Form_Open

2. Form_Load

3. Form_Resize

4. Form_Activate

5. Form_Current

6. *FirstControl*_Enter

What's significant is that the form isn't displayed on the screen until after the fifth event, Form_Current. Because the form doesn't become part of the screen object until after it is displayed, a reference to the Screen.ActiveForm object doesn't refer to the form that is being opened until after the Form_Current event concludes.

In this example, the Form_Current procedure calls the Sections_AfterUpdate procedure, which refers to Screen.ActiveForm. Assuming that you opened the form with the Open button in the database window, the result is the error message in Figure 12-4.

When the error occurs, Access pauses the execution of the procedure. To continue with the form opening process, you must terminate execution with the **Reset** command:

Select **Run** | **Reset** to terminate the procedure.

The form will appear on the screen and function correctly.

You can solve this problem by removing the Screen.ActiveForm reference and replacing it with a reference to this particular form using its form name, *Pages*. In the following procedure, the required change is shown in **bold**.

```
Sub Sections_AfterUpdate ()
    Forms![Pages].GotoPage [Sections]
    Select Case [Sections]
        Case 1
            [Text101].Caption = "Name Information"
        Case 2
            [Text101].Caption = "Address Information"
        Case 3
            [Text101].Caption = "Telecom Information"
        Case 4
            [Text101].Caption = "Notes"
    End Select
End Sub
```

The Screen.ActiveForm object is a convenient shortcut that circumvents the need to write the exact name of a form into the Access Basic code. However, this object is available only after the form appears on the screen. If you are writing event procedures for any of the six events that occur before the form is physically on the screen, you cannot use the Screen.ActiveForm object to refer to the form that is being opened.

Changing the Record Order

The record order is one of the key characteristics for navigating through a record set with a form. In Access, the order of the records displayed in a form is determined by their order in the record set (either a table or a query) used as the Record Source for the form.

You will notice that the terms *Record Source* and *RecordSource* both appear in the text. *Record Source* (two words) refers to the property you see listed on the property sheet that is displayed in the form design mode. When you address the same property from Access Basic, the name of the property is *RecordSource* (one word). ■

The record order is usually determined by the primary key, which is established in the table's structure. If no primary key is defined, the records appear in the order they were added to the table — that is, the natural order of the table.

A convenient navigation feature involves sorting the records into a different order. When using the Invoice form from the previous chapters, you may find it useful to view records in different orders. For instance, you might want to switch between records sorted by invoice number, company name, date, product, or another field.

You can sort the records in a form's record set by using the **Records** I **Edit Filter/Sort** and **Records** I **Apply_Filter/Sort** commands. But how can you build different sort orders into the layout of a form?

You can solve this problem by using Access Basic to modify the RecordSource property of the form. The RecordSource property defines the set of records that will be displayed. This property is usually set automatically when a form is created, based on the table or query name selected at that time.

Like most object properties, this property can be changed using an Access Basic procedure. The trick is to set the RecordSource property so that the records are re-sorted based on a selection the user makes on the form. Figure 12-6 shows an option box control with three buttons. Each button represents a different sort order for the records in the table: invoice number, company name, or product (that is, vehicles listed by year, make, and model).

Figure 12-6: An option group can be used to change the sort order of a form.

When the user makes a selection in the option group, which is called *Sort Order*, the AfterUpdate procedure for this control modifies the RecordSource property of the form to sort the records in the desired order.

The most direct method of doing this is with a SQL statement that defines the form's record set. A common technique for assigning a record set is to use the name of a table in the Record Source property. The following property assigns the Invoices table as the source of the form's record set:

```
Record Source:   Invoices
```

However, Access allows you to use a SQL statement in place of an identifier (a table or query name). The following SQL statement is equivalent to entering the table name, Invoices, as the Record Source:

```
Select * From Invoices;
```

The asterisk (*) following Select stands for *all fields*. This means that all the fields in the table are included in the record set. The advantage of using a SQL statement becomes obvious when you add an Order By clause. The Order By clause allows you to specify a sort order for arranging the records. For example, the following SQL statement sorts the record set by company:

```
Select * From Invoices Order By Company;
```

If this statement is used as the Record Source, the form will display the records in company name order. The Order By clause can perform multiple field sorts. The following statement sorts the records by year, by make within each year, and by model within each make:

```
Select * From Invoices Order By Year, Make, Model;
```

By default, items are sorted in ascending order. You can specify descending order for any of the sort fields by placing the keyword *Desc* after the field name. The following statement reverses the sort order for the *Year* field so that the latest year vehicles appear first. The *Make* and *Model* fields are sorted in an alphabetical (ascending) order.

```
Select * From Invoices Order By Year Desc, Make, Model;
```

If desired, you can order records by an expression. The following example sorts records by the day of the week — that is, all Sunday records, followed by Monday records, and so on:

```
Select * From Invoices Order By Weekday([Date]);
```

You can apply these SQL statements to the Invoice form by setting the RecordSource property equal to the SQL statement. When the following statement is executed, Access changes the record set of the specified form to match the SQL statement, which tells Access to sort the records by company:

```
Forms![Invoice].RecordSource = "Select * From Invoices Order By
          Company;"
```

You can also eliminate the reference to the specific name of the form by using the Screen object:

```
Screen.ActiveForm.RecordSource = "Select * From Invoices Order By
                Company;"
```

Note that the SQL statement is enclosed in quotation marks, indicating that it is a text value. In other words, the RecordSource property will accept only text as a value. However, the text value doesn't have to be a literal. It can be a variable or any other identifier that refers to a text value.

The following example shows how this works. The first statement defines a variable named *SQLText* as having *Select * From Invoices Order By Company;* as its text value. The second statement assigns the *SQLText* variable to the RecordSource property.

```
SQLText = "Select * From Invoices Order By Company;"

Screen.ActiveForm.RecordSource = SQLText
```

These two statements have the same effect as the single statements in the previous examples. Why bother breaking up the operation into more than one statement? The two-statement example simply shows that you can arrive at the text of the SQL statement in a number of different ways.

I have a habit of using the variable name *SQLText* in procedures that use SQL statements as arguments. The name has no special significance to Access Basic. It could just as well be *X, QueryText,* or *MyAuntTillie.* However, I find that my code is more understandable when I always use the same name for the same basic function. Anyone reading my code also will catch on to my habits, which should help them recognize a standard technique when it pops up in different places.

In this example, the goal is to sort the record set in three orders: invoice number, company, or product. With the exception of the field names that follow the Order By clause, the SQL statements that correspond to each sort order are identical:

```
Select * From Invoices Order By Invoice;
Select * From Invoices Order By Company;
Select * From Invoices Order By Year Desc, Make, Model;
```

You can express this difference using a Select case structure. In the following example, the value of the option group control *Sort Order* is used to select one of the three values:

```
Select Case [Sort Order]
   Case 1
      SortKey = "Invoice;"
```

continued

```
        Case 2
           SortKey = "Company;"
        Case 3
           SortKey = "Year Desc, Make, Model;"
     End Select
```

The last character in any SQL statement *must* be a semicolon (;). In this example, the last character in each SortKey alternative is a semicolon. This assumes that the SortKey text will be placed at the end of the assembled SQL statement. The semicolon is not very visible and can easily be forgotten when you are creating long, complex SQL statements. Make a mental note to check for the semicolon before executing any SQL operations. ■

Next, you can combine the SortKey text with the portion of the statement that is the same in all cases. This forms a single SQL statement, which is then used to set the RecordSource property. The resultant procedure stores the standard part of the SQL statement in the variable *SQLText*. The Select Case structure selects a field list that is stored in SortKey. The two pieces are assembled in the last statement in the procedure, which sets the RecordSource property to the selected sort order:

```
Sub Sort_Order_AfterUpdate ()
    SQLText= "Select * From Invoices Order By" & Chr(32)
    Select Case [Sort Order]
        Case 1
           SortKey = "Invoice;"
        Case 2
           SortKey = "Company;"
        Case 3
           SortKey = "Year Desc, Make, Model;"
    End Select
    Screen.ActiveForm.RecordSource = SQLText & SortKey
End Sub
```

Figure 12-7 shows a form that uses an option group control to change the sort order of the records in the form's record set.

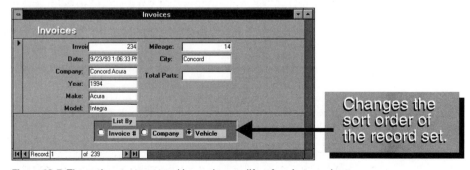

Figure 12-7: The option group control is used to modify a form's record set.

Chr(32)? Huh?

You may wonder what the expression *Chr(32)* is doing at the end of the first statement in the Sort_Order_AfterUpdate procedure. The answer reveals some of the problems involved in writing about programming. In this case, I had to figure out how to show you that a space must be added to the end of the text that is assigned to the *SQLText* variable.

First, technically speaking, why is the space needed? Because there must be a space between the words *by* and the field name in the SQL statement. If you combine two text items — for example, "Order By" and "Company;" — you get *Order ByCompany;*. Access can't process this statement because it doesn't understand the word *ByCompany.* You need to insert a space either at the end of the first part ("Order By ") or at the beginning of the second part (" Company;") so that when they are combined they form the correct phrase (*Order By Company;*).

Okay, why not simply add the space to the text as I did in the preceding paragraph? Spaces are simply too hard to see when they are tacked on the beginning or the end of a phrase. The propor-

tionally spaced type used in this book and on the Windows screen display increases the chances that such leading or trailing spaces will be missed.

My solution in this case is to use the Chr() function. With this function, I can add a space to the end of the phrase in a way that can't be overlooked. Chr() inserts characters based on their ASCII value. (ASCII — American Standard Code for Information Interchange — and Chr are discussed in Chapter 2.) In the ASCII system, a space is character 32. Hence, Chr(32) is equal to a space.

This is a small point and the explanation may seem like overkill. But I think it's useful to point out that when you are communicating complex ideas about programming, you can often get hung up on annoying (but important) details, such as a missing space or semicolon. In subsequent sections of this book and in Access documentation, Chr(34) is used in a similar way. For example, the insertion of quotation marks (") using Chr(34) is described in the section on filtering records.

Remember that when you alter the sort order of the records, Access needs time to calculate the specified order. If the table is large, changing the sort order may cause a lengthy delay. In such cases, you might be able to improve performance by creating an index for the field on which the record set is sorted. Indexes are discussed in Chapter 1.

Filtering the Record Set

The technique I just described for sorting records also can be applied to filtering the records. *Filtering* refers to using logical criteria to limit which records are available for display. For example, suppose you want to limit the displayed records to one company at a time. The following SQL statement limits the set of records to those with the company name *Mark Smith Nissan:*

```
Select * From Invoices Where Company = "Mark Smith Nissan"
```

Limiting the form to a specific company probably won't be useful because it requires a separate form for each company. However, you can accomplish the same thing using one form by linking the Record Source property to a control that can display any of the available company names. Figure 12-8 shows a form that uses this approach. Each time a company name is selected in the control in the form's header, the record set is filtered to allow only invoices for that company.

Figure 12-8:
The company name in the control is used to filter the form's record set.

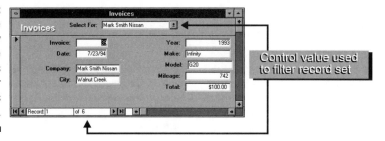

To implement this filter, you need to create a list or combo box control that displays the values that are to be used as criteria for filtering the record set. In this example, the invoices are filtered according to company name. In Chapter 3, this type of control was used to locate records that matched the selection. The list was defined by a SQL statement similar to the following example:

```
Select Distinct Company From Invoices Where Company Is Not Null;
```

Recall that the *Distinct* keyword eliminates duplicate names from the list. The *Where* clause eliminates any records that don't have an entry in the *Company* field. Each time a new name is selected, the record set of the form should be changed to match the selected company name. This can be accomplished by the AfterUpdate procedure for the combo box control, which in this example is called *RecordFilter.*

The following procedure uses the value in the *RecordFilter* control on a form called Invoices to select for one company at a time:

```
Sub RecordFilter_AfterUpdate ()
    SQLText = "Select * From Invoices Where Company =
            Forms![Invoice]![RecordFilter];"
```

```
        Screen.ActiveForm.RecordSource = SQLText
    End Sub
```

There is another approach to this procedure that avoids entering a specific form and control identifier. As such, it can be used in a variety of situations. In the following procedure, the first variable, *SQLText*, contains the part of the SQL statement that remains the same no matter which company is selected. *FilterText* is defined in part by the value of the combo box control, *RecordFilter*. The two segments are combined and used to set the form's RecordSource property. When the code is written in this way, you can change the source of the company name by simply changing the name of the control in the second statement.

```
    Sub RecordFilter_AfterUpdate ()
        SQLText = "Select * From Invoices Where Company = " & Chr(34)
        FilterText = [RecordFilter] & Chr(34) & ";"
        Screen.ActiveForm.RecordSource = SQLText & FilterText
    End Sub
```

One interesting aspect of the procedure involves the use of Chr(34). The *Chr( )* function inserts characters based on their ASCII value. Character 34 is a quotation mark ("). Figure 12-9 shows why Chr(34) is needed to create a valid SQL statement.

Figure 12-9: Quotation marks are not included when text is combined.

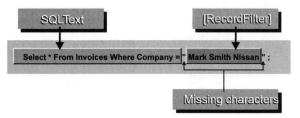

The quotation marks used to enclose a text literal are not stored as part of the text. To create a complete SQL statement, you must specifically insert quotation marks with Chr(34). If you don't, Access evaluates the combined text in the last statement of the procedure as follows:

```
    Select * From Invoices Where Company = Mark Smith Nissan ;
```

This statement won't execute properly because *Mark Smith Nissan*, without quotation marks, looks like an invalid identifier, not a text literal. When the Chr(34) functions are inserted in the text, the assembled SQL statement has the correct syntax:

```
Select * From Invoices Where Company = "Mark Smith Nissan" ;
```

This alternative technique can be used in many situations where no single identifier contains the exact text you need for the *Where* clause criteria. This technique is used later in the book for creating more advanced procedures.

When either of these methods is employed, the result is the same. Each time a selection is made from the list box, Access filters the record set of the form to include only those records that match the selection.

You should note that altering the Record Source of the form also redefines the record set for any aggregate summary functions used on the form. In practice, this means that controls having expressions with functions such as *Count( )*, *Sum( )*, or *Avg( )* will update each time the record set is filtered. Figure 12-10 shows a form that has *Count( )*, *Sum( )*, and *Avg( )* functions in the form footer. The values in these functions summarize the entire record set of the form. In this case, however, the form's record set is limited to one company at a time. As a result, these controls summarize the currently displayed company.

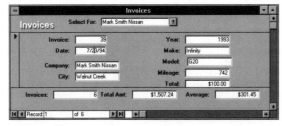

Figure 12-10: The aggregate summary functions Count( ), Sum( ), and Avg( ) change to match the new record set.

The techniques used to sort and filter the form's record set suggest some interesting possibilities for Access Basic. For example, in Figure 12-10, two separate and independent SQL statements are in operation. One statement is used as the Row Source of the combo box control. This statement reflects all the records in the Invoices table, even though the record set of the form may be limited to one specific company.

There is no limit to the sources of information available to a single form. In this example, the same underlying table, Invoices, is accessed independently by two SQL statements on a single form. This suggests that record sets can be manipulated independently from the form that is currently active.

The next chapter introduces the powerful tools that Access offers for defining, manipulating, and modifying sets of information through Access Basic procedures. Unlike macro actions, which closely mirror the way a user interacts with the Access interface, Access Basic allows these operations to take place without requiring any visible change in the screen display. This allows you to perform some remarkable operations with a relatively small amount of Access Basic code.

Chapter 13

Using Record Sets

Chapter 12 showed you how to use Access Basic procedures to manipulate the record sets that are assigned to a form. In particular, you saw how a change in the Record Source property of a form enables you to change the selected records or the sort order while still displaying the same form on the screen. This chapter takes the next logical step and shows you how to manipulate record sets drawn from a database's source, not just from the form's record set.

This chapter also introduces object variables. Up to now, all the variables I've discussed have been used to store individual text, numbers, or date values. These uses of variables are common to all programming languages, and Access Basic uses the same syntax as many other versions of the Basic language.

The term *object variables* combines the concept of data — such as tables, record sets, forms, reports, and controls — with the concept of variables defined as part of an Access Basic procedure.

This chapter details the characteristics and behavior of object variables. They are important because all Access Basic procedures can use and manipulate information stored in any database object, in any available Access database. The phrase *any database* refers not only to the currently loaded database, but also to any database stored on any available disk in the system.

Related Defaults

Both forms and tables allow you to define default values for controls or fields. A default value is inserted into a field or control whenever a new record is added to the record set.

However, this use of default values is limited to values that you expect to be the same for most of the records in your record set. For example, if you do business in only one state, the *State* field always remains the same.

A more useful type of default value is one I refer to as a related default value. A *related default value* can be filled in automatically as soon as the user fills in another related field. In the invoice table example from the previous chapters, when you select the name of the customer or company, you can assume that such values as street address, state, zip code, work phone, fax, contact name, and account number are the same as those entered on any previous invoice for the same customer or company.

The difference between a related default and a standard default has to do with which event triggers the insertion of the default values. The standard default method, which is built into Access, is triggered as soon as a new record is displayed. A related default value is inserted *after* the new record is displayed. The related default entry is delayed until a key item, such as the name of the company, is entered. Once that key value is entered, the default values related to that item can be inserted into other controls. Figure 13-1 shows how this type of default might work.

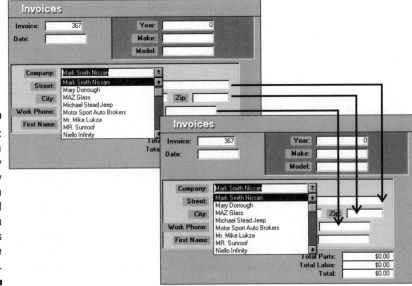

Figure 13-1: Selecting a company automatically fills in related fields from a previous entry for the same name.

The *Company* control is a combo box that lists the names of all previously entered companies. This is accomplished by a SQL statement in the Row Source property. When a selection is made in this control, an Access Basic procedure, Company_AfterUpdate, is triggered. This procedure locates the previous entry for that company and inserts all other items — address, phone numbers, and so on — related to that selection.

If the company entry is a new name, the procedure simply leaves the related controls blank. However, once you fill in the data for a new company or customer, that record can serve as the basis for any future records entered for that name. In other words, you have to enter the items related to a given name only once. From then on, the Access Basic procedure automatically fills in the related default values.

The usual approach is to create a customer or company table containing information that doesn't change from invoice to invoice, such as the address and phone number. With this approach, the data is displayed on the invoice form or report by means of a link between tables, or a form-subform relationship (which is described later in this book). However, if the standard information is similar to the example, it's probably too cumbersome for the user to enter addresses and phone numbers in a separate form or table. The method shown in this chapter achieves similar results within a simple form by manipulating the form's record set.

Cloning a Record Set

To create the procedure described in the preceding section, you need to clone a record set. The cloning technique is important for two reasons. It is

- ✔ **Practical.** Cloning a record set represents the next logical step in learning how to use Access Basic to solve problems through the customization of forms and reports. The related defaults procedure can't be implemented without these techniques.

- ✔ **Conceptual.** By examining how cloning works and why it is needed to create the proposed related defaults procedure, you'll gain a clearer understanding of how Access treats records, tables, and record sets. (To understand cloning, you need a more precise understanding of what is meant by *record sets* than has been discussed to this point.)

The Access Basic code for the related defaults procedure isn't much longer than any of the examples you have already encountered. However, some statements in this procedure require a more sophisticated use of Access database objects and the Access Basic tools that manipulate them. In fact, the cloning technique serves as an introduction to the most sophisticated aspects of Access Basic.

Before answering the question, *What is a clone?*, you need to ask again, *What is a record set?* So far, I've answered this question by saying that a record set consists of all the records that are related to an object, such as a table, query, form, or report. Although this is perfectly true, it's now important to make a distinction between the physical records stored in the tables and the record sets that are manipulated through the use of objects. In other words, there is a difference between the underlying record source that consists of the tables in which information is ultimately stored, and the record set that is assigned to an object such as a form.

Figure 13-2 shows two different forms — Form 1 and Form 2 — that have the same record source. The record source is a table named Invoices, which is pictured at the bottom of Figure 13-2. When the forms are first opened, they display information from the same record in the Invoices table.

What happens to the record displayed in Form 2 if you edit the record in Form 1? As soon as the first change is made in Form 1, the record displayed in Form 2 is locked — that is, no change is allowed. When the changes in Form 1 are saved, Form 2 is updated with those changes before you can edit that record. Access

Figure 13-2:
Several objects can have separate record sets based on the same underlying table.

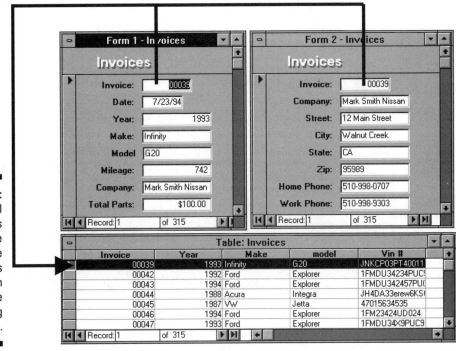

uses this same record locking procedure when users on a network access the same table. The lock applies only when the same record is displayed. If desired, you can edit two different records in the same record set at the same time. ■

In this example, both forms have a common record source — the Invoices table. But each form has its own record set. Once the forms are opened, the user is free to navigate among records in either form independently. For example, Figure 13-3 shows that Form 1 displays invoice 47 while Form 2 still shows invoice 39. In other words the *current* record in Form 1 is different from the current record in Form 2, even though they have the same underlying record source. Each form must have a current record, but it doesn't have to be the same record.

In some cases, you may want to synchronize the record sets of two or more forms so that the same record is current in the individual record sets. ■

You can use this concept to solve the problem of related defaults. In Figure 13-4, two forms with the same record source are displayed at the same time. The form on the right displays a new record with the name of the company, *Mark Smith Nissan*, entered into a text box. The form on the left shows a previously entered record for the same company. The older record contains items, such as the address and phone numbers, that need to be copied into the new record.

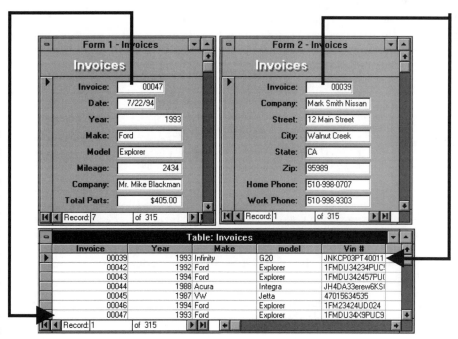

Figure 13-3:
Each record set has its own properties, even when the record sets are based on the same underlying table.

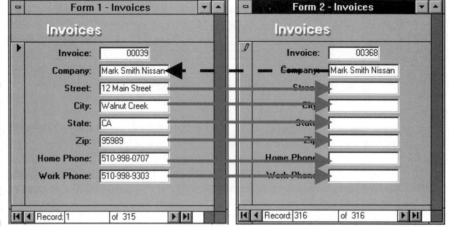

Figure 13-4:
Related
default
values can
be copied
from a
different
record set.

How can you copy the data from one form to another? You could manually
highlight, copy, and paste each control. But a better solution is to use SetValue
actions or Access Basic Let statements to change the values of the controls in
the new record to match the values displayed in the other form window. The
following procedure transfers the values displayed in Form 1 to the corresponding controls in Form 2:

```
Sub Company_AfterUpdate()
    Forms![Form 2]![Street] = Forms![Form 1]![Street]
    Forms![Form 2]![City] = Forms![Form 1]![City]
    Forms![Form 2]![State] = Forms![Form 1]![State]
    Forms![Form 2]![Zip] = Forms![Form 1]![Zip]
    Forms![Form 2]![Home Phone] = Forms![Form 1]![Home Phone]
    Forms![Form 2]![Work Phone] = Forms![Form 1]![Work Phone]
End Sub
```

As you can see, copying the values is a rather simple procedure. However, it
will work only if you create a duplicate form with the same record set and controls, open that form, and locate the record matching the company name in the
new record. After the values are copied, Form 2 can be closed. These actions,
shown in bold, should be added to the procedure as follows:

```
Sub Company_AfterUpdate()
    DoCmd OpenForm "Form 1"
    DoCmd FindRecord Forms![Form 2]![Company]
    Forms![Form 2]![Street] = Forms![Form 1]![Street]
    Forms![Form 2]![City] = Forms![Form 1]![City]
```

```
         Forms![Form 2]![State] = Forms![Form 1]![State]
         Forms![Form 2]![Zip] = Forms![Form 1]![Zip]
         Forms![Form 2]![Home Phone] = Forms![Form 1]![Home Phone]
         Forms![Form 2]![Work Phone] = Forms![Form 1]![Work Phone]
         DoCmd Close A_FORM, "Form 1"
     End Sub
```

Creating a record set clone

There is no functional need to see the previous record displayed in a form. The only reason Form 1 appears in the procedure is because you need to access its record set in order to find a previous entry for the same company. You could eliminate Form 1 if you had some way to manipulate the record set without creating an extra form.

The solution involves creating a duplicate of the record set of the current form without actually creating a new form. In the current example, the set of records you want to manipulate is already defined as the record set of the current Invoices form. You may recall from Chapter 12 that each form has a RecordSource property that displays the name of the table or query on which the form is based. The following statement displays the record source for the Invoices form — that is, the Invoices table:

```
    Msgbox Forms![Invoices].RecordSource
```

Access recognizes the exclamation point (!) as a separator if it precedes a user-defined name, such as the name of a form, field, or control. The period can be used with identifier names, as well as Access properties and methods. ∎

You can generalize this statement by substituting the screen object for the specific form name:

```
    Msgbox Screen.ActiveForm.RecordSource
```

Of course, the RecordSource property displays only the name of the record source. Access Basic provides a special property called *RecordSetClone* that lets you create a new record set that is identical to the record source of the current form. The identifier in the following example refers to a copy of the current form's record set. The Screen object is used in place of any specific form name, so this identifier can be used in any form:

```
    Screen.ActiveForm.RecordSetClone
```

The clone set has the same properties as the original record set. For example, you would use the following identifier to refer to the Invoice field in the clone set:

```
    Screen.ActiveForm.RecordSetClone.[Invoice]
```

The text values of the RecordSource and RecordSetClone properties are identical within the same form. If you use a MsgBox statement to display the value of either property (*The Msgbox ScreenActive.Form.RecordSource* property or the *Msgbox ScreenActive.Form.RecordSetClone* property), you get the same results. However, you can't use RecordSource in a Set statement. (The Set statement is described later in this chapter, in Defining an object variable.) You must use RecordSetClone to define a Record Set object. ∎

So? How does making a copy of the current record set solve the problem?

It's important to remember that even though a record set clone has the same contents (that is, the same records and fields) as the original record set, it can be manipulated independently from the form's record set. This means that you can change the current record in the clone without changing the current record in the form's record set. Conversely, any navigation among records in the form doesn't affect the clone.

The following procedure can be entered into the Click property of a command button control that you have added to the form:

```
Sub Button99_Click ()
    Debug.Print "Form: " & Screen.ActiveForm.[Invoice]
    Debug.Print "Clone: " & Screen.ActiveForm.RecordSetClone.[Invoice]
End Sub
```

This procedure prints the contents of the Invoice field from both the form's record set and the clone's record set to the Immediate window. You can use the results to monitor the behavior of the two record sets.

If you click this button immediately after opening the form, you get an identical value for each Invoice number:

```
Form:   000039
Clone:  000039
```

What happens if you change the form's current record by clicking on the Next Record button? The form's record set advances to the next record, but the clone is still at the first record:

```
Form:   000040
Clone:  000039
```

If you move to the last record in the form, the form's invoice number changes again, but the clone remains exactly where it was — at the first record:

```
Form:   000378
Clone:  000039
```

The process also works in reverse; You can navigate through the clone set without affecting the form. By using the move methods listed in Table 13-1 within an Access Basic procedure, you can duplicate the functions of the First, Last, Next, and Previous buttons that appear on the form.

Table 13-1: Move methods

Method	*Function*
MoveFirst	Makes the first record current
MoveLast	Makes the last record current
MoveNext	Makes the next record current
MovePrev	Makes the previous record current

For example, the following statement makes the last record in the clone record set current:

```
Screen.ActiveForm.RecordSetClone.MoveLast
```

Note that the statement consists of an object name and a method. Methods use the same syntax as properties. However, because a method represents an action such as "go to the last record," no other command is needed to make an executable statement. The following procedure adds a MoveLast statement before the invoice number is displayed:

```
Sub Button99_Click ()
    Debug.Print "Form: " & Screen.ActiveForm.[Invoice]
    Screen.ActiveForm.RecordSetClone.MoveLast
    Debug.Print "Clone: " & Screen.ActiveForm.RecordSetClone.[Invoice]
End Sub
```

When this procedure is executed, the current record of the clone record set changes. For example, if the procedure is executed immediately after the form is opened, the form shows the first invoice number while the clone shows the last record in the set:

```
Form:   000039
Clone:  000378
```

The find method

Moving to the first or last record in a set demonstrates how you can navigate within the clone record set. A more useful method of navigation involves the find methods listed in Table 13-2.

Table 13-2: Find methods

Method	Function
FindFirst *CriteriaExpr*	Finds the first matching record
FindLast *CriteriaExpr*	Finds the last matching record
FindNext *CriteriaExpr*	Finds the next matching record
FindPrev *CriteriaExpr*	Finds the previous matching record

These methods search the specified record set and locate the first, last, next, or previous record that matches a specified *criteria expression*. For example, the following statement searches the clone record set of the Invoice form for the first record in which *Company* contains Concord Ford:

```
Forms![Invoice].RecordSetClone.FindFirst "Company = 'Concord Ford' "
```

You can insert the Screen object name in place of the specific name of the form:

```
Screen.ActiveForm.RecordSetClone.FindFirst  Company = "Concord Ford"
```

Before applying the find method to the related defaults problem, it is useful to examine what Access means by a criteria expression. Criteria expressions are closely related to the *Where* clause used in SQL statements. Suppose you want to write a SQL statement that selects the same record as the FindFirst method shown in the previous example — that is, the first record in the table with the company name *Concord Ford*. The following SQL statement locates that record by using the criteria expression, which is shown in bold in the *Where* clause of the statement:

```
Select * From Invoices Where Company = "Concord Ford";
```

You may have noticed that the SQL statement doesn't specifically find the first record that matches the criteria expression. Rather, it returns a record set of all records in the source that match the criteria. Of course, the first record in this set would be the first matching record. ■

When using a find method in Access Basic, you don't need to specify all the details that would appear in an equivalent SQL statement. The object to which the find method is attached — the form's record set clone — already defines a record source for the search. All you need as an argument is the criteria expression used with the *Where* clause.

However, it's important to remember that this portion of the SQL statement is a text phrase. This means the entire phrase must be enclosed in a set of quotation marks. Because the phrase already contains a set of quotation marks around the company name — "Concord Ford" — you must change the quotation marks inside the phrase to single quotes. This change allows Access to correctly interpret the criteria expression. Therefore:

```
Company = "Concord Ford"
```

must be changed to

```
" Company = 'Concord Ford' "
```

As long as the criteria expression uses a literal criteria such as *Concord Ford* or *Hillside Nissan,* this technique isn't too complicated. However, suppose the actual name of the company isn't known in advance, and is meant to be entered into a control on the form, for example, *[Company].* The following statement appears to solve this problem by substituting a control identifier, *[Company],* for the literal name of the company:

```
" Company = [Company] "
```

As explained at the end of Chapter 12, however, this won't work because Access evaluates the criteria as an expression in which a name is simply inserted without quotation marks. As such, it appears as though *Concord* or *Ford* is an identifier name rather than a literal name:

```
Company = Concord Ford
```

You can solve this problem by using Chr(34) to insert quotation mark characters at the necessary locations in the statement:

```
" Company = " & Chr(34) & [Company] & Chr(34)
```

Access can understand this criteria expression, which would be evaluated in the example as *Company = "Concord Ford".* When you put all this together, you arrive at the following statement:

```
Screen.ActiveForm.RecordSetClone.FindFirst "Company=" & Chr(34) &
              [Company] & Chr(34)
```

You may find this statement a bit mind-boggling at first. It might be helpful to break down the statement into more manageable pieces. As shown in Figure 13-5, the statement consists of four distinct parts: the object, the property, the method, and the criteria expression.

It also helps to remember that this single statement accomplishes a lot. In a single statement, you access a duplicate of the record set, locate a specific record, and make it the current record of the clone set. Later in this chapter, you learn how to simplify this type of statement through the use of object variables.

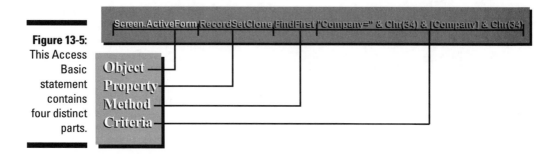

Figure 13-5:
This Access
Basic
statement
contains
four distinct
parts.

In the Access manuals and help files, a complicated statement such as the example in Figure 13-5 is often broken up into different statements. In such cases, the criteria expression is assigned to a variable. The following pair of statements perform the same function as the statement in Figure 13-5:

```
Criteria = "Company=" & Chr(34) & [Company] & Chr(34)
        Screen.ActiveForm.RecordSetClone.FindFirst Criteria
```

The two statements are related by the *Criteria* variable. First, *Criteria* is assigned the text of the criteria expression. Then the variable name is inserted into the FindFirst statement in the position of the criteria expression. The variable name *Criteria* is commonly found in the Access manuals and help screens. My personal preference is to use a name like *CritText*, because it emphasizes that the text being manipulated forms a criteria expression.

The Related Defaults Procedure

Although it may seem like a long, torturous journey since you started with the problem of entering related default values, the time has finally come when you can put all the elements together and write the required procedure. The following discussion assumes that you have a combo box control that displays a list of values that have been entered into this field in previous records. In this example, the control is bound to the *Company* field, and the following SQL statement is used to create a list of unique company names:

```
Select Distinct Company From Invoices Where Company is Not Null;
```

The AfterUpdate event property for the combo box control uses the following procedure to locate and insert the related default values:

```
Sub Company_AfterUpdate ()
    CritText = "Company=" & Chr(34) & [Company] & Chr(34)
    Screen.ActiveForm.RecordSetClone.FindLast CritText
    [Street] = Screen.ActiveForm.RecordSetClone![Street]
    [City] = Screen.ActiveForm.RecordSetClone![City]
```

```
        [State] = Screen.ActiveForm.RecordSetClone![State]
        [Zip] = Screen.ActiveForm.RecordSetClone![Zip]
        [Home Phone] = Screen.ActiveForm.RecordSetClone![ Home Phone]
        [Work Phone] = Screen.ActiveForm.RecordSetClone![ Work Phone]
   End Sub
```

You might notice that the procedure uses the FindLast method instead of FindFirst. This allows for changes in the address or the phone numbers that take place after a user has entered the initial record for the company. In other words, FindLast allows you to use the most recently entered values for the related fields. As a result, a new record will reflect any changes made to that company's information.

The related values are inserted into the form's current record by a series of statements that have the following general form:

```
   FieldName = Screen.ActiveForm.RecordSetClone!FieldName
```

Access assumes that the field (or control) name used by itself refers to the form's record set and current record. The preceding statement works because the clone's record set operates independently from the form's record set. Even though *FieldName* is used twice in the same statement, it refers to two different objects. The *FieldName* that appears to the left of the equal sign is assumed to refer to the field (or control) related to the record displayed on the current form. The *FieldName* that appears after *RecordSetClone* refers to the current record in the clone record set. This is true even if the same name, for example, *Wholesale,* appears in both places. The following statement transfers the value of *Wholesale* in the clone record set into the *Wholesale* field (or control) on the current form:

```
   Wholesale = Screen.ActiveForm.RecordSetClone!Wholesale
```

Remember that the field name and the control name don't have to be the same. You can store any field value in any control (assuming they are the same data types) using this type of statement. However, because of the way forms are usually created, a control that is bound to a field usually has the same name as the field.

Also keep in mind that identifiers in the clone record set are limited to the field names only. However, the form can include unbound controls that appear on the form as well as all of the fields from the form's record set. This allows you to perform two operations on the form that you cannot do with the clone record set:

✔ You can insert values into fields that aren't on the form. If a form's record set includes a field called *Wholesale* that doesn't appear on the form, you can update the field from the clone record set.

✔ You can update unbound controls that appear on the form by inserting a field from the clone record set.

The technique outlined in this section allows you to apply any Access Basic method or record set property to the clone record set.

Working with Object Variables

In the previous section, you created a procedure that can locate and copy sets of values from a record other than the one displayed on the form, without requiring the use of other form or table windows. As you know, this is all made possible by cloning a form's record set.

When looking at the code used to implement this procedure, you probably noticed that the same rather cumbersome object name is repeated in all but one of the statements:

```
Sub Company_AfterUpdate ()
    CritText = "Company=" & Chr(34) & [Company] & Chr(34)
    Screen.ActiveForm.RecordSetClone.FindLast CritText
    [Street] = Screen.ActiveForm.RecordSetClone![Street]
    [City] = Screen.ActiveForm.RecordSetClone![City]
    [State] = Screen.ActiveForm.RecordSetClone![State]
    [Zip] = Screen.ActiveForm.RecordSetClone![Zip]
    [Home Phone] = Screen.ActiveForm.RecordSetClone![ Home Phone]
    [Work Phone] = Screen.ActiveForm.RecordSetClone![ Work Phone]
End Sub
```

You could eliminate a lot of typing and make the code easier to read and understand by replacing this awkward name with something simpler, such as the letter *C* for clone:

```
Sub Company_AfterUpdate ()
    CritText = "Company=" & Chr(34) & [Company] & Chr(34)
    C.FindLast CritText
    [Street] = C![Street]
    [City] = C![City]
    [State] = C![State]
    [Zip] = C![Zip]
    [Home Phone] = C![ Home Phone]
    [Work Phone] = C![ Work Phone]
End Sub
```

This substitution doesn't affect the meaning of the statements but it does greatly simplify both the writing and reading of the code. Access Basic supports the use of *object variables,* which allow you to make such a substitution and write more streamlined code.

Of course, object variables do much more than simplify code. These other capabilities and functions are discussed later in this chapter and throughout the remainder of the book.

When you use an ordinary variable in an Access Basic procedure, you can assign the variable name a single value, such as a text phrase, a numeric value, or a date:

```
Overdue = [Date Shipped] + 90
```

Object variables can be defined as any valid Access database object, such as a form, a control, a report, or even a record set. An object variable has all of the characteristics and properties you would normally associate with an object of the same type. For example, a record set variable has all of the same characteristics as a record set associated with a form, except a screen display component.

This description of object variables should sound familiar because this is exactly how a clone record set behaves. In fact, the name *Screen.ActiveForm.RecordSetClone* operates like an object variable. The only differences are that there can be only one *Screen.ActiveForm.RecordSetClone* at a time, and the name (cumbersome as it is) is always the same. Object variables allow you to assign user names to objects such as clone record sets. This means you aren't stuck using a name like *Screen.ActiveForm.RecordSetClone* over and over each time you want to refer to a record set.

In theory, you can create multiple clones of the form's record set and assign a different object variable name to each clone. However, regardless of the names you select, all of the clones operate on the same record set. This means that if you create several clones of the same record set, each time you change the current record in one clone, all of the other clones will immediately change to the same current record. If you want to create multiple object variables that can each access *different* records in the same record set used by the form, you have to use the CreateRecordSet() method. ■

Defining an object variable

An object variable is defined by two separate but related statements:

- ✔ **Dim...As**. The Dim statement *must* be used to declare which type of database object the variable will be.
- ✔ **Set**. The Set statement assigns information to a database variable.

The Dim...As statement has the following general form:

```
Dim VariableName As ObjectType
```

If you want to create a record set, you would use *RecordSet* as the type. The following statement defines *C* as a RecordSet type variable:

```
Dim C As RecordSet
```

Controls and fields

When a control is bound to a field through its Control Source property, you usually treat the control as if it is synonymous with the field in the underlying table. In most cases, there's no need to split hairs about the difference between a bound control and the field to which it is bound.

However, as shown by the technique used in this chapter to copy data from a record in the clone set to the record displayed on the form, the controls displayed on the form isn't actually part of the form's record set. The form consists of a set of controls. All of the information that appears on these controls is stored in a memory buffer. Although the memory buffer is related to the underlying record set, it is independent of the record set. This explains why unbound controls can temporarily store information even though they have no connection to the form's record set.

When you select a company name from the drop list, the text is inserted into the Company control, which stores the text in the *editing buffer* area of the computer's memory. The fact that the control may be bound to a field — for example, the *Company* field in the Invoices table — doesn't come into play until the form is saved. At that moment, Access uses the Control Source property of the bound controls to copy the information from the editing buffer to a record in the form's record set.

The editing buffer allows you to move around the form's record set without disturbing the information displayed on the screen. The techniques described in this chapter work because the control and the record set are two different objects that use different storage areas.

As is the case with standard variables, the Dim statement doesn't assign any values or data to the variable name. It simply indicates to Access Basic which object type uses this variable name in the current procedure.

The Set statement has the following general form:

```
Set VariableName = ObjectExpression
```

VariableName is the name of a variable whose type has already been defined by a **Dim...As** statement. *ObjectExpression* is an identifier, a function, or an object method that produces a database object such as a form, a control, or a table.

The following statement assigns the current form's record set clone to the object variable name *C:*

```
Set C = Screen.ActiveForm.RecordSetClone
```

Unlike Let, which is optional, the keyword Set must appear at the beginning of each Set statement.

Object variable names aren't limited in size any more than the names of standard variables. They can be up to 40 characters. However, one of the advantages of using object variables is that they can reduce the verbosity of Access Basic statements. As such, it's appropriate to use short — even single-letter — names. ∎

As shown in the following example, you can use object variables to simplify the names used in the related defaults procedure (the changes are shown in bold):

```
Sub Company_AfterUpdate ()
    Dim C As RecordSet
    Set C = Screen.ActiveForm.RecordSetClone
    CritText = "Company=" & Chr(34) & [Company] & Chr(34)
    C.FindLast CritText
    [Street] = C![Street]
    [City] = C![City]
    [State] = C![State]
    [Zip] = C![Zip]
    [Home Phone] = C![ Home Phone]
    [Work Phone] = C![ Work Phone]
End Sub
```

The first two statements in the procedure create the object variable _C_, which is a RecordSet type variable. In the remaining statement, this variable is used in place of _Screen.ActivateForm.RecordSet_ .

The RecordSet variable type is new in Version 2.0. This variable type is used in place of the snapshot, dynaset, and table objects found in Version 1.0. The reason for this change is to create a more consistent way of dealing with record set objects. Access still maintains the distinction between table, snapshot, and dynaset objects. ∎

The use of the object variable in this procedure doesn't change the operation of the procedure — that is, the procedure still inserts default values from the previous matching record. However, the change greatly simplifies the code.

Using _Screen.ActiveForm.RecordSetClone_ is useful for learning how record sets are related to objects such as forms, but it is much too cumbersome to be used repeatedly in a procedure or group of procedures. SQL statements can also be a bit unwieldy. As you learn more about object variables, you'll see that the results of a SQL statement can be assigned to an object variable. Once that assignment is made, you can perform any number of operations with the record set by referring to the object variable.

The NoMatch property

Many records added to a table such as Invoices will be companies that are already entered into the table, but some will be new entries. For new company names, the procedure should skip the statements that copy values.

Each record set has a *NoMatch* property, which is either True (-1) or False (0). The find methods listed in Table 13-2 set the value of the NoMatch property based on the results of the last find. You can use the NoMatch property to evaluate the success or failure of a find method and thereby control how the procedure operates.

The following procedure uses the NoMatch property of the record set C to determine whether the name in the *Company* control matches any previous company names:

```
Sub Company_AfterUpdate ()
    Dim C As RecordSet
    Set C = Screen.ActiveForm.RecordSetClone
    CritText = "Company=" & Chr(34) & [Company] & Chr(34)
    C.FindLast CritText
    If Not C.NoMatch Then
            [Street] = C![Street]
            [City] = C![City]
            [State] = C![State]
            [Zip] = C![Zip]
            [Home Phone] = C![ Home Phone]
            [Work Phone] = C![ Work Phone]
    Endif
End Sub
```

The statements that set values operate only if the FindLast method is successful in locating a matching record. Records with new company names will skip that section of the procedure.

You might notice that the expression used in the *If* structure is *Not C.NoMatch*. This sounds like a double negative (*not no match*), which in English can cause some confusion.

In this procedure, the *If* structure is used to execute a group of statements only when a find is successful. Access defines the NoMatch property as False when a find succeeds, and True when it fails. In this example, you want to execute the statements within the *If* structure when a find succeeds. Because the *If* structure requires a true value to activate the *Then* portion, the *Not* operator is used to reverse the value of NoMatch from False (the find was successful) to True. Table 13-3 shows the different ways that you can use NoMatch.

Table 13-3: How the NoMatch property is evaluated

	True Expression	*False Expression*
Find succeeds	Not *Object*.NoMatch	*Object*.NoMatch
Find fails	*Object*.NoMatch	Not *Object*.NoMatch

If you get confused about the use of the NoMatch property, it might be helpful to read the property not as *No Match* (a negative) but as *failed*. Thus, you would read the statement *If Not C.NoMatch Then* as *if not failed then*. After all, the phrase *if not no match then* would make any English teacher wince. ∎

Updating List Controls

One of the keys to solving the related defaults problem involves using the combo box list to display the names of the companies that are already entered into the record set. However, you need to be aware that Access calculates the values for the combo box list only once. This occurs the first time you display the drop list associated with the combo box control. On some systems, you may notice a delay the first time you open this list because Access must process the SQL statement before the list can be displayed.

But what happens to this list when you add new company names to the record set? Nothing. The list reflects only names that were entered when you first opened the combo box list. As you add new companies to the record set, the combo box list becomes incomplete because it is missing these new names.

Access sets the contents of a combo box drop list the first time the list is displayed, not when the form is opened. This is because Access doesn't perform the SQL selection statement (or query) associated with the control until you open the drop list. If you add new names *before* you open the list for the first time, the new entries will appear on the list because they have been added to the record source (the Invoices table) before the control's Row Source is processed.

It's interesting to note that list box controls behave differently. Because list boxes must display a list of values as soon as the form is opened, the Row Source for list boxes is retrieved *before* the form is displayed. Any new names added to the record set won't appear in a list box control until the Row Source is required. ∎

The solution is to *requery* the control. The requery operation prompts Access to perform the Row Source property — a SQL statement — again. In doing so, the list is updated to reflect any changes made to the record set used by the Row Source. In the example used throughout this chapter, you need to requery the *Company* control after each new company name is added to the record set.

Access supports both a requery action and a requery method. The action can be used in a macro or, by means of the DoCmd statement, in an Access Basic procedure. The following statement updates the *Company* control:

```
DoCmd Requery "Company"
```

Keep in mind that Requery accepts only control names as arguments, and they must be either text or variables that have a text value.

You shouldn't use the DoCmd Requery action without specifying the name of a control. The action is valid without a control name, but it requeries the Record Source of the form instead of updating the row source of a control. Although this will update the row sources of all combo box and list controls on the form, it also has the undesired effect of changing the current record to the first record in the record set. ∎

How can you implement the requery action in the example form? As shown in the following procedure, which is assigned to the form's AfterUpdate property, the simplest way is to update the control's list each time a record is updated,

```
Sub Form_AfterUpdate ()
    DoCmd Requery "Company"
End Sub
```

However, Access will update the control even when no change has taken place. This causes frequent delays because Access must execute the SQL statement each time the drop list is opened. A more efficient approach links the update to the entry of a new company name.

Recall that you have already created a procedure that can determine, by use of the FindLast method and the NoMatch property, when a new name is added to the record set. You can use that procedure to set up an update of the company list. The following procedure adds a requery action as the *Else* portion of the existing *If* structure. In this procedure, the requery action takes place when no match is found for the company name:

```
Sub Company_AfterUpdate ()
    Dim C As RecordSet
    Set C = Screen.ActiveForm.RecordSetClone
    CritText = "Company=" & Chr(34) & [Company] & Chr(34)
    C.FindLast CritText
    If Not C.NoMatch Then
            [Street] = C![Street]
            [City] = C![City]
            [State] = C![State]
            [Zip] = C![Zip]
            [Home Phone] = C![ Home Phone]
            [Work Phone] = C![ Work Phone]
    Else
            DoCmd Requery "Company"
    Endif
End Sub
```

Unfortunately, this approach is flawed. If you were to use this procedure, you would find that sometimes it works and other times a new name would fail to appear on the drop list. Why?

The answer involves the difference between the two types of AfterUpdate event properties that occur on a form. Each control has its own AfterUpdate property that is triggered when the control is updated — that is, when the focus changes to another control or record. The form's AfterUpdate event doesn't take place until the entire record is saved.

Figure 13-6 shows what happens (and what doesn't happen) when a new company name is entered into the *Company* control on a form.

Figure 13-6:
The underlying record set isn't updated until the form's AfterUpdate event.

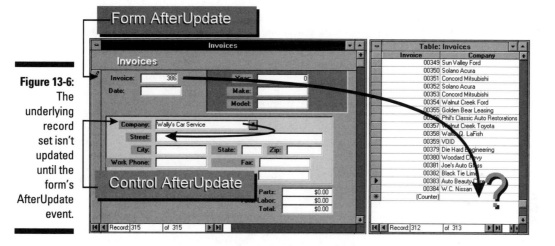

The control's AfterUpdate event is triggered, which causes Access to execute any procedure linked to that event (such as the example). If the procedure executes a requery action at this point, it will fail to add the name that appears in the *Company* control.

Figure 13-6 shows why this is the case. Remember that the records in the underlying record set (in this example, a table called Invoices) are the source of names for the combo box. The figure shows that the record that is currently on the Invoices form has not yet been added to the Invoices record set — that is, the Invoices table. The record set isn't updated until the form's AfterUpdate event takes place. In other words, the requery action won't work while the pencil icon appears in the form's record selector box.

Using a Flag Variable

You can solve this problem by delaying the action needed to update the list until the record that contains the new company name is added to the record set. This seems to imply that you should move the requery action into the Form_AfterUpdate procedure so that it executes after the new or modified record is added to the form's underlying record set.

This solution works, but it also updates the *Company* control after *every* record update, regardless of whether a new company name is used. Ideally, you want to perform the requery action only when it's necessary — that is, only when a new company name is added to the form's record set.

You are facing a problem that occurs in many programming efforts: the event that indicates the need for an action occurs *before* that action can be carried out. To solve this problem, you need a method that delays the execution of the requery action until after the record set is updated.

The technique used to solve this type of problem is called a *register* or a *flag*. Figure 13-7 shows the normal sequence of events in which an action is immediately triggered by the event to which it is related.

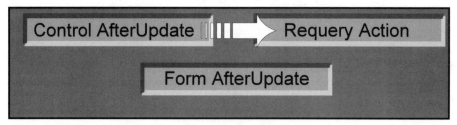

Figure 13-7: Control AfterUpdate immediately triggers the Requery action.

A register or flag is a variable that typically has a true or false value. The purpose of this variable is similar to the flag attached to a mailbox. When the flag is down (false), it indicates that no action is needed. When the flag is up (true), it indicates that an action is necessary.

The diagram in Figure 13-8 shows how a flag variable is used to solve the problem of updating the company list. The control's AfterUpdate procedure is used to set the flag up (true) if a new company name is entered into the form. Note that setting the flag is a simple matter of changing the variable's value. It does not execute the action at that time.

When the form's AfterUpdate event takes place (that is, when the record is saved) that procedure checks the value of the flag variable. If the flag is set to true, the action (in this case a requery) is executed. This ensures that the next time the company drop list is displayed, it will provide an up-to-date list of company names.

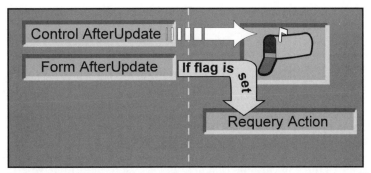

Figure 13-8: A flag variable is set by the control's AfterUpdate procedure and later controls an action executed by the form's AfterUpdate procedure.

The flag variable, sometimes called a register, allows you to record the need to perform an action without immediately performing the action. Another procedure that executes at a later point can check the flag or register to see if some action is needed. This technique allows you to avoid unnecessary actions and correctly identify when it is necessary to update the control list.

To implement this technique, you need to use the declarations section of the form's Access Basic module. The declarations section is used to define variables that are used by more than one procedure. A variable that is defined in the declarations section is available to all of the form's procedures, and it retains its value until the form is closed.

Open the declarations section of the form's module and define a variable called *UpdateCompanyList*:

```
Options Compare Database   'Use database order for string comparisons
Dim UpdateCompanyList
```

The Company_AfterUpdate procedure no longer performs the Requery action. Instead, the following procedure sets the value of the *UpdateCompanyList* flag variable to True when a new company name is entered:

```
Sub Company_AfterUpdate ()
    Dim C As RecordSet
    Set C = Screen.ActiveForm.RecordSetClone
    CritText = "Company=" & Chr(34) & [Company] & Chr(34)
    C.FindLast CritText
    If Not C.NoMatch Then
            [Street] = C![Street]
            [City] = C![City]
```

continued

```
                    [State] = C![State]
                    [Zip] = C![Zip]
                    [Home Phone] = C![ Home Phone]
                    [Work Phone] = C![ Work Phone]
         Else
                    UpdateCompanyList = True
         Endif
    End Sub
```

The list is updated when the form is updated. This means you need to add a
Form_AfterUpdate procedure to the module. The requery action is now located
in this procedure. The requery action is controlled by an *If* structure that uses
the value of the flag variable *UpdateCompanyList* to determine whether the action should be performed:

```
    Sub Form_AfterUpdate ()
        If UpdateCompanyList Then
                DoCmd Requery "Company"
                UpdateCompanyList = False
        Endif
    End Sub
```

Note that the flag variable is changed to False after the requery action is performed.
This statement is equivalent to the mail carrier putting down the flag on the
mailbox after picking up the mail. Once the list is updated, you need to make
sure that the flag doesn't trigger another requery action until the entry of a new
name makes it necessary.

Resetting the flag variable is an important part of the flag technique. For the flag
to work correctly, there must be at least one way to set the flag to True and at
least one way to set it to False. If you forget to reset the flag after the action is
performed, it simply repeats the action each time, regardless of the conditions.

The Requery Method

As discussed earlier in this chapter, Access supports both a requery action and
a requery method. The requery method can be used in Access Basic, and it
eliminates the need for a DoCmd (macro action) statement in an Access Basic
procedure.

In this example, there is no obvious functional difference between the requery
action and the requery method. However, it is useful to see how you would
write this procedure using only Access Basic variables, properties, and methods.

Recall that object variables can be used to represent any of the objects in an
Access database. In this case, the object to be manipulated is not a record set
but a control. You can create an object variable for a control just as you would

for any other type of object. First, you use a Dim statement to define the variable type. Then, you use a Set statement to assign an object value to that variable.

The following procedure shows how to assign the *Company* control on the active form to an object variable named *Ctrl*. The control is updated using the requery method.

```
Sub Form_AfterUpdate ()
    Dim Ctrl As Control
    Set Ctrl = Screen.ActiveForm![Company]
    If UpdateCompanyList Then
            Ctrl.Requery
            UpdateCompanyList = False
    Endif
End Sub
```

It is useful to recognize how the use of object variables changes the style of Access Basic code. For example, specific identifier names are placed at the beginning of the procedure. As a result, the first group of statements in the procedure gives you a general idea of the types of objects that are involved in the operation.

Conversely, when you encounter a name within a procedure, you can clarify what that name stands for by looking at the variables defined in the first few statements. For example, by looking at the statements at the beginning of the following procedure, you can easily determine that the name *Ctrl* refers to a control:

```
Sub Form_AfterUpdate ()
    Dim Ctrl As Control
    Set Ctrl = Screen.ActiveForm![Company]
    If UpdateCompanyList Then
            Ctrl.Requery
            UpdateCompanyList = False
    Endif
End Sub
```

Another benefit of this style of code is that object variable names can be used to simplify the names of objects. In the previous example, the name *Ctrl* is used as a substitute for the object named *Screen.ActiveForm![Company]*. Using the shorter variable name *Ctrl* simplifies the rest of the code, making it easier to write and read.

In contrast, DoCmd statements often require a long list of arguments whose meaning can become obscure. You might recall from Chapter 10 the complicated syntax of the FindRecord action, in which several commas are required as placeholders to ensure that the last argument, False, is in the correct position:

```
DoCmd FindRecord [Company], , , , , , False
```

The Screen Object and the Immediate Window

There is one more reason why object variables are preferable to using the Screen object in procedures. This reason relates to the use of the Immediate window for debugging.

The Immediate window allows you to display the values of various expressions, properties, and objects while you are debugging a procedure. However, when the Immediate window is selected, Access recognizes it as the Screen object. As a result, Access can't evaluate the object *Screen.ActiveForm* because the current Screen object — the Immediate window — isn't a form and doesn't support the ActiveForm property.

If you try to display the value of a control or property from the form you are debugging, Access displays the error message *No form is active.* This error also occurs when you step through a procedure that uses the *Screen.ActiveForm* object.

This is admittedly a bit of a quirk. If you are debugging a module attached to a form, you would expect that any reference in the code or the Immediate window to the *Screen.ActiveForm* object would pertain to that form. Currently, Access doesn't work that way.

The solution is to use object variables as early in the procedure as possible. Why? There's no sure-fire method for debugging statements that use the *Screen.ActiveForm* object. However, once that object is assigned to an object variable, you can operate in the code and Immediate windows. For example, suppose you use a breakpoint to pause a procedure so that you can determine which is the current invoice in the clone record set. The following entry in the Immediate window would produce an error because Access wouldn't recognize the ActiveForm object:

```
? Screen.ActiveForm.RecordSetClone.[Invoice]
```

The alternative is to assign the clone record set to a variable and then break execution after those statements are processed. The following code places a breakpoint after the clone record set is assigned to the variable C:

```
Dim C As RecordSet
Set C = Screen.ActiveForm.RecordSetClone
<breakpoint>
```

You can then obtain the desired information — that is, the current value of *Invoice* in the clone record set — by referring to the variable C in the Immediate window:

```
? C.[Invoice]
```

Chapter 14

Working with Collections

*T*he simplest solution to a programming problem is to create a macro or a function in which specific details are *hardwired* into the procedure. For example, the related defaults procedure from the previous chapter includes several statements that insert values from the clone record set into the current form. In this example, six fields are involved, and each uses one statement to copy information from a field into a control:

```
Sub Company_AfterUpdate ()
    Dim C As RecordSet
    Set C = Screen.Active Form.RecordSetClone
    CritText = "Company=" & Chr(34) & [Company] & Chr(34)
    C.FindLast CritText
    If Not C.NoMatch Then
            [Street] = C![Street]
            [City] = C![City]
            [State] = C![State]
            [Zip] = C![Zip]
            [Home Phone] = C![ Home Phone]
            [Work Phone] = C![ Work Phone]
    Else
            UpdateCompanyList = True
    Endif
End Sub
```

Suppose you also want to copy the *Contact* or *Account Number* fields. To do so, you would have to add two more statements. In fact, every time you change your mind about whether or not you want to copy a particular field, you have to rewrite the code.

In practice, you have to make changes like this all the time. Making this kind of change is one of the most time-consuming, tedious aspects of programming. The essential structure of the procedure remains the same, but you must repeatedly edit the code to get the right set of items. Because users often change their preferences as they become more familiar with a program, it's more efficient to build procedures in which you can modify operations without rewriting the code.

This chapter shows you how to design procedures that can adjust to a different set of specifications without being rewritten. The details aren't specified directly in the procedure code.

Instead, the procedure relies on lists maintained automatically by Access. These special lists are called *collections*. For example, when you design a form, you do so by placing controls on the form. When you save a form, it's really a collection of controls. An important part of any form must be a list of its components — in this case, controls.

Containers and Collections

To gain an understanding of the techniques available in Access Basic for creating more flexible procedures, let's go back to the related defaults problem posed in the previous chapter. How can you copy a group of values from a previous entry into a new record? The solution involves manipulating the form's record set without changing the displayed form.

Instead of writing a procedure in which specific fields are copied, suppose you want to create a procedure that copies all the entries from the previous record into the new or current record. In other words, you want to ditto the last record entered for the same company.

You can solve this problem by simply expanding the related defaults procedure to include the names of all the controls on the form. However, what if you need to add or delete one of those controls? You would have to edit the code to reflect those changes.

Can you create a procedure that automatically adjusts to changes in the form and still inserts the default values from a previous record? Of course. That's what this chapter is all about.

The solution presented in this chapter involves the concepts of containers and collections:

✔ **Containers**. A *container* is an object that contains other objects. For example, a form is an object that is composed of controls — which are themselves objects. The form is considered a container because it contains controls.

✔ **Collections**. A *collection* is a group of objects that are stored in a container. For example, if the container is a form, all the controls on the form make up a collection.

The objects in Access are organized in a series of relationships in which each object contains a collection of smaller objects:

✔ **Workspace.** The workspace object refers to all the items that can be used by a single user during an Access session. Each time you load Access, you create a default workspace object that automatically includes any open databases.

✔ **Database.** Within each workspace may be one or more open databases. When you work strictly from the Access program menus, you work with one database at a time. However, Access Basic does allow you to open multiple databases and perform operations in which a single workspace has more than one database object.

✔ **Database collections.** Within each database are collections of such familiar objects as tables, forms, and reports.

The diagram in Figure 14-1 begins with the Workspace object and illustrates how other Access objects are organized within that workspace.

Figure 14-1:
Access objects are organized into multiple level containers.

Numbered Objects in Collections

The concepts of containers and collections are useful, in an abstract way, to help you envision the relationships between various objects. Databases contain forms, forms contain controls, and so on.

There is also an important practical reason why these concepts are relevant to creating procedures in Access. So far, you have used identifier *names* for all the references to objects in your macros and Access Basic procedures. For example, the following statement displays the name of the record source (table, query, or SQL statement) for the form named Invoices:

```
MsgBox Forms![Invoices].RecordSource
```

If the statement refers to the currently active form, you can replace the specific form name with the Screen object. Assuming that Invoices is the active form, the following statement yields the identical result:

```
MsgBox Screen.ActiveForm.RecordSource
```

However, Access provides another way to refer to open forms. Access maintains a list called the *forms* collection of all open forms. In this list, each form is assigned a number, starting with 0. As shown in the following example, the forms that are open in a database can be referred to by number:

```
Forms(0)
Forms(1)
Forms(2)
```

When referring to an object in a collection, you can use the function form of the identifier. In the function form of the identifier, the list number is entered as an argument of the object. In other words, the list number is enclosed in parentheses. For example, the following statements have the same meaning and produce identical results:

```
MsgBox Screen.ActiveForm.RecordSource
```

```
MsgBox Forms(0).RecordSource
```

The numbering sequence of forms within the forms collection is *dynamic*. This means that, Access changes the number of the form in the collection when the user performs an action such as opening a new form or selecting another form as the active form. The active form is always 0. For example, if the Invoice form is active, it is Form 0. If you then open the Inventory form, Inventory becomes 0 and Invoices becomes 1. If you then switch back to Invoices, the numbers change again so that Invoices (the current form) is now 0 and Inventory is now 1.

It's important to remember that most lists and series in Access begin with 0, not 1. If a collection contains three objects, they are numbered 0, 1, and 2 — not 1, 2, and 3. Lists that begin with 0 are called *zero-based* lists. This distinguishes them from the more common practice of starting a sequenced list with 1. Zero-based lists reflect the fact that the default state of any byte of computer memory is 0 (0000 0000 in binary notation). As soon as you turn on your computer, its memory is automatically filled with 0 values. When you start to number a list, it makes sense to start with the number that is already there, 0. Contrast this with a manual system in which you write numbers on a piece of paper. Because a blank sheet of paper is devoid of values, it is just as easy to start a handwritten list with 1 as with 0. ■

All Access objects exist in collections that can be referenced by number. To create the ditto procedure described at the beginning of the chapter, you need to be concerned with two other collections:

- **Controls.** Each form is composed of controls. All the controls on the form are part of a collection in which the controls are listed in sequence, starting with 0.

- **Fields.** Each record source is a collection of fields. In the fields collection list, the fields are listed in sequence, starting with 0.

A form typically contains one or more connections in which a member of the form's control collection is bound to a member of the record source's field collection. To create the ditto procedure, you need to understand how to transfer data from one collection to another without using specific identifier names in the Access Basic statements.

Working with Control Collections

Before discussing the code that solves the ditto problem, you need to know how to write Access Basic statements that work with elements in a collection rather than specific object names. Specifically, you need to understand the techniques for manipulating the collection of controls contained in any form.

For example, the simple form in Figure 14-2 contains four controls, each with a unique name. When you add a data-oriented control such as a text box to a form, you need to remember that you are actually adding a second control — that is, the label control that identifies the text box. Access automatically generates a name for these label controls, such as *Text1* or *Text3*.

When Access generates a control name, it combines the control type with a number. The result is a name like *Text1* or *Button57*. The number is generated by a counter, similar in function to the counter field type. However, the number is consecutive for the total number of controls of any type. If you begin a form by placing a text box bound to a field, the first control is *Text1* and the text box matches the name of the field. When you place the next field, the label control is *Text3*, not *Text2*, because the label is the third control placed on the form. Access doesn't bother to keep a separate counter for each field type. If you delete and add fields to a form, the counter doesn't recycle. It continues counting like a counter field. If you delete the first 100 fields from a form, the next label placed will be *Text101*, even though it may be the only control on the form. ■

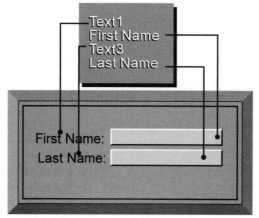

Figure 14-2:
Each control
on a form
has a unique
name.

Alternatively, each control on a form can be treated as an element in the form's control collection. The diagram in Figure 14-3 shows that each of the controls could be referenced by a number value starting with 0 and moving consecutively through the form's collection.

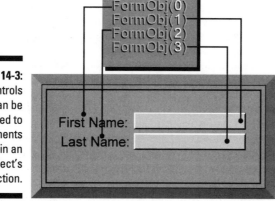

Figure 14-3:
Controls
also can be
referred to
as elements
in an
object's
collection.

It is important to remember that the numbers assigned to the elements in a collection are dynamic. Unlike the control names, which remain fixed, Access automatically renumbers the elements in the form's collection each time a control is added or deleted.

How would you use collection elements in a procedure? First, you need to create an object variable for the container. In this case, the container is a form, so you need to define an object variable as a form type object. The following statement defines the object variable *F* as a form type variable:

```
Dim F As Form
```

As previously mentioned, even though object variable names can be up to 40 characters in length, you should choose names that are as simple as possible in order to cut down on the length of statements that use these variables. For example, the single letter *F* is often used for a form variable.

After defining the variable name, you can use a Set statement to assign an object of the corresponding type to the variable. In this example, the active form is assigned to the variable *F*.

```
Set F = Screen.ActiveForm
```

You can now use *F* as the name of the container and refer to any element in its collection by number. For example, if the form contains the controls shown in Figure 14 -2 and Figure 14 -3, you would use the following element names:

```
F(0)
F(1)
F(2)
F(3)
```

However, an element name such as *F(0)* isn't a complete Access Basic statement. To use the element name, you must place it in the context of a statement that manipulates the control. For example, every control has a Name property. The following statement displays the name of the first control in the form's collection:

```
Msgbox F(0).Name
```

Technically, you aren't required to use an object variable. You can refer to a control in the form's collection by using either the form name or the screen object. If the active form is named Invoices, either *Forms![Invoices](0).Name* or *Screen.ActiveForm(0).Name* would be a valid reference to the name of the first control on the form. The object variable *F* is used to simplify the code. ■

If you put all the statements together, you get the following procedure, which is attached to the Click property of a command button control *(Button5)*:

```
Sub Button5()
    Dim F As Form
    Set F = Screen.ActiveForm
    MsgBox F(0).Name
    MsgBox F(1).Name
    MsgBox F(2).Name
    MsgBox F(3).Name
End Sub
```

Each time the procedure is triggered by clicking the button, it displays a series of message boxes that show the names of the first four controls on the current form.

But what have you accomplished with this technique? What if the form contains ten controls? You would have to expand the procedure with six more statements. This is exactly the type of editing you want to avoid!

The goal is to write a procedure that automatically adjusts to the number of controls found on the form. To reach this goal, you have to use another type of programming structure called a loop.

A Counting Loop

A *loop* is a structure in which two statements are used to repeat a group of statements within a procedure. The diagram in Figure 14-4 shows how loops work.

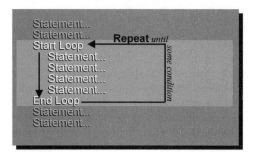

Figure 14-4: A loop uses two statements to repeat a block of statements until some condition is met.

Inside a procedure are two statements. The first statement marks the beginning of the loop and the second marks the end. The loop structure forces the program to execute the statements within the loop over and over until some condition occurs that stops the loop. When that condition is met, the program continues with the statement that follows the end of the loop.

The simplest type of loop is a counting loop. In a *counting loop*, the statements are repeated a specified number of times. Counting loops are created using the For and Next statements:

- **For.** The For statement serves three functions. First, it marks the beginning of the loop structure within a procedure. Second, it initializes a counter variable. Third, it sets the upper limit for the counter variable.

- **Next.** This statement marks the end of the loop within the procedure. When the Next statement is encountered, the value of the counter variable specified in the For statement is incremented. When the counter value reaches the upper limit set in the For statement, the loop terminates and the procedure continues with the statement following Next, if any. The Next statement does not use any arguments.

The For statement has the following general form:

```
For CounterVariable = StartValue To Limit
```

The Next statement doesn't use any arguments:

```
Next
```

The following code is a simple For...Next loop:

```
For k = 1 To 4
    MsgBox k
Next
```

The For statement initializes a variable named k with the starting value at 1. The first time through the loop, the MsgBox statement displays the value of k, which is 1. When the Next statement is encountered, the program compares its current value, 1, to the upper limit, 4. Because 1 is less than 4, the procedure returns to the For statement, increases the value of k from 1 to 2, and executes the loop again. During the second pass, the MsgBox statement displays 2, which is the current value of k.

The process continues until k reaches the upper limit set for the variable — in this case, 4. When this occurs, the Next statement terminates the loop, and the procedure moves on to any statements following the Next statement.

For...Next loops are not limited to counting by ones. You can specify a different increment value with the *Step* argument. The statement *For k = 1 To 10 Step .5* adds .5 to *k* each time — that is, 1, 1.5, 2, 2.5, and so on. You can even count backward by using a negative step value. The statement *For k = 10 to 1 Step -1* assigns *k* the values 10, 9, 8, 7, 6, 5, 4, 3, 2, 1. ■

You can apply the For...Next loop to the problem of using the elements in a collection. In the following example, a For...Next loop is used to execute the MsgBox statement four times. The variable *k* starts at 0 and changes to 1, 2, and 3 as the loop repeats. The variable *k* is then used to indicate which element in the form's collection is displayed:

```
Sub Button5()
    Dim F As Form
    Set F = Screen.ActiveForm
    For k = 0 To 3
        MsgBox F(k).Name
    Next
End Sub
```

Figure 14-5 shows how the series of Msgbox statements in the original procedure can be replaced with a For...Next loop structure.

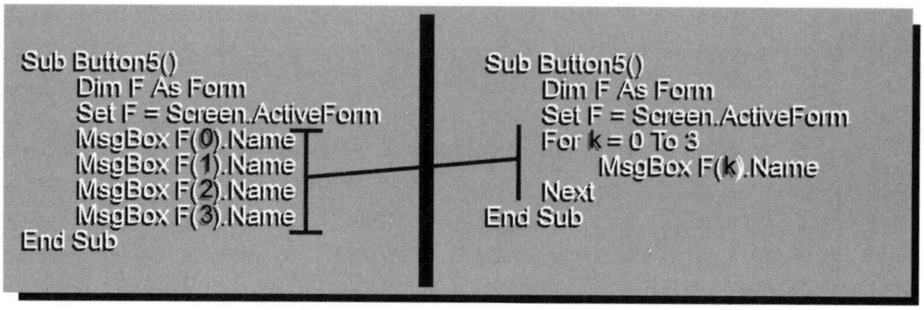

Figure 14-5:
A For...Next loop cycles through the elements in a collection.

```
Sub Button5()
    Dim F As Form
    Set F = Screen.ActiveForm
    MsgBox F(0).Name
    MsgBox F(1).Name
    MsgBox F(2).Name
    MsgBox F(3).Name
End Sub
```

```
Sub Button5()
    Dim F As Form
    Set F = Screen.ActiveForm
    For k = 0 To 3
        MsgBox F(k).Name
    Next
End Sub
```

What's most significant about the loop structure is that it works with a collection of any size. If the form contains 100 controls, you simply change the upper limit from 3 to 99:

```
Sub Button5()
    Dim F As Form
    Set F = Screen.ActiveForm
    For k = 0 To 99
        MsgBox F(k).Name
    Next
End Sub
```

Because collections are zero-based lists, the upper limit of the loop is one less than the number of items in the collection.

For *k*?

As with other variables, Access places no special limits on the name of the variable used as the counter in a For statement. You can use any valid name up to 40 characters in length. As in mathematics, however, tradition sometimes affects the choice of variable names used with certain programming structures and techniques. For example, the letter *i* is typically used as the counter variable. I don't know why, but my guess is that it stands for *increment*. You will find *i* used in most of the For...Next examples in the Access manual and help screens. When For statements are nested inside one another, the letter *j* is typically used for the second variable.

Okay, why did I use *k*? Because *i* is so commonly used, I find that many people think it's part of the For statement. Using *k* serves as a reminder that you can use any variable name in the For statement.

In addition, on systems that use proportionally spaced fonts (such as Windows), the letter *k* is easier to read than the letter *i* because *k* is larger.

The letter k also reminds me of *kounter,* which stands for the counter variable. Why not *c* for counter? First, the word Count is a reserved word in Access. There is a Count function and a Count property. To avoid confusion on that score, I make the phonetic switch to *k*. Therefore, in this book, the letter *k* is used as the counter variable in For statements.

The Count property

This leaves one last problem. How can you get the number of items in a collection automatically inserted into the For statement? The answer is provided in the form of the Count property for forms or reports:

Form.Count

Report.Count

In the following procedure, the Count property automatically calculates the correct upper limit for the For...Next loop. The expression *F.Count-1* is used because the collection is a zero-based list. If *F.Count* is 100, the loop in the following procedure will process controls 0 through 99.

```
Sub Button5()
    Dim F As Form
    Set F = Screen.ActiveForm
    For k = 0 To F.Count-1
        MsgBox F(k).Name
    Next
End Sub
```

In testing this concept, you might find it cumbersome to deal with a message box for each element in the collection. An alternative is to direct the output to the Immediate window, whose contents can be seen from the code window. The following example prints the number of the element followed by the name:

```
Sub Button5()
    Dim F As Form
    Set F = Screen.ActiveForm
    For k = 0 To F.Count-1
            Debug.Print k & ".  " &  F(k).Name
    Next
End Sub
```

The following result appears in the Immediate window:

```
0. Text12
1. Text13
2. Button18
3. First Name
4. Text15
5. Last Name
6. Text17
7. Field19
8. Text20
```

The procedure can be used with any form and achieve the same result — that is, it displays one message box with the control name for each control on a form. Of course, this doesn't solve the ditto problem. A number of other problems still must be overcome. However, the use of the For…Next loop is a critical step because it provides a technique for accessing the elements in any form by means of the form object collection. It's no longer necessary to use specific names in the procedure. In fact, neither the name of the container (the form's name) or the collection (the control names) appear in the procedure. The logic of the procedure is no longer tied to a specific form. Instead, it can be applied to any form in the database's forms collection.

The Fields Collection

All forms that display records have a second collection of objects that are related to the operation of the form. This collection belongs to the record set that is associated with the form. The record set container consists of a collection of fields from the underlying table, query, or SQL statement.

To access and manipulate the collection of fields contained in the form's record set, you use the same general techniques that you employed to manipulate the form's control collection:

1. Define an object variable for the container object. In this case, the container object is the record set associated with the form. As such, the object variable should be a record set type variable:

```
Dim C as RecordSet
```

2. Assign the container object to the variable. In a form, the object is accessed through the form's RecordSetClone property:

```
Set C = Screen.ActiveForm.RecordSetClone
```

3. Manipulate the elements in the object's collection. The following code includes a loop that prints the names of the field in the Immediate window:

```
For k = 1 To C.Fields.Count-1
  Debug.Print k & ".   " & C(k).Name
Next
```

Note that the Fields.Count property gives us the total numbers of fields in the record set. Like the form's control collection, the fields collection is zero-based, so the first item in the collection is item zero.

To refer to the value of the field instead of the name of the field, you can leave off the element property, *C(k)*, or use the value property, *C(k).Value*. The following code prints a numbered list of fields, along with the value of the current record for each field:

```
Dim C as RecordSet
Set C = Screen.ActiveForm.RecordSetClone
For k = 1 To C.Fields.Count-1
    Debug.Print k & ".   " & C(k).Name & ": " & C(k)
Next
```

Filling a Monitor Box

Access provides the Immediate window so that you can monitor the effects of various Access Basic statements during the debugging process. In many circumstances, however, directing the data output to the Immediate window is a bit cumbersome. An alternative is to create a monitor box control. A *monitor box* is simply an unbound text box control in which an Access Basic procedure writes information while the form is active. The box functions as a mini Immediate window, displaying information from the form you want to monitor.

Figure 14-6 shows a form that uses a monitor box to display the values from the last record entered for the selected company name. The monitor box allows you to observe the values located by the procedure without actually having them inserted into the new record. When you are sure that the procedure is locating the desired records, you can remove the monitor box.

As mentioned, the monitor box is simply a text box control in which the procedure writes information. The following procedure is a modified version of the related defaults procedure. Notice that the For...Next loop is used to access the entire fields collection of the record set variable *C*. The modifications to the related defaults procedure are shown in bold:

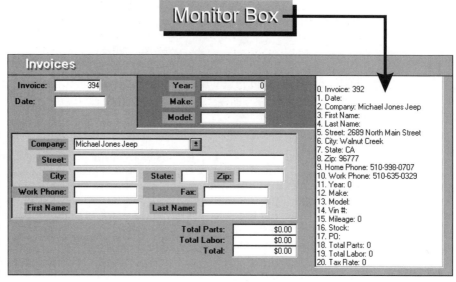

Figure 14-6:
A monitor box displays data obtained from the fields collection.

```
Sub Company_AfterUpdate ()
    Dim C As Recordset
    Set C = Screen.Activeform.RecordSetClone
    [Monitor Box] = ""
    Nl = Chr(13) & Chr(10)
    CritText = "Company = " & Chr(34) & [Company] & Chr(34)
    C.FindLast CritText
    If Not C.NoMatch Then
        For k = 0 To C.Fields.Count - 1
            FInfo = & k & ". " & C(k).Name & ": " & C(k)
            [Monitor Box] = [Monitor Box] & Nl & FInfo
        Next
    End If
End Sub
```

The following is a detailed explanation of each change:

✔ **[Monitor Box] = " "**. This statement sets the value of the *Monitor Box* control to a null value. Each time the procedure is executed, the box begins as a blank.

✔ **Nl = Chr(13) & Chr(10)**. This statement defines a variable named *Nl* — NewLine. Access recognizes ASCII characters 13 (carriage return) and 10 (line feed) as the equivalent of pressing Ctrl-Enter when typing in a text box. Each time *Nl* is added to the text, it forces the text to be printed on a new line.

✔ **For k = 0 To C.Fields.Count - 1**. This statement initiates a For…Next loop that cycles through the entire fields collection of *C*, which is the variable assigned to the form's record set clone. Notice that the collection is a zero-based list.

✔ **FInfo = & k & "." & C(k).Name & ":" & C(k)**. This statement gathers several items into a single string variable called *FInfo* (Field Information). *k* is the number of the item in the collection. *C(k).Name* is the Name property of the element. *C(k)* inserts the value of the element.

✔ **[Monitor Box] = [Monitor Box] & Nl & FInfo**. This statement combines the text that is already in the monitor box with *FInfo* for the current element. The *Nl* variable inserts a new line before each new item, so the contents of *Monitor Box* take the form of a list rather than paragraph text.

This statement uses a special form called an accumulator. An *accumulator* is a Let statement in which the same identifier appears on both sides of the equal sign. The effect of an accumulator statement is to add or append data onto an existing item rather than replace it. To understand how an accumulator statement works, you need to remember that Let statements are *not* mathematical equations but are statements that assign values to items. You should read the statement as *let Monitor Box equal the contents of Monitor Box plus new line and field information*. Each time this statement is executed, the field information is appended onto the previous entry, instead of replacing it.

You can use Access Basic to set the ScrollBars property of the box to show a vertical scroll bar. In the following example, an *If* structure (shown in bold) has been added to check the number of items in the collection. If that number exceeds 20, the scroll bars are displayed in the monitor box.

```
Sub Company_AfterUpdate ()
    Dim C As Recordset
    Set C = Screen.Activeform.RecordSetClone
    [Monitor Box] = ""
    Nl = Chr(13) & Chr(10)
    If C.Fields.Count > 20 Then
            [Monitor Box].ScrollBars = 2
    End If
    CritText = "Company = " & Chr(34) & [Company] & Chr(34)
    C.FindLast CritText
    If Not C.NoMatch Then
        For k = 0 To C.Fields.Count - 1
                FInfo = & k & ". " & C(k).Name & ": " & C(k)
                [Monitor Box] = [Monitor Box] & Nl & FInfo
        Next
    End If
End Sub
```

The monitor box technique can be useful in developing procedures because information is placed directly on the form, revealing how the procedure is operating. This provides more immediate feedback than the Immediate window. In addition, you can control the contents directly from the procedure. For example, you can clear the box when desired.

In terms of the ditto problem, you have almost established methods of accessing the two collections involved in the task: the collection of controls on the form and the collection of fields in the form's record set. The last hurdle is to find a means for copying the data from one collection into the other collection. The goal is to transfer the data without writing a specific statement for each piece of data transferred. Instead, you want to create a procedure that automatically handles the transfer, regardless of the specific fields and controls involved. Chapter 15 completes the solution to the ditto problem.

Chapter 15

Using One Collection to Update Another Collection

··

In This Chapter

▶ Linking items in different collections

▶ Using the parentheses identifier style

▶ Determining control types

▶ Using control object variables

▶ Creating user-defined functions

··

*1*n the previous chapter, you created two separate procedures that can access objects in a collection by cycling through the collection using a For...Next loop. The first procedure accesses all the controls on the displayed form. The second procedure locates a record in the form record set — for example, the last entry for the selected company name — and accesses the values stored in the fields of that record.

In this chapter, you continue working with collections. By the end of this chapter, you will have solved the ditto problem posed at the beginning of Chapter 14 and learned how one collection can be used as a road map to the data in other collections.

Linking Two Collections

The procedure for solving the ditto problem requires the use of two collections: controls and fields. You need to set up a structure in which data from the fields collection can be copied into the corresponding controls in the controls collection. In Chapter 14, this is accomplished with a separate statement for each field.

In the solution to the related defaults problem, the following statements are used to copy the values from the previous record into the current form:

```
[Street] = C![Street]
[City] = C![City]
[State] = C![State]
[Zip] = C![Zip]
[Home Phone] = C![ Home Phone]
[Work Phone] = C![ Work Phone]
```

For example, the *Street* field in the clone data set — *C.[Street]* — is copied into the *Street* control on the form — *[Street]*. The statements follow a pattern in which the same name appears on both sides of the equal sign. In other words, the name of the item is the same in both collections (for example, Street = Street, and City = City).

Is there some way to create a procedure that automatically matches the names in one collection with the names in another collection? There is indeed. The key to this technique is a third method for writing object identifier names. So far, you have used two methods:

- ✔ **! or . (dot) style.** This style of identifier uses an exclamation point (!) or a period to connect parts of the identifier. For example, you can refer to the *Street* item in the *C* object as either **C![Street]** or **C.Street**.

- ✔ **Parentheses style.** You use the parentheses style when you want to refer to an item in the collection by its number value. For example, you refer to the first item — that is, item 0 — in the *C* object collection as **C(0)**.

However, the parentheses style isn't limited to numbers. You can also use the parentheses style to refer to an item by name. The following identifier is equivalent to *C![Street]*:

```
C("Street")
```

Note that the name used inside the parentheses is enclosed in quotation marks. This indicates that the name is specified by a text value.

You can use either form in Access Basic statements. For example, the following statements produce the same result — that is, they display the *Street* item in the collection represented by the object variable C:

```
MsgBox C![Street]

MsgBox C("Street")
```

The real significance of the parentheses style becomes clear when you realize that the text literal used in the previous example can be replaced by a variable that has a text value. The first statement in the following example stores the text *Street* in a variable called *NameText*. The variable is then used inside the parentheses to specify the element in the collection:

```
NameText = "Street"
Msgbox C(NameText)
```

But how does this help you solve the problem of transferring data between two different collections? The answer lies in the fact that the same names are used for the controls into which the data is copied and the fields in the underlying record set. It's important to remember that this isn't always the case.You can create a form in which the control names don't match the names of the fields to which they are bound. In most cases, however, the field names and control names will match because Access automatically uses the field name as the control name when you place a control on a form by dragging the field name from the field list box in the form design mode. This is also true if you create a form with the Form Wizard.

Assume that the columns in Table 15 -1 represent the items in two collections. The left column lists the names of the items in the form control collection, which is assigned to the variable *F*. The right column lists the fields in the form's record set collection, which is assigned to the variable *C*. Note that some of the names in the control collection match the names in the fields collection.

Table 15-1: Items in a form's control collection and record set collection

Control Collection	*Fields Collection*
Set F=Screen.ActiveForm	Set C=Screen.ActiveForm.RecordSetClone
F(0).Name = "Text12"	C(0).Name = "Invoice"
F(1).Name = "Text13"	C(1).Name = "Date"
F(2).Name = "Box50"	C(2).Name = "Company"
F(3).Name = "Box44"	C(3).Name = "First Name"
F(4).Name = "Invoice"	C(4).Name = "Last Name"
F(5).Name = "Text15"	C(5).Name = "Street"
F(6).Name = "Date"	C(6).Name = "City"
F(7).Name = "Text17"	C(7).Name = "State"
F(8).Name = "Year"	C(8).Name = "Zip"
F(9).Name = "Text19"	C(9).Name = "Home Phone"
F(10).Name = "Make"	C(10).Name = "Work Phone"
F(11).Name = "Text21"	C(11).Name = "Year"
F(12).Name = "model"	C(12).Name = "Make"
F(13).Name = "Text23"	C(13).Name = "Model"
F(14).Name = "Street"	C(14).Name = "Vin #"

In this example, you can assume that a control and a field with the same name represent elements in the two collections that are bound together. For example, *F(14).Name* is the name of the control that is bound to the field *C(5).Name*.

Before going on, I want to explain why I chose the names *F* and *C* for the collections listed in the table. The *F* collection lists all of the items that appear on the *Form*. The *C* collection lists all of the items that appear in the *Clone* record set. You might have chosen to do it the other way around, where *C* would stand for the *controls* on the form and *F* would stand for the *fields* in the Clone record set. My preference was to use a name that I felt emphasized the *source* of the item, either the form or the clone, since that concept is at the heart of this programming technique.

The goal of the ditto procedure is to copy the value from the fields collection into the corresponding control. For example, the *Street* field should be copied into the *Street* control. Starting with the type of statement used in the previous chapter — *[Street] = C("Street")* — you replace the identifier for the *Street* control with the corresponding element in the form control collection.

Because you want to set the value of the control, you need to specify the Value property:

```
F(14).Value = C("Street")
```

Moving to the right side of the statement, the literal "Street" can be replaced with the name of the control, *F(14).Name*:

```
F(14).Value = C( F(14).Name )
```

This statement has the same meaning as the original statement, in which *Street* appears as a literal value. Figure 15-1 summarizes the steps you take to arrive at the statement that uses items from the form's collection rather than a literal name.

If the statements have the same meaning, what have you accomplished? The answer becomes clear when you realize that the collection version of the statement works regardless of which text box you select from the form collection.

For example, item 6 in the form's control collection is *Date*. If you change the number in the statement, it transfers the date field's value to the *Date* control:

```
F(6).Value = C( F(6).Name )
```

Moving from specific values to a more general approach, you can replace the numbers with a variable whose value is controlled by a *For...Next* loop. The following statements cycle through all the items in the form collection and execute the transfer statement for each item:

```
For k = 0 To F.Count -1
    F(k).Value = C( F(k).Name )
Next
```

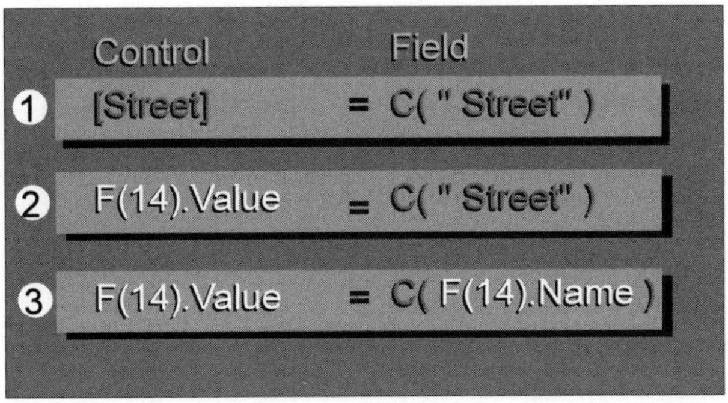

Figure 15-1:
Collection
items
replace
control and
field names.

Determining a Control's Type

If you have been paying attention, you've already spotted a glaring flaw in the previous example. Although some of the items in the form control collection do correspond to fields in the record set — for example, 6 and *Date*, 14 and *Street* — many items in the form collection have nothing to do with data stored in the record set. Such items as text label controls and command buttons are part of the form control collection but are not bound to the fields in the form's record set.

As a result, you can't simply run through all the elements in the form control collection with the loop *For k = 0 To F.Count-1*. Unlike fields, which all have the same set of properties, the property list of a control varies depending on the type of control. Although all controls share some properties, such as Name, some controls may have properties that other controls lack. For example, some controls do not have a Value property.

Assuming that the first item in the form's control set is a label called *Text12*, the following statement results in an error when the code is executed:

```
F(0).Value = C( F(0).Name )
```

The error results because there is no Value property for a Label type control. To solve this problem, you need to determine the type of each control *before* Access executes any statements involving the control's value. Access provides a special form of the *If* statement that is designed to deal with just this problem. In the following statement, *ControlType* represents a reserved word — such as TextBox, Label, CheckBox, or CommandButton — that specifies the type of control:

```
If Typeof ControlName Is ControlType Then
```

This structure is included in Access Version 2.0 specifically to address the problem you've encountered here. Table 15-2 lists the contents of a typical form's control collection. The controls shown in bold are textbox controls that are bound to specific fields. As you can see, they are interspersed among the other types of controls on the form.

Table 15-2: A sample control collection

Item	Name	Type
F(0)	Text12	Label
F(1)	Text13	Label
F(2)	Box50	Rectangle
F(3)	Box44	Rectangle
F(4)	**Invoice**	**TextBox**
F(5)	Text15	Label
F(6)	**Date**	**TextBox**
F(7)	Text17	Label
F(8)	**Year**	**TextBox**
F(9)	Text19	Label
F(10)	**Make**	**TextBox**
F(11)	Text21	Label
F(12)	**Model**	**TextBox**
F(13)	Text23	Label
F(14)	**Street**	**TextBox**

For the procedure to work properly, it must include a mechanism that selects only the textbox controls. The following example uses an *If Type* of structure to select only textbox controls for updating. Using Table 15-2 as an example, the following code updates items 4, 6, 8, 10, 12, and 14, and skips all the other controls contained in the collection:

```
For k = 0 To F.Count -1
   If Typeof F(k) Is TextBox Then
```

```
        F(k).Value = C( F(k).Name )
    Endif
Next
```

This change allows you to loop through the entire collection of controls, but the procedure updates only those controls that are related to fields in the record set's field collection.

Avoiding controls that can't be updated

Unfortunately, selecting only the textbox controls doesn't solve all the problems with looping through the control collection. Various conditions preclude copying data from the previous entry into a new record. The most common conditions include:

- ✔ **Counter fields.** If a control is bound to a counter type field, it cannot be updated with a value because Access automatically generates the values that appear in a counter field.

- ✔ **Control source expressions.** If the control source of the field bound to the control is an expression, the control cannot be updated because the expression is used to determine its value.

How can you account for these special cases? I'll start with the problem posed by counter type fields. One solution is to check the type of field before you execute the statement that copies a value. Each field has a Type property that returns a value indicating the type of field. The values, which are listed in Table 15-3, are similar, but not identical, to the field types listed in the table design mode. The constants listed on the right side of the table are predefined names that you can use in any Access Basic procedure.

Table 15-3: Values of the type property

Field Type	Constant
Date/Time	DB_DATE
Text	DB_TEXT
Memo	DB_MEMO
Yes/No	DB_BOOLEAN
Integer	DB_INTEGER
Long Integer	DB_LONG
Currency	DB_CURRENCY
Single	DB_SINGLE
Double	DB_DOUBLE

The list of values in Table 15-3 doesn't include a field type for OLE objects because OLE objects on forms are placed in BoundObjectFrame controls. Although it is possible to specify an OLE object field as the control source for a textbox (or another control), the contents of such a textbox wouldn't make sense. ■

You might notice that Table 15-3 doesn't list Counter as one of the field types. In Access, counter type fields are automatically defined as long integer numeric fields. If you want to test for a counter field, you can use DB_LONG as the value that indicates a counter field.

Using DB_LONG to determine counter fields isn't entirely foolproof. A table might include a numeric long integer field that isn't a counter. (This would be unusual, however.) Like almost all programming techniques, this method relies on some assumptions that are usually, but not absolutely, true. ■

To exclude any counter fields from the ditto process, the following code adds an *If* structure to the *If Type* of structure:

```
For k = 0 To F.Count -1
   If Typeof F(k) Is TextBox Then
            If C(F(k).Name).Type <> DB_LONG Then
                 F(k).Value = C( F(k).Name )
            End if
   End if
Next
```

Note that the value tested is *C(F(k).Name).Type*. This identifier stands for the Type property of the field in the collection *C()* with the name that matches *F(k).Name*, which is the name of a control in the form's control collection.

The other problem — controls with expressions — can be handled by checking the control's ControlSource property to see it matches the control's name. Remember that the ditto procedure is based on the assumption — which is usually true — that a control bound to a field will have the same name as the field to which it is bound. If you put that idea into an Access expression, it takes the form of the following expression:

```
F(k).Name = F(k).ControlSource
```

In the ditto procedure, you want to update only the controls for which this expression is true. If the ControlSource is anything other than the same text as the control's name, you can assume that it is an unbound control and should not be updated.

If you plug the preceding expression into an *If* structure, you get the following section of code in the procedure:

```
For k = 0 To F.Count -1
    If Typeof F(k) Is TextBox Then
            If F(k).Name = F(k).ControlSource Then
                    F(k).Value = C( F(k).Name )
            End if
    End if
Next
```

Because you need to avoid two conditions, you can create a compound expression with an *And* operator. This creates the following rather long If statement shown in bold:

```
For k = 0 To F.Count -1
    If Typeof F(k) Is TextBox Then
            If C(F(k).Name).Type <> DB_LONG  And F(k).Name =
                F(k).ControlSource Then
                    F(k).Value = C( F(k).Name )
            End if
    End if
Next
```

The *If Typeof* and *If* structures eliminate the conditions under which the key statement, *F(k).Value = C(F(k).Name)*, would cause an error.

Completing the Ditto Procedure

At long last, you can put together all the pieces and write the *ditto* procedure. You may be surprised to find that this much more sophisticated procedure is about the same length as the one you created in Chapter 13. You can't judge the power or the significance of a routine by its length. The compete procedure is as follows (the statements added in this chapter are shown in bold):

```
Sub_Company_AfterUpdate ()
    Dim F As Form, C As RecordSet
    Set F = Screen.ActiveForm
    Set C = Screen.ActiveForm.RecordSetClone
    CritText = "Company=" & Chr(34) & [Company] & Chr(34)
    C.FindLast CritText
    If Not C.NoMatch Then
            For k = 0 To F.Count -1
                    If Typeof F(k) Is TextBox Then
                            If C(F(k).Name).Type <> DB_LONG  And
                            F(k).Name = F(k).ControlSource Then
                                    F(k).Value = C( F(k).Name )
                            End if
                    End if
            Next
    Endif
End Sub
```

When executed, this procedure fills in all the controls on the current form that are bound to the underlying table. In doing so, it uses the values from the last record entered for the same company name — that is, it creates a *ditto* of the previous entry. However, this isn't accomplished with references to specific fields and controls. Instead, the procedure uses the collections of objects related to the form and record set containers.

This might seem like a long way to go for a simple task. However, this procedure is important because it illustrates the techniques required to manipulate objects in collections. These techniques are fundamental to almost all of the advanced features you can create using Access Basic.

Defining a Control Object Variable

As mentioned, the ditto procedure is significant because it isn't linked to a specific set of controls. The only assumption made by the procedure is that textbox controls bound to fields have the same names as the fields to which they are bound — for example, the *Street* control is bound to the *Street* field. This is a reasonable assumption because this is how bound controls are defined by the Form Wizard and by default when they are dragged from the field list in the form design mode.

With this structure, you can add or remove bound controls from the form, and the procedure will still operate correctly. You can also use the same code in another form and it will operate correctly, as long as it is used with the *Company* field. This raises another question. Can you eliminate the specific reference to the *Company* control? No problem.

This is accomplished by defining an object variable for the control from which the selection is made. In the modified procedure, an object variable named *Key* is defined as a Control type variable. *Key* is assigned to the *Screen.ActiveControl*. This means that the control that is selected when the procedure is triggered is defined as *Key*. Remember that your goal is to allow this procedure to work with any list or combo box control, not just one named *Company*.

The CritText statement is modified to use the name of the current control, *Key.Name*, and its value, *Key.Value*, to form the search criteria for the FindLast method. The modified procedure is as follows:

```
Sub_?_AfterUpdate ()
    Dim F As Form, C As RecordSet, Key As Control
    Set F = Screen.ActiveForm
    Set C = Screen.ActiveForm.RecordSetClone
    Set Key = Screen.ActiveControl
    CritText = Key.Name & " = "& Chr(34) & Key.Value & Chr(34)
    C.FindLast CritText
```

```
      If Not C.NoMatch Then
          For k = 0 To F.Count -1
              If Typeof F(k) Is TextBox Then
                      If C(F(k).Name).Type <> DB_LONG  And
                      F(k).Name = F(k).ControlSource Then
                              F(k).Value = C( F(k).Name )
                      End if
              End if
          Next
      Endif
  End Sub
```

This procedure works with any list or combo box control in any form. The procedure uses the screen object to pick up the names of the form, record set, and control involved in the operation. The procedure then uses collections and properties associated with those objects to guide the ditto process.

Making the procedure a user-defined function

The question mark (?) in the procedure name *Sub_?_AferUpdate()* indicates that the procedure can be executed from controls on any form. If you want to access this procedure from any part of your database, you need to change the procedure from a subroutine to a function and place that function in a standalone module rather than in a module attached to a particular form. (This is discussed in Chapter 10.)

Standalone modules are listed in the Modules list of the Database window when the module icon is selected. To create a function, open a new or existing module. Type the name of the function you want to create — *Function Ditto* — and press **Enter**. Access opens a new procedure window with the Function and End Function statements automatically entered. You can copy and paste code from another module window into the new function. In this case, the code doesn't need any modification:

```
  Function Ditto ()
      Dim F As Form, C As RecordSet, Key As Control
      Set F = Screen.ActiveForm
      Set C = Screen.ActiveForm.RecordSetClone
      Set Key = Screen.ActiveControl
      CritText = Key.Name & " = "& Chr(34) & Key.Value & Chr(34)
      C.FindLast CritText
      If Not C.NoMatch Then
          For k = 0 To F.Count -1
              If Typeof F(k) Is TextBox Then
                      If C(F(k).Name).Type <> DB_LONG  And
                      F(k).Name = F(k).ControlSource Then
                              F(k).Value = C( F(k).Name )
                      End if
              End if
          Next
      Endif
  End Function
```

To use the Ditto function, enter *=Ditto( )* into the AfterUpdate property of the control you want to use as the key value:

Name	Control Source	After Update
Company	Company	=Ditto()

Remember that it doesn't matter which module you use for storing the function.

You might have the mistaken impression that this chapter and Chapter 14 involve a lot of work for little gain. Although the starting and ending examples aren't radically different in effect — they both copy values from an older record into a new record — they are light years apart in terms of technique.

Both examples involve the same task, copying data. The initial example does so in a way that can be applied to only one specific form linked to one specific table. In this chapter, you have created a generalized procedure that you can apply to any number of forms and tables. You have created a single tool that you can apply to any number of specific problems. That is truly a gain in productivity.

In a larger sense, the final procedure also represents a compact but very powerful example of what Access Basic is all about. To work effectively with Access Basic, you need to understand the use of objects, collections, properties, and methods. Now that you understand how they work, you are well on your way to being able to solve almost any problem you encounter with Access.

Chapter 16
Form Letter Reports

*F*orm letters are produced by combining standard blocks of text with individual items of data that are unique to each copy of the form letter. Form letters are usually associated with word processing programs. However, the data that is inserted into the form letter is often stored in a database. This chapter shows you how to produce form letters in Access by manipulating text blocks that are printed on reports.

Producing Form Letters

To generate form letters, you start with a document that contains primarily standard paragraph text. However, in addition to that standard text, certain tokens are inserted at various points in the text. A *token* is a placeholder that indicates the location in the text where specific items of information — for example, a company name or balance amount — should be inserted. By inserting different sets of items for each token, the same basic form letter can be used to produce any number of specific letters. The basic theory behind form letters is illustrated in Figure 16-1.

This type of substitution goes on all the time in Access forms and reports. Values are frequently inserted into controls either from existing record sets or as the result of an Access Basic procedure.

Form letters present a problem only when you want to insert an Access Basic item into an existing paragraph instead of into a specific control. However, it is possible to create an Access Basic function that updates the tokens in a paragraph with actual values.

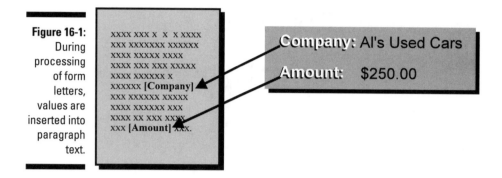

Figure 16-1:
During
processing
of form
letters,
values are
inserted into
paragraph
text.

For example, the form in Figure 16-2 lists members of an organization and the amounts they pledged. By looking at the *Pledge Paid Date* box on any member's form, you can tell whether the pledge has been fulfilled. Based on this, you might want to print form letters reminding members of their pledge.

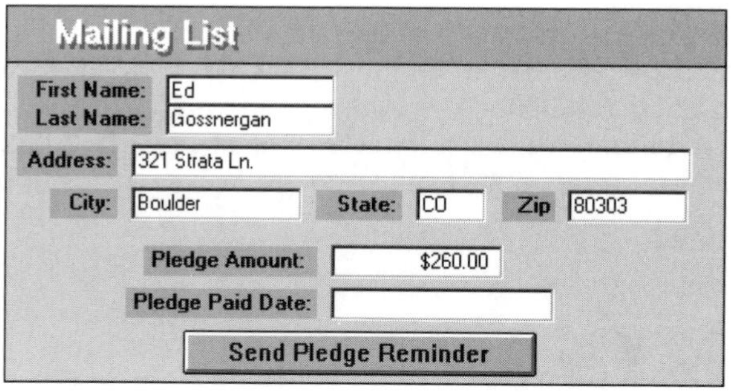

Figure 16-2:
The Send
Pledge
Reminder
button
generates a
copy of a
form letter.

The *Send Pledge Reminder* button triggers the printing of that form letter. Figure 16-3 shows how you can create a control on a report that can function as a form letter. The control is a Label type control in which you type your form letter as text. To start a new line inside a Label control, you press **Ctrl-Enter**.

You also need to insert tokens where information is to be inserted into the printed form letter. In this example, the tokens are enclosed in brackets to differentiate them from the standard text. The brackets have no special meaning. You can mark tokens in any way you like.

Why use a Label control? Wouldn't a text box be just as good or better? An unbound text box wouldn't retain the form letter after the form is closed. A Label control stores the text you enter into it as its Label property. This text is retained along with all other properties of the form, so the form letter is there every time you open the report.

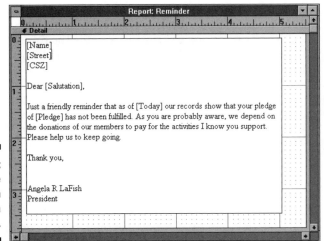

Figure 16-3:
A Label type
control can
be used as a
form letter.

The Replace () function

The key to producing form letters is an Access Basic function called *Replace()*. This function locates a token in a block of text and replaces it with some other text.

The first line in the procedure for the Replace() function lists three arguments:

```
Function Replace (Block, Token, ReplaceText)
```

The Block is the overall block of text that will be modified. In the current example, the block is all the text in a Label control on a report. This text can be referenced by using the Caption property, for example, *Reports![Reminder].[Text1].Caption.*

The Token is a text value that indicates the portion of the block that will be changed. In Figure 16-3, the tokens are items such as [Name] or [Pledge]. The text in the tokens doesn't matter very much. The tokens simply mark locations in the text where various replacement values should be inserted.

Replace Text is the information inserted in the block. In the current example, this information is obtained from the form displayed when the form letter is printed for example, *Forms![Mail List]![PledgeAmount].*

How does this procedure insert text at some location within the block of text? The technique is fairly simple. First, the block of text is divided into two parts. Front is all the text from the beginning of the block to the the token. Back is all the text after the token to the end of the block. Then Front and Back, are combined with ReplaceText to create the new block of text.

The first step in the procedure is to calculate the location of the token in the text. The *InStr ( )* (inside string) function locates the first occurrence of one item (the token) within another (the block). The function locates a character or group of characters within a larger text (string) item. To ensure that the *InStr( )* value doesn't include the first character in the token itself, the following statement subtracts 1 from the *InStr ( )* value:

```
StartToken = InStr(Block, Token) - 1
```

StartToken is then used to locate the beginning of the Back section of the text. This is accomplished by adding the length of the token, *Len(Token)*, plus 1:

```
EndToken = StartToken + Len(Token) + 1
```

With these two values you can use the *Left( )* and *Mid( )* functions to break the text into the two parts: the text before the token and the text after the token. The *Left( )* function is used to select a portion of a text(string) item starting with the first character on the left side of the text. *Mid( )* is used to select a portion of the text beginning at any location within the text (string).

Left( ) starts with the first character in the block and ends at the character indicated by the StartToken value. *Mid( )* begins at EndToken and includes the remainder of the block:

```
Front = Left(Block, StartToken)
Back = Mid(Block, EndToken)
```

In the final statement, the pieces are reassembled by inserting ReplaceText between the two parts:

```
Replace = Front & ReplaceText & Back
```

Because the reassembled text is assigned to the variable *Replace* (the name of the function), the value returned by the function is the modified text.

The entire *Replace* procedure is as follows:

```
Function Replace (Block, Token, ReplaceText)
    StartToken = InStr(Block, Token) - 1
    EndToken = StartToken + Len(Token) + 1
    Front = Left(Block, StartToken)
    Back = Mid(Block, EndToken)
    Replace = Front & ReplaceText & Back
End Function
```

You can put the Replace function to work in a procedure that specifies how to replace tokens included in the Label control pictured in Figure 16-3 with actual text. In this procedure, a function called *FillOutReminder( )* links the tokens in the Reminder Report with the data in the form pictured in Figure 16-2. The procedure uses two objects:

```
Function FillOutReminder ()
    Dim F As Form, C As Control
    Set F = Forms.[Mail List]
    Set C = Reports.[Reminder].Letter
```

F is the form that contains the information needed to fill out the form letter. *C* is the Label control on the report that contains the form letter with the tokens that need to be replaced.

The rest of the procedure is simply a matter of executing one *Replace( )* function for each token:

```
FormLetterControl = Replace(FormLetterControl, Token, FormControl)
```

Because there are six tokens in the example form letter, six *Replace( )* functions are needed:

```
C.Caption = Replace(C.Caption, "[Name]", F.[First Name] & " " &
        F.[Last Name])
C.Caption = Replace(C.Caption, "[Street]", F.[Address])
C.Caption = Replace(C.Caption, "[CSZ]", F.City & ", " & F.State & "
        " & F.Zip)
C.Caption = Replace(C.Caption, "[Salutation]", F.[First Name])
C.Caption = Replace(C.Caption, "[Today]", Date)
C.Caption = Replace(C.Caption, "[Pledge]",
        Format(F.PledgeAmount,"Currency"))
```

Note that the modifications are being made to a Label control, which has no value. It's actually the Caption property of the control that is being modified. Also note that the [Today] token is replaced with the current system date instead of a value from the form. The entire function looks like this:

```
Function FillOutReminder ()
    Dim F As Form, C As Control
    Set F = Forms.[Mail List]
    Set C = Reports.[Reminder].Letter
    C.Caption = Replace(C.Caption, "[Name]", F.[First Name] & " " &
            F.[Last Name])
    C.Caption = Replace(C.Caption, "[Street]", F.[Address])
    C.Caption = Replace(C.Caption, "[CSZ]", F.City & ", " & F.State
            & " " & F.Zip)
    C.Caption = Replace(C.Caption, "[Salutation]", F.[First Name])
    C.Caption = Replace(C.Caption, "[Today]", Date)
    C.Caption = Replace(C.Caption, "[Pledge]",
            Format(F.PledgeAmount,"Currency"))
End Function
```

The form letter is implemented by two-event-related procedures. First, you need to set the OnClick property of the *Send Pledge Reminder* button in the form to print the Reminder report. You can do this with an OpenReport macro action or an Access procedure that uses DoCmd to execute the same action:

```
Sub Reminder_Click ()
    DoCmd OpenReport "Reminder", A_NORMAL
End Sub
```

Next, you need to set the OnFormat property of the report section (typically the Detail1 section) to execute the *FillOutReminder( )* function:

Name	OnFormat
Detail1	=FillOutReminder()

The OnFormat event is triggered before the report is sent to the printer. This enables the *FillOutReminder( )* function to modify the text of the report before it is printed. The OnFormat event is discussed in greater detail in Chapter 17.

Now you can print a simple form letter, with data inserted in standard paragraph text, by clicking the *Send Pledge Reminder* button in the form. There is no record set to manipulate in this case because the report isn't bound to any record set. As shown in Figure 16-4, the procedure copies the values from the form and inserts them into the report in place of the tokens you inserted in the Label control. The changes made to the control by the Access Basic procedures aren't saved as part of the report, so you can reuse the same form to print any number of reminder letters.

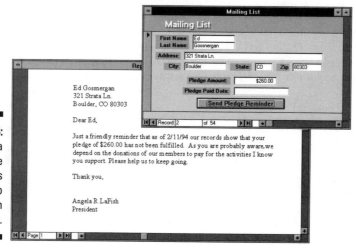

Figure 16-4:
The data
from the
form is
inserted into
the form
letter.

Building Maps for Form Letters

If you find it handy to use the form letter operation described in the previous section, you might also want to consider using a form letter map table like the one shown in Figure 16-5. This table lists the names of the tokens used in a form letter report and matches them with the names of the fields or controls that contain the values that should be used to replace the tokens. Notice that asterisks are used to mark the tokens.

Figure 16-5:
The form letter map table links tokens to fields or controls.

ID	Letter Name	Token	Replace With
1	Reminder	*FName*	First name
2	Reminder	*LName*	Last Name
3	Reminder	*Salutation*	First Name
4	Reminder	*Street*	Address
5	Reminder	*City*	City
6	Reminder	*State*	State
7	Reminder	*Zip*	Zip
8	Reminder	*Pledge*	PledgeAmount
(Counter)			

Table: Form Letter Map

Record: 1   of 8

The form letter map table also contains a field called *Letter Name*. This field allows you to enter the token setup for any number of different form letter reports. The *Letter Name* field is then used in processing each form letter to select the tokens that apply to a specific form letter.

The form letter map is an example of a resource table. A *resource table* contains lists of information used by particular procedures. Resource tables appear on the database list of tables just like tables that contain user data. The only difference is that resource tables are not normally intended to be edited or updated by the user. To indicate that a table is part of the programmer's system, you may want to add a prefix such as *zsys* to all resource table names, for example, *zsysForm Letter Map*. Why *zsys* and not just *sys*? Starting with *z,* you force Access to list these tables at the bottom of the table list, following any tables that have conventional names. ■

The form letter map makes it easy to revise the contents of a form letter without changing the Access Basic code. When you add another token to the form letter, simply update the form letter map by adding another record with the information about the new token.

Figure 16-6 shows a Label control containing a form letter that uses the tokens from the form letter map table in Figure 16-5. The [Today] token is a special case because it is the current system date. Instead of appearing on the form as a control, it is obtained directly from the system's clock/calendar.

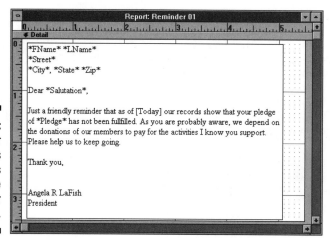

FName *LName*
Street
City, *State* *Zip*

Dear *Salutation*,

Just a friendly reminder that as of [Today] our records show that your pledge
of *Pledge* has not been fullfilled. As you are probably aware, we depend on
the donations of our members to pay for the activities I know you support.
Please help us to keep going.

Thank you,

Angela R LaFish
President

Figure 16-6:
A form letter
control uses
the tokens
listed in the
form letter
map table.

Working Through a Record Set

To use the data stored in the form letter map table, you need a way to work
through the records in that table one by one until you reach the end. Earlier
examples used a For...Next loop to cycle through record sets. This approach is
adequate for small record sets. However, in operations with larger record sets,
you may find two potential weaknesses in using a For...Next loop:

- **MoveLast delay**. As mentioned, the For...Next approach relies on the
  RecoundCount property to set the number of repetitions for the loop. For
  RecordCount to perform this function correctly, you must force Access to
  read the entire record set once by executing a MoveLast method. If the
  record set is large or complex (based on a complex query of SQL
  statement), this method might cause a significant delay before the loop
  starts.

- **No random navigation**. The For...Next method permits each record to be
  current once since the number of repetitions corresponds to the total
  number of records in the set. In some applications, you may find that after
  the loop starts, you may need to access various records multiple times in a
  random fashion. Since the For...Next loop sets the number of repetitions
  before the loop begins, it cannot accommodate any navigation except
  MoveNext inside the loop. Conversely, some procedures might advance
  more than one record at a time during each pass through the loop. This
  means that less passes than the RecordCount are needed to reach the end
  of the record set.

For these reasons, For...Next structures are usually not applied to looping through record sets. The alternative is a Do Until loop structure. In this type of structure, which is illustrated in Figure 16-7, the loop begins with a *Do Until* statement that contains a condition expression. A *condition expression* evaluates to either a True or False value.

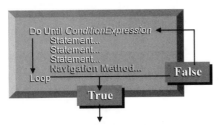

Figure 16-7: A Do Until loop repeats until a specified condition is true.

At the bottom of the structure is a *Loop* statement. When Access encounters this statement, it evaluates the condition specified in the *Do Until* statement. If the condition is False, Access returns to the *Do Until* statement and repeats the statements in the loop. If the expression is True, the loop is terminated and Access executes any statements that follow the *Loop* statement.

What sort of condition expression should be used when you want to loop through a record set? The most commonly used condition is to test the value of the Eof property of the record set. *(end of file)* In a record set, the end of file property is always False—with one exception. The exception occurs when the current record is the last record in the set and a MoveNext method is executed. Since there is no next record to move to, the end-of-file is encountered, which changes the Eof property to True. The property remains true until another navigation method moves to a new current record.

Remember the following when you work with the Eof property:

✔ The MoveLast method selects the last record in the set as the current record. MoveLast will never reach the end-of-file marker. To set the Eof property to True, you must use MoveNext to attempt to move past the last record.

✔ When the Eof property is True, there is *no current record*. None of the fields in the record set's field collection are available when there is no current record. The following sequence of statements will always generate an error because the Msgbox statement occurs when Eof is True and there is no current record:

```
R.MoveLast
R.MoveNext
Msgbox R(0)
```

> ✔ It is possible to create a record set that contains no records. This can occur when the source table is empty, or a query (or SQL statement) fails to select any records. A record set with no records is called a *null* set. When a null set is defined with the Set statement, the Eof property is immediately set to True without the need for any move methods. Since a null set contains no records, it can contain a current record. Any references to fields in the null set's collection will result in an error.

Using the *Do Until* approach, the code needed to loop through a record set would typically look like the following:

```
Do Until R.Eof
   MsgBox R.Ditto
   R.MoveNext
Next
```

Pay careful attention to the fact that the loop *must* have a statement that will eventually result in the *Do Until* condition becoming True. If the condition is Eof equals True, there must be a move method in the loop that will eventually result in reaching the end of the record set. Otherwise, the loop will repeat endlessly until you press **Ctrl-Break**. ■

The *Do Until* method avoids the problems that can occur with a *For...Next* loop. In a *Do Until* loop, it doesn't matter how many or how few repetitions of the loop occur because the value of the condition expression controls the termination of the loop. If the record set turns out to be empty (no records are selected from the source tables), no error will occur. The loop never gets started because Eof is True when the *Do Until* statement is encountered. The *Do Until* method also tends to improve performance because it avoids the need to read the entire table before the loop begins.

If you put all the pieces together, you arrive at a general form for a procedure that will process the records in any record set drawn from any source in the current database:

```
Dim D As Database, R As RecordSet
Set D = DBEngine.Workspaces(0).Databases(0)
Set R = D.OpenRecordSet("Related Defaults")
Do Until R.Eof
MsgBox R(0)
R.MoveNext
Loop
```

This procedure has seven basic steps.

1. **Define the Variables.** The Dim statement is used to define variable names for the object needed. Note that a record set also requires that a database variable be defined. You can define several variables with one statement, as shown in this example, or you can use separate Dim statements.

2. **Set the database.** The Set D statement establishes the source for the record sets. Assuming that you are working with data in the current database, this statement will be the same in all procedures.

3. **Open the record set.** The Set R statement defines a record set drawn from the specified database. The first record in the set, assuming it is not a null set, is set as the current record.

4. **Start the loop.** The Do Until statement establishes the condition expression that will be used to control repetition of the loop. If the expression is false when this statement is executed, the loop will begin and continue until the expression is true.

5. **Process.** The MsgBox statement represents one or more potential statements that should be executed using the current record. In this example, the contents of the first field in the record set's collection, *R(0)*, are displayed in a message box.

6. **Advance the record**. The R.MoveNext statement advances to the next record in the set, if any.

7. **Loop**. This statement marks the end of the loop. In this example, the loop will terminate when the end of record set R is encountered. The procedure will continue with any statements following Loop.

Using the Map To Fill in the Form Letter

You can use the form letter map table concept to create a new procedure called FillOutFromMap. This procedure is a variation of the FillOutReminder procedure described earlier in this chapter. The procedure begins with an argument, *LetterName,* that specifies which form letter report is being printed:

```
Function FillOutFromMap (LetterName)
```

The procedure then uses the same statements as the previous version to replace the [Today] token with today's date:

```
Dim F As Form, C As Control, D As Database, R As Recordset
Set F = Forms.[Mail List]
Set C = Reports.[Reminder].Letter
Set D = DBEngine.Workspaces(0).Databases(0)
C.Caption = Replace(C.Caption, "[Today]", Date)
```

The main change is the use of a *Do Until* loop that converts the form letter tokens into actual text. The procedure defines a record set R, which contains the map table information for the form letter that is specified by the argument variable *LetterName*. The procedure then moves through the record set and executes one *Replace( )* operation for each record in the set:

```
SQLText = "Select * From [Form Letter Map] Where [Letter Name] =
          '" & LetterName & "';"
Set R = D.OpenRecordset(SQLText)
Do Until R.Eof
    C.Caption = Replace(C.Caption, R.Token, F(R.[Replace With]))
    R.MoveNext
Loop
```

The *Do Until* loop eliminates the need to modify the procedure because of changes in the structure of the form letter. Furthermore, the same procedure can be used for any number of different form and form letter combinations:

```
Function FillOutFromMap (LetterName)
    Dim F As Form, C As Control, D As Database, R As Recordset
    Set F = Forms.[Mail List]
    Set C = Reports.[Reminder].Letter
    Set D = DBEngine.Workspaces(0).Databases(0)
    C.Caption = Replace(C.Caption, "[Today]", Date)
    SQLText = "Select * From [Form Letter Map]
          Where [Letter Name] = '" & LetterName & "';"
    Set R = D.OpenRecordset(SQLText)
    Do Until R.Eof
        C.Caption = Replace(C.Caption, R.Token, F(R.[Replace With]))
        R.MoveNext
    Loop
End Function
```

This procedure takes a slightly different approach to the use of tokens in the form letter report. In the FillOutReminder procedure, some of the tokens are replaced by expressions that combine data from several fields or controls. For example, the [Name] token is replaced with [First Name] & " " & [Last Name]. In the FillOutFromMap procedure, each token must represent data from a single field or control. Instead of the single token [Name], the form letter in Figure 16-6, uses two tokens, *FName* and *LName*. These tokens correspond to two controls, *First Name* and *Last Name*, on the form.

You might also want to make some modifications to the *Replace( )* function procedure. In the following procedure, an *If* structure (in bold) is added to skip the Replace operation if the specified token isn't included in the form letter:

```
Function Replace (Block, Token, ReplaceText)
If InStr(Block, Token) Then
    StartToken = InStr(Block, Token) - 1
    EndToken = StartToken + Len(Token) + 1
    Front = Left(Block, StartToken)
    Back = Mid(Block, EndToken)
    Replace = Front & ReplaceText & Back
End If
End Function
```

You should also keep in mind that numeric values don't retain their formatting when they are used by Access Basic. For example, even though *PledgeAmount* appears as $1,000 in the control, it will appear as 1000 in the form letter. You can correct this by using the *Format( )* function. For example, you can specify the currency format with *Format(ReplaceText, "Currency")*. However, this particular change applies only to Currency type fields. You can use the *VarType( )* function to test ReplaceText for the data type. (The values returned by this function were listed in Table 2-3.)

The additions to the procedure that are needed to account for the formatting of currency values are shown in bold:

```
Function Replace (Block, Token, ReplaceText)
If InStr(Block, Token) Then
    StartToken = InStr(Block, Token) - 1
    EndToken = StartToken + Len(Token) + 1
    Front = Left(Block, StartToken)
    Back = Mid(Block, EndToken)
    If VarType(ReplaceText) = 6 Then
        Replace = Front & Format(ReplaceText, "Currency") & Back
    Else
        Replace = Front & ReplaceText & Back
    End If
End If
End Function
```

Two more changes are necessary. The OnFormat property of the form letter report must execute the *FillOutFromMap( )* function with the name of the form letter as an argument:

Name	On Format
Detail1	= FillOutFromMap("Reminder")

Finally, if you assume that the actual name of the report matches the name used in the *Letter Name* field;

Name	On Format
Detail1	= FillOutFromMap(Screen.ActiveReport.Name)

you can use the ActiveReport object to insert that name automatically.

Chapter 17
Bills, Statements, and Invoices

· ·

In This Chapter

▶ Formatting reports as they print

▶ Billing one customer at a time

▶ Billing selected customers

▶ Generating an aging table

· ·

*M*ost databases do a good job of producing column reports. Such reports contain record-by-record listings of table information as well as summary totals and subtotals. In business, these column reports usually are intended primarily for *internal* use.

Bills, statements, and invoices represent a different type of business communication. Although these items may differ in appearance, they are all meant for *external* use — that is, they are distributed to your customers.

For bills, statements, and invoices, the focus of each printed document is one set of related records rather than the contents of an entire table. This chapter introduces a number of special techniques that allow you to produce these customer- oriented documents using the Access report feature.

Format and Print Events

For the most part, the printing of forms and reports is determined by the controls and properties you have designed. However, you can alter the contents or appearance of a form or report by writing Access Basic procedures that execute when the form or report is printed. For example, such procedures might perform special operations to solve problems that may occur when printing business forms such as invoices.

The printing of all Access reports is a two-stage process. The first stage involves formatting. The second stage is the printing process.

1. **Formatting.** The formatting process takes place before Access sets the layout of each section of a report. You can use the OnFormat event to alter any part of the section's layout before it is printed. The most common use of the OnFormat event is to hide or display controls using the Visible property. You can also change the size, position, font, and other attributes of the controls. The default layout is determined by the layout you created in the report design mode.

2. **Printing.** The OnPrint event immediately follows the OnFormat event. At this point, you can no longer change the section's layout characteristics prior to printing. However, you can use the OnPrint event to alter the value of the controls included in the section. You can also use the current values to determine whether the section should be printed. All OnPrint event procedures recognize the *Cancel* variable. If this variable is set to True when the event procedure is completed, Access skips the printing of the current section.

Which event you select — format or print — depends on the type of change you want to make to the report. If you merely want to change the value of a control — for example, change the text from *Invoice* to *Customer Copy* — you can do so with either the OnFormat event or the OnPrint event. Layout properties such as Visible, FontSize, or Width, must be changed during the OnFormat event. For example, if you want to stop boxes and lines from appearing on a copy, you must change the Visible property of the appropriate controls during the OnFormat event, not the OnPrint event.

Reports are printed section by section. For each section there is a format event and then a print event. A simple page usually contains a page header, a detail section, and a page footer. Because each section has both a format event and a print event, six events are generated during the printing of a single page:

1. PageHeader0_Format
2. PageHeader0_Print
3. Detail1_Format
4. Detail1_Print
5. PageFooter2_Format
6. PageFooter2_Print

If more than one record is printed on a page, the printing of that page will include separate detail events for each record.

Most of the examples in this section apply to reports. However, you can apply the same logic to the printing of forms. All form sections have OnFormat and OnPrint events that you can use to control how the information is printed. ∎

Although most simple reports output information that is already stored in tables, some circumstances call for *smart* reports — that is, reports that need to calculate, modify, or manipulate existing information in order to produce the desired report. The following sections describe how to create a smart report.

The Detail Summary Problem

When you create a form or a report, you can use three different types pf controls, depending on the contents of each control:

- **Bound.** The data in the field is linked to a field that is contained in a table or a query.

- **Unbound.** The control has no permanent value. Any value entered into the control is lost when the form or report is closed.

- **Calculated.** The value that appears in the control is the result of an expression that can use any available object, function, or operator to arrive at a value.

Many business forms lend themselves to calculated controls. For example, Figure 17-1 shows a typical invoice form. It is composed of information that is stored in several tables and linked by a common item. In this example, the common item is the invoice number. The invoice number is used to establish a one-to-many relationship between the main invoice record and the Parts Details and Labor Details subforms.

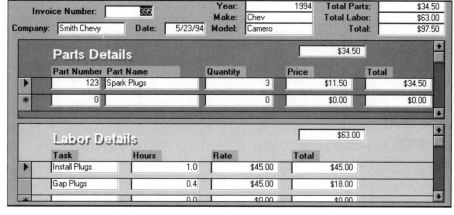

Figure 17-1: A typical invoice form with a one-to-many relationship.

You could set up the form in Figure 17-1 without Access Basic programming. However, the controls on the form and the subforms suggest that many of the values displayed on the invoice are the results of expressions rather than values bound to fields.

For example, the *Total* control in the Parts Details subform is the result of an expression that multiplies *Price* times *Quantity*. This ensures that the displayed value in *Total* is accurate. The same is true of the *Total* field in the Labor Details subform — that is, it's the result of an expression that multiplies *Rate* times *Hours*.

In addition, the values that appear on the main form for *Total Parts, Total Labor,* and *Total,* depend directly on the values in the *Total* controls on the subforms. As such, they too are the results of expressions that evaluate values from summary controls located on the subforms.

This means that a lot less information is stored in the tables than appears on the form. The only values that really need to be stored are *Price, Quantity, Rate,* and *Hours*. All the other numeric values can be calculated from those values. Is this a problem?

It isn't a problem as long as the invoice data is accessed using the same form/subform relationships. You might have a problem, however, if you try to produce a bill or a statement that is supposed to summarize multiple invoice records for each customer. Figure 17-2 shows a report that prints billing or statement information. The report lists each invoice and the totals for parts, labor, and the invoice, without showing any other details.

The original invoice form in Figure 17-1 uses expressions to calculate the values that are printed on the bill in Figure 17-2. In other words, these fields don't have information stored in them. If you simply place bound controls on the report for the *Total Parts, Total Labor,* and *Total fields,* you will get a blank report.

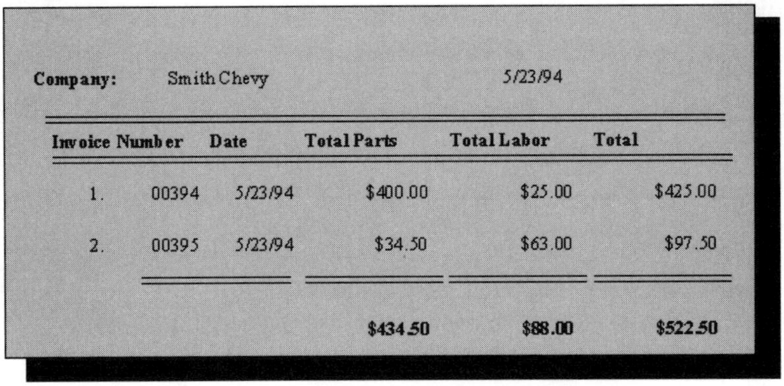

Figure 17-2: Bill or statement reports summarize multiple invoices.

Company:	Smith Chevy			5/23/94	
Invoice Number	Date	Total Parts	Total Labor	Total	
1. 00394	5/23/94	$400.00	$25.00	$425.00	
2. 00395	5/23/94	$34.50	$63.00	$97.50	
		$434.50	$88.00	$522.50	

To create a summary form such as Figure 17-2, you need to create a report that can calculate these values. You can do this by using the OnFormat event for the report's Detail section. Remember that Access reports can do more than simply spit out data stored in other parts of the system. An OnFormat event takes place *before* each section of the report is printed. You can attach procedures to these events to calculate the required information as each section is formatted for printing. In this case, you need to create a procedure that calculates the *Total Parts, Total Labor,* and *Total* values for each invoice as the report is being formatted for printing.

Calculating Report Details

A bill or statement report like the one pictured in Figure 17-2 contains three sections:

- ✔ **Page header.** This section contains information about the customer to whom the bill is being sent. It also contains the column headings that appear above the invoice information.

- ✔ **Detail.** This section lists the totals for each invoice. In this example, the information in this section must be generated when the report is printed, because it isn't stored in any tables related to this report.

- ✔ **Report footer.** This section lists the overall totals for the bill. Because these totals are summaries of the values printed in the Detail section, they must also be generated by a procedure during the printing of the report.

Because the *Total Parts, Total Labor*, and *Total* fields in the underlying invoice table don't contain values, the controls on the form that list these values are unbound controls. The values are inserted into the controls during the OnFormat procedure.

The procedure that calculates the totals for each invoice printed in the Detail section must do the following:

- ✔ Re- establish links to the records in the detail tables (parts and labor).

- ✔ Summarize the parts details by multiplying *Price* times *Quantity* for each item related to the current invoice.

- ✔ Summarize the labor details by multiplying *Rate* times *Hours* for each item related to the current invoice.

The Detail section of a report is formatted once for each record included in the report. The procedure assigned to the OnFormat property of the Detail section is also executed once for each record.

The first task in the procedure is to create two record sets: one for parts details and the other for labor details. Both of these record sets are defined by the same criteria: a matching value in the *Invoice Number* field. This field is assumed to be common to the three tables involved in the procedure.

The procedure begins by defining two record set variables, *Parts* and *Labor*. The relationship between the current table and the detail tables is stored in a variable called *SQLCrit*. This is done because the same criteria is used to define both record sets.

```
Sub Detail1_Format (Cancel As Integer, FormatCount As Integer)
    Dim D As Database, Parts As Recordset, Labor As Recordset
    Set D = DbEngine.Workspaces(0).Databases(0)
    SQLCrit = "Where [Invoice Number] = " & [Invoice Number] & ";"
```

The next two statements create record sets that draw the records needed to calculate the total for the current invoice. Both statements use the same criteria — *SQLCrit* — but the two statements draw records from different tables — Parts Details and Labor Details:

```
Set Parts = D.OpenRecordset("Select * From [Parts Details] " &
            SQLCrit)
Set Labor = D.OpenRecordset("Select * From [Labor Details] " &
            SQLCrit)
```

Before you can get the records that contain the values used to calculate the invoice totals, you need to initialize the controls on the report to 0. This is necessary because Access treats the unbound text box controls on the form as nulls. If you attempt to add a value to a null — for example, *[Total Parts]* + 100 — Access returns a null for that expression. The following statements set the values of the controls to 0:

```
[Total Parts] = 0
[Total Labor] = 0
```

This establishes the controls as Numeric type values so that they will work properly in the expression that follows. *Total Parts* is calculated by looping through the Parts record set and accumulating the total in the control *Total Parts*:

```
Do Until Parts.Eof
    [Total Parts] =[Total Parts] + Parts.[Price] * Parts.[Quantity]
    Parts.MoveNext
Loop
```

The same type of loop is used to loop through the Labor record set to accumulate the total for *Total Labor*:

```
Do Until Labor.Eof
    [Total Labor] =[Total Labor] + Labor.[Rate] * Labor.[Hours]
    Labor.MoveNext
Loop
```

The final step is to add the parts and labor (and any other fields, such as tax) to arrive at the overall total of the invoice:

```
[Total] = [Total Parts] + [Total Labor]
End Sub
```

The completed procedure calculates the values needed for each item that is printed on the bill as part of the report formatting process:

```
Sub Detail1_Format (Cancel As Integer, FormatCount As Integer)
    Dim D As Database, Parts As Recordset, Labor As Recordset
    Set D = DbEngine.Workspaces(0).Databases(0)
    SQLCrit = "Where [Invoice Number] = " & [Invoice Number] & ";"
    Set Parts = D.OpenRecordset("Select * From [Parts Details] " &
            SQLCrit)
    Set Labor = D.OpenRecordset("Select * From [Labor Details] " &
            SQLCrit)
    [Total Parts] = 0
    [Total Labor] = 0
    Do Until Parts.Eof
        [Total Parts] =[Total Parts] + Parts.[Price] * Parts.[Quantity]
        Parts.MoveNext
    Loop
    Do Until Labor.Eof
        [Total Labor] =[Total Labor] + Labor.[Rate] * Labor.[Hours]
        Labor.MoveNext
    Loop
    [Total] = [Total Parts] + [Total Labor]
End Sub
```

Passing Values to Other Report Sections

Printing the details is only half of what's required to complete the bill. The second part involves accumulating a total for the bill by adding values from each record in the Detail section. To accomplish this, you need to define module-level variables for the report. Remember that after each Detail section is printed, Access discards the variables that are defined when the OnFormat procedure runs. To accumulate the totals for the entire report, you need variables that remain active for the duration of the report.

This can be accomplished by defining the details in the declarations section of the report's Access Basic module. In this example, the variables *GtParts* and *GtLabor* are used to calculate the grand totals for all the invoices included in the report, and *ICount* is used to number the items on the report, — 1, 2, 3, and so on. These variables are declared in the following statements:

```
Option Compare Database   'Use database order for string comparisons
Dim ICount As Integer, GtParts As Double, GtLabor As Double
```

These module-level variables are used in two places. First, as shown in bold in the following code, they are used at the end of the Detail section formatting procedure, to keep a running sum of the parts and labor values:

```
Sub Detail1_Format (Cancel As Integer, FormatCount As Integer)
    Dim D As Database, Parts As Recordset, Labor As Recordset
    Set D = DbEngine.Workspaces(0).Databases(0)
    SQLCrit = "Where [Invoice Number] = " & [Invoice Number] & ";"
    Set Parts = D.OpenRecordset("Select * From [Parts Details] " &
            SQLCrit)
    Set Labor = D.OpenRecordset("Select * From [Labor Details] " &
            SQLCrit)
    [Total Parts] = 0
    [Total Labor] = 0
    Do Until Parts.Eof
        [Total Parts] =[Total Parts] + Parts.[Price] *
                Parts.[Quantity]
        Parts.MoveNext
    Loop
    Do Until Labor.Eof
        [Total Labor] =[Total Labor] + Labor.[Rate] * Labor.[Hours]
        Labor.MoveNext
    Loop
    [Total] = [Total Parts] + [Total Labor]
    GtParts = GtParts + [Total Parts]
    GtLabor = GtLabor + [Total Labor]
    ICount = ICount + 1
    [Item Number] = ICount & "."
End Sub
```

In this same bold section of the code, the *ICount* variable counts the records as they are formatted and inserts the current number at the start of each detail line.

When the report reaches the Report Footer section — the final part of the report to print — the accumulated totals stored in the module-level variables are inserted into the controls in the Report Footer so they can be printed to summarize the bill:

```
Sub ReportFooter4_Format (Cancel As Integer, FormatCount As Integer)
    [GrandTotal_Total Parts] = GtParts
    [GrandTotal_Total Labor] = GtLabor
    [GrandTotal_Total] = GtLabor + GtParts
End Sub
```

If you use the Wizard to lay out a report, the summary controls in the Report Footer section are automatically filled with an expression. If you want to determine the value of these controls using Access Basic, you must delete the Control Source expression, leaving these summary controls unbound.

Using the Bill Report

The bill report discussed in the previous section can be used in three ways:

- ✔ **Printing one bill.** You can use the bill report to print the current bill for one selected customer.
- ✔ **Printing all bills.** You can print an entire bill cycle by generating a bill for every customer who has an open invoice.
- ✔ **Printing selected bills.** You can choose one or more customers from a list and print bills for only the selected customers.

Printing one bill

After you have created a report form that correctly calculates the values needed for the bill, you can print a single bill for any customer using a form like the one shown in Figure 17-3. This form contains a combo box control that lists the names of the customers.

Figure 17-3: A combo box is used to select a customer for bill printing.

When you make a selection, the following AfterUpdate event procedure uses the OpenReport action to print the bill:

```
Sub Customer_AfterUpdate ( )
    CritText = "Company = Screen.ActiveControl And Not Paid"
    DoCmd OpenReport "Bill", A_NORMAL, , CritText
End Sub
```

The record set for the report is restricted to records that match the selected customer name and are not marked as paid. This procedure assumes that the Invoice table includes a field called *Paid*, that is True for all paid invoices and False for all outstanding invoices.

Printing all bills

A second way to print bills is to output a complete bill cycle. This means that you want to print a bill for every customer who has at least one unpaid invoice.

At the heart of this procedure are the same statements — shown in bold — that were used in the previous example to print one bill at a time. The difference here is that the company name is drawn from the R record set, which contains the names of all the companies that have unpaid invoices in the Invoices table.

The following procedure loops through that record set, executing an Open-Report action for each company included in the record set:

```
Sub Button6_Click ()
    Dim D As Database, R As Recordset
    Set D = DbEngine.Workspaces(0).Databases(0)
    SQLText="Select Distinct Company From Invoices Where Company Is
            Not Null;"
    Set R = D.OpenRecordset(SQLText)
    Do Until R.Eof
        Ok = SysCmd(4, "Printing Bill for : " & R.Company)
        CritText = "Company= " & Chr(34) & R.Company & Chr(34) &" And
            Not Paid"
        DoCmd OpenReport "Bill 01", A_NORMAL, , CritText
        R.MoveNext
    Loop
End Sub
```

Figure 17-4 shows a button labeled *Print All Bills,* which triggers the execution of the procedure for printing a full cycle of bills.

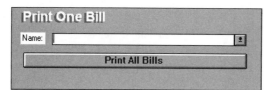

Figure 17-4: The Print All Bills button triggers the printing procedure.

Printing selected bills

A third method of printing bills involves the use of a *pick list* to select one or more companies for which bills should be printed. Figure 17-5 shows a form that lists the company names and the number of open invoices for each company. A check box lets you select companies included in the bill printing cycle that is initiated when you click the *Print* button.

You can implement a pick list like the one shown in Figure 17-5 by creating a table with three fields:

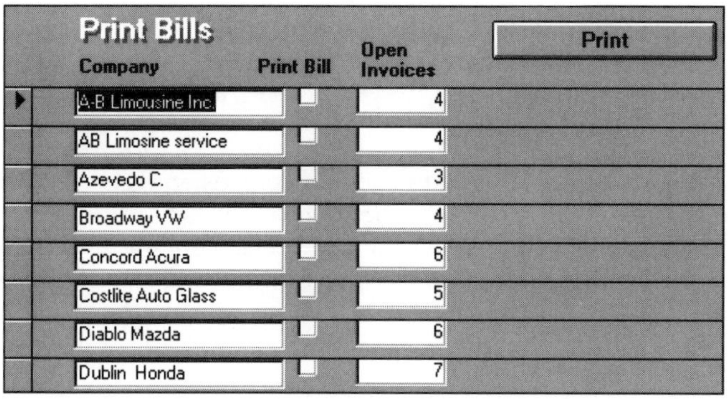

Figure 17-5:
This form
displays a
pick list of
company
names for
bill printing.

Field	Type
Company	Text
Print Bill	Yes/No
Out	Number

These fields contain the information that is displayed in the form shown in Figure 17-5. However, because this information can change, it must be updated each time the bill printing form is displayed. This can be accomplished by adding a procedure to the OnLoad event of the form's Access Basic module. OnLoad events take place after the form is opened. The procedure begins by defining a database and two record sets:

```
Sub Form_Load ()
    Dim D As Database, R As Recordset, N As Recordset
    Set D = DbEngine.Workspaces(0).Databases(0)
```

The source of the first record set is the table — I'll call it *Print Bills* — that contains the three fields *Company*, *Print Bill*, and *Out*. The record set is opened by referring to the RecordSource property of the current form:

```
Set R = D.OpenRecordset(Me.RecordSource)
```

This example uses the Me object. Depending on where it is used, the Me object is usually the same as the Screen.ActiveForm object or the Screen.ActiveReport object. The only difference is that the Me object retains it meaning when the object (form or report) in which it is used doesn't have the focus.

This means that the Me object has two advantages over the Screen objects. First, it's a lot simpler to enter. Second, it can be used in the Immediate window during the debugging process. If you try to refer to the Screen.ActiveForm object in the Immediate window, an error occurs and Access tells you there is no active form. The Me object works in the Immediate window of a form or report module because it still refers to the form or report object you are working with, even though the system's focus is on the Immediate window.

The other record set involved is the invoice source, *Invoices.* In this example, you want to retrieve a list of unique company names and a count of the open invoices for each company. The number of invoices isn't critical to the printing process. It is included here as an example of the information you may want to display on the pick list. It gives you an idea of which bills need printing. You can assume that the company names with numerous open invoices are the ones that need to be printed.

To retrieve this data, a SQL statement is composed that uses the *GROUP BY* clause to group by company name:

```
SQLText = "SELECT Company, Count([Invoice Number]) AS Out FROM
           Invoices WHERE Not Paid GROUP BY Company;"
Set N = D.OpenRecordset(SQLText)
```

The grouping process produces one record for each unique company name. The *Count( )* function is used to count the invoices for each company. The *WHERE* clause selects only unpaid invoices. The expression *Not Paid* is equivalent to *Paid=False.*

Once the two record sets are established, you need to be sure that the form's record set is empty. Records left over from the last printing (if any) must be deleted so the set can be refilled with accurate data. The following Do loop deletes all records from the form's record set:

```
Do Until R.Eof
    R.Delete
    R.MoveNext
Loop
```

Note that a Delete All loop must contain a MoveNext method to advance to the next record. Without MoveNext, the loop would endlessly delete the same record.

Once the old records have been removed, the record set can be filled with up-to-date information:

```
Do Until N.Eof
   R.AddNew
   R.Company = N.Company
   R.Out = N.Out
   R.Update
   N.MoveNext
Loop
```

The last step is to requery the form to ensure that it displays the updated records. Once again, the Me object is used to refer to the current form:

```
    Me.Requery
End Sub
```

Each time the form is opened, the completed loading procedure ensures that the list of companies and open invoices is accurate:

```
Sub Form_Load ()
    Dim D As Database, R As Recordset, N As Recordset
    Set D = DbEngine.Workspaces(0).Databases(0)
    Set R = D.OpenRecordset(Me.RecordSource)
    SQLText = "SELECT Company, Count([Invoice Number]) AS Out FROM
              Invoices WHERE Not Paid GROUP BY Company;"
    Set N = D.OpenRecordset(SQLText)
    Do Until R.Eof
        R.Delete
        R.MoveNext
    Loop
    Do Until N.Eof
        R.AddNew
        R.Company = N.Company
        R.Out = N.Out
        R.Update
        N.MoveNext
    Loop
    Me.Requery
End Sub
```

When the form is displayed with the newly updated list of companies and open invoices, a printing cycle is initiated with a command button control. The OnClick event procedure for the button is similar to the procedure used to print all the bills. The only difference in the OnClick procedure is that company names used in the OpenReport action are those that are checked off on the current form.

The procedure obtains the current form's record set using the RecordSetClone method on the Me object. The procedure then loops through the record set looking for True values in the *Print Bill* field. If one is found, the company name is inserted into the OpenReport action and a bill is printed for that company. The complete OnClick event procedure for the command button is as follows:

```
Sub Button14_Click ()
    Dim R As Recordset
    Set R = Me.RecordSetClone
    R.MoveFirst
    Do Until R.Eof
```

continued

```
If R.[Print Bill] Then
    Ok = SysCmd(4, "Printing Bill for : " & R.Company)
    CritText = "Company = " & Chr(34) & R.Company  & Chr(34) &
                  " And Not Paid"
    DoCmd OpenReport "Bill", A_NORMAL, , CritText
End If
R.MoveNext
Loop
End Sub
```

All the printing methods shown — one bill at a time, all bills, a selected list of bills — simply select the companies to print. The procedures for calculating the billing information and summary totals are contained in the Access Basic module of the report. Instead of a report that is simply an output template for data already stored in a table, your report can be a smart object that performs any sort of operation necessary to produce the required results.

Creating an Aging Table

A bill usually shows detailed information for the current financial period, typically the current month. As shown in Figure 17-6, outstanding charges or invoices older than the current period are summarized in an aging table, which is typically printed at the bottom of the bill or statement.

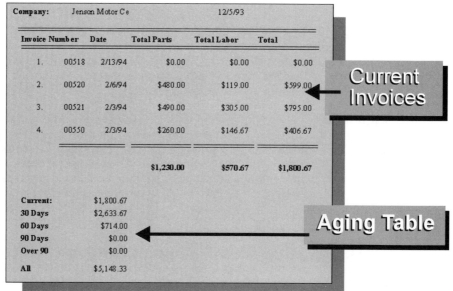

Figure 17-6: An aging table summarizes outstanding invoices from previous periods.

The first step in producing an aging table is to add unbound controls to the Report Footer section of the bill or statement report. In this example, the controls are named *Current, Days30, Days60, Days90,* and *Over90.* These names correspond to the current period and periods that are 30, 60, 90, and more than 90 days prior to the current billing date.

This report is based on the report used in the previous sections of this chapter to produce bills on which each outstanding invoice is listed. When the aging table is added, the report must perform the following additional tasks:

✔ Distinguish between current period invoices, which are printed in the Detail section on the bill , and previous period invoices — which are summarized in the aging table at the end of the bill.

✔ Accumulate totals for previous period invoices.

✔ Separate previous period invoices into groups of 30, 60, 90, and over 90 days.

✔ Print the accumulated totals in the bill's aging table for the 30, 60, 90, and over 90 day periods.

The first step in implementing the aging table is to create module-level variables for each of the aging periods. These variables are defined in the declarations section of the report's Access Basic module so that they are available to all procedures included in the report. This is necessary because the aging totals are calculated in the Detail section but aren't printed until the Report Footer section. Because each section executes different event procedures, module-level variables are needed to pass values between separate event procedures. In the following code, the variables added for this example are shown in bold:

```
Option Compare Database    'Use database order for string comparisons
Dim ICount As Integer, GtParts As Double, GtLabor As Double
Dim D30 As Double, D60 As Double, D90 As Double, Ovr90 As Double
```

The next change is in the Detail section's OnFormat event procedure. This procedure is executed once for each record in the report's record set. However, because the age of the invoice is now significant, the procedure that is triggered by formatting the Detail section must distinguish between current period invoices and older invoices. Current period invoices should be printed in the Detail section. Older invoices should not. Further, even though the older invoices are not printed, you must still calculate their value because their totals are included in the aging table that appears at the bottom of the bill. The problem is solved with the following:

✔ **DateDiff( ).** This built-in Access function returns a number that is the difference between two dates. The DateDiff( ) function allows you to specify the unit of time — days, weeks, months, quarters, or years to be calculated. In this case, you can simplify the calculation by using *m* (month) as the unit of time. The following expression compares the invoice date — *[Date]* — to the current system date — *Now( )* — by month:

```
DateDiff("m", [Date], Now() )
```

If the expression returns 0, the invoice is a current period charge. If the value is greater than 0, the invoice shouldn't be included in the Detail section, but its value should be calculated for the appropriate period in the aging table.

✔ **Cancel.** The OnFormat event supports the use of the *Cancel* variable. If *Cancel* is True when the procedure ends, the Detail section is not printed.

The *DateDiff( )* function and the *Cancel* variable can be used to solve the aging table problem. First, *DateDiff( )* is used to differentiate current invoice dates from older invoice dates. All current invoices are processed with a procedure called CurrentPeriod. All older invoices are directed to a Select Case structure that uses *DateDiff( )* to match the invoice with its proper aging category — that is, 30, 60, 90, or over 90 days — based on the number of months calculated by *DateDiff( )*.

The Select Case structure includes a function procedure named PreviousPeriod, which is used to calculate the value of the older invoice. Following the Select Case structure, the statement *Cancel=True* is used to cancel the OnFormat event so that no Detail section is printed for the older invoices. In the following code, the modifications made to the Detail1_Format procedure are shown in bold:

```
Sub Detail1_Format (Cancel As Integer, FormatCount As Integer)
    Dim D As Database, Parts As Recordset, Labor As Recordset
    Set D = DbEngine.Workspaces(0).Databases(0)
    SQLCrit = "Where [Invoice Number] = " & [Invoice Number] & ";"
    Set Parts = D.OpenRecordset("Select * From [Parts Details] " &
            SQLCrit)
    Set Labor = D.OpenRecordset("Select * From [Labor Details] " &
            SQLCrit)
    If DateDiff("m", [Date], Now()) = 0 Then
        CurrentPeriod Parts, Labor
    Else
        Select Case DateDiff("m", [Date], Now())
            Case 1
                    D30 = D30 + PreviousPeriod(Parts, Labor)
            Case 2
                    D60 = D60 + PreviousPeriod(Parts, Labor)
            Case 3
                    D90 = D90 + PreviousPeriod(Parts, Labor)
            Case Else
                    Ovr90 = Ovr90 + PreviousPeriod(Parts, Labor)
        End Select
        Cancel = True
    End If
End Sub
```

Object variables are used as arguments — in this case, the record sets Parts and Labor — in both the CurrentPeriod and PreviousPeriod procedures. Object variables can be passed to subroutines and functions just as you would pass single-value variables. In this example, the record sets are defined once in the Detail1_Format procedure and then passed as arguments to the other procedures.

The CurrentPeriod procedure is identical to the Detail1_Format procedure used in the previous section. It calculates and prints the totals for each invoice. Note that the Parts and Labor arguments are reassigned to the RecordSet variable:

```
Sub CurrentPeriod (Parts As Recordset, Labor As Recordset)
    [Total Parts] = 0
    [Total Labor] = 0
    Do Until Parts.eof
        Me.[Total Parts] = Me.[Total Parts] + Parts.[Price] *
            Parts.[Quantity]
        Parts.MoveNext
    Loop
    Do Until Labor.eof
        Me.[Total Labor] = Me.[Total Labor] + Labor.[Rate] *
            Labor.[Hours]
        Labor.MoveNext
    Loop
    Me.[Total] = Me.[Total Parts] + Me.[Total Labor]
    GtParts = GtParts + [Total Parts]
    GtLabor = GtLabor + [Total Labor]
    ICount = ICount + 1
    Me.[Item Number] = ICount & "."
End Sub
```

The PreviousPeriod procedure is a function type procedure that calculates the total amount for any invoice date not in the current period:

```
Function PreviousPeriod (Parts As Recordset, Labor As Recordset)
    P = 0
    Do Until Parts.eof
        P = P + Parts.[Price] * Parts.[Quantity]
        Parts.MoveNext
    Loop
    Do Until Labor.eof
        P = P + Labor.[Rate] * Labor.[Hours]
        Labor.MoveNext
    Loop
    PreviousPeriod = P
End Function
```

The final modification is to add statements to the Report Footer OnFormat procedure to insert the accumulated totals for each aging period into the controls that make up the aging table. These additions to the Report Footer OnFormat procedure are shown in bold in the following code:

```
Sub ReportFooter4_Format (Cancel As Integer, FormatCount As Integer)
    [GrandTotal_Total Parts] = GtParts
    [GrandTotal_Total Labor] = GtLabor
    [GrandTotal_Total] = GtLabor + GtParts
```

continued

```
        [Current] = [GrandTotal_Total]
        [Days30] = D30
        [Days60] = D60
        [Days90] = D90
        [Over90] = Ovr90
        [All] = [Current]+D30+D60+D90+Ovr90
    End Sub
```

The report will now produce the bill shown in Figure 17-6, which includes details for current invoices and totals for any aged invoices.

Chapter 18

Special Printing Techniques

*T*he preceding chapter showed you how to use the OnFormat event to create smart reports. These reports use Access Basic procedures to calculate and summarize information, and then output that data as part of a report. This chapter presents tips and techniques for controlling the printing and layout of your reports.

Page and Pages

During printing, Access automatically maintains two special values (referred to as report or form properties):

- **Page.** This is the value of the current page number.
- **Pages.** This is the value of the total number of pages that will be printed in the report.

These values are typically used in controls to add page numbering to a form or report. The following expression uses both values to print information in the format *Page # of #* on a report (for example, Page 1 of 5):

```
= "Page " & Page & " of " & Pages
```

Of the two values, Pages is the most interesting and, in terms of the problem presented here, the most useful. Whereas the Page value simply increases each time a new page is printed, Pages must evaluate the overall size of the report before the pages are actually printed. This doesn't happen by magic. By placing a reference to the Pages property in any part of a report, you force Access to process the report differently. For example, to print information such as *Page 1 of 5* on a report, Access must determine the total number of pages before printing the first page of the report. In other words, Access must scan the entire record set used by the report before it can format and print the first page.

This becomes clear when you print a report that uses a large record set. If the report doesn't use the Pages value, the first page is immediately formatted and printed. However, by simply adding Pages, you force Access to scan the entire record source prior to formatting and printing the first page. In a large record set — for example, 20,000 records — the delay is noticeable. In such cases, a progress meter is displayed at the bottom of the window.

The Pages property also affects the event sequence of a report. The Print event for each section usually follows immediately after the Format event for that section. However, if you add Pages to the report, Access adds a series of events. Before the normal Format and Print events take place, Access runs a complete set of Format events for the entire report in order to obtain the value for the total number of pages.

It's important to remember that the Page and Pages properties operate only when they are included in the Control Source property of one of the controls on the report. If you want to refer to either value in Access Basic, your form must include a control that uses the property as well. Simply using Page or Pages in an event procedure won't cause Access to calculate the correct values for these properties. If you don't want to print the numbers on the report, you can hide the control by setting the Visible property to No.

Manually Feeding the First Page

Before attacking the problem of printing multiple copies, we'll look at a simpler printing problem. Suppose you want to print a report and the first page requires special handling. You want to print the first page on company stationery that you manually feed into the printer, and print the remainder of the report on plain paper. The solution is to create an event procedure that pauses the printing by displaying a message box before the first page prints. The following procedure is associated with the Print event of the Page Header section of the report:

```
Sub PageHeader0_Print (Cancel As Integer, PrintCount As Integer)
    If Page = 1 Then Msgbox " Place letterhead in manual feed bin."
End Sub
```

This section is evaluated before each page is printed. The expression *Page = 1* ensures that the message box is displayed only before the first page is printed. All other pages are printed without pause.

Printing for Two-Sided Copying

Most word processing and desktop publishing programs allow you to format separate page headers and footers for odd and even pages. This is done primarily so that page elements are positioned correctly when documents are reproduced as two-sided copies. For example, page numbers are traditionally located on the outside edge of the page. As shown in Figure 18-1, page numbers are usually printed on the right side of an odd-numbered page. On the other hand, when an even-numbered page is printed on the back of an odd-numbered page, the outside is the left side of the page.

Figure 18-1:
The placement of the page number changes for odd and even pages.

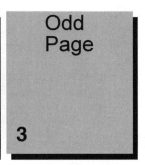

You can duplicate this effect with the following Format event procedure, which is used with the Format event for the Page Footer section. Depending on whether the page being formatted is even or odd, this procedure switches the location of the *PageNumber* control from 5 inches from the left side of the report to .5 inches:

```
Sub PageFooter2_Format (Cancel As Integer, FormatCount As Integer)
    If Page Mod 2 Then
        [PageNumber].Left = 5 * 1440
    Else
        [PageNumber].Left = .5 * 1440
    End If
End Sub
```

The value 1440 converts twips into inches. The *Mod* operator returns the remainder when two numbers are divided. In this procedure, *Page Mod 2* divides the page number by 2. If the page number is even, the value is 0, which is treated as a False value. For an odd-numbered page, the expression yields 1, which is a True value.

Keep in mind that this procedure must be associated with a Format event because it involves a change in the section's layout — that is, the left position of a control. If the same statements are executed in a Print event, they won't affect the placement of the control because the section's layout is already set by then.

Printing Non-Identical Copies

What in the world is a non-identical copy? Aren't copies supposed to be identical? The term *non-identical copy* refers to the fact that most business forms are produced in several copies — for example, duplicate or triplicate. However, each copy of the bill, invoice, or statement is meant for a slightly different purpose. Business forms usually include the original, a customer copy, and an office copy.

Although computers are supposed to eliminate the need for all these copies, business customs and traditions still require the printing of forms in duplicate or triplicate. Each copy is usually differentiated from the others in some way. The most common practice is to use multiple-ply forms in which each ply of paper is a different color such as white, yellow, and pink. You can purchase multiple-ply forms that are designed for use with impact printers (for example, a dot matrix or a daisy wheel printer).

You can even purchase blank 8.5-by-11 inches multiple-ply forms and print any type of business form you want by designing an Access form or report. However, you should remember that printing boxes, lines, and graphics slows down the printing process. Preprinted invoices, statements, and other forms eliminate the need to print these elements.

This is all very nice if you have an impact printer, but what about non-impact printers? Because of their combination of high quality and high speed, laser and ink-jet printers are the most popular types of printers today. These printers create printed images by placing toner or ink on the surface of the page so you can't produce carbon copies with non-impact printers.

It's often assumed that if you want to print business forms in duplicate or triplicate you *must* use an impact printer. By taking advantage of the OnFormat property associated with the sections of a report, however, you can create duplicate or triplicate type forms with a laser or ink-jet printer.

The OnFormat property lets you vary the style of a report so that each copy is slightly different. For example, as illustrated by the diagram in Figure 18-2, an invoice report might have *Invoice* as the heading on the first copy, *Customer Copy* on the second, and *Office Copy* on the third.

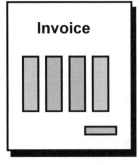 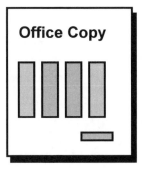 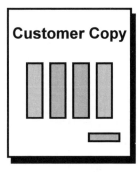

Figure 18-2:
Multiple
copies of a
form are
printed with
different
headings.

Keep in mind that the changes can be as subtle or dramatic as you desire. For example, the first copy might include lines, boxes, and shading while the subsequent copies would be printed without these graphic items.

Although changing the print of each copy isn't as noticeable as a change in the color of the paper, it does give you some capablities that aren't possible when printing duplicates on standard multiple-ply forms. For example, you might want to suppress the printing of sensitive information on some of the copies. For instance, Federal Express forms consist of a complicated set of carbons of different lengths and special patterns. The design of these forms eliminates from several of the duplicate copies the account numbers that are entered on the top copy. By using the OnFormat property, you can achieve the same result without purchasing expensive or complicated paper forms.

Changing a Control When Printing Copies

The examples in the previous sections controlled a report by using the Page property to obtain the value of the current page. Printing different headings on each copy of a report is a bit more complicated.

Suppose you elect to print three copies of a report that consists of three invoices. Each invoice appears on a separate page, so the process generates nine pages. By default, Access prints *collated* copies. As shown in Figure 18-3, this means that Access produces the three copies by printing pages 1 through 3 and then returning to the first page to produce the next copy. When you produce three collated copies, you are executing the page printing sequence three times in a row.

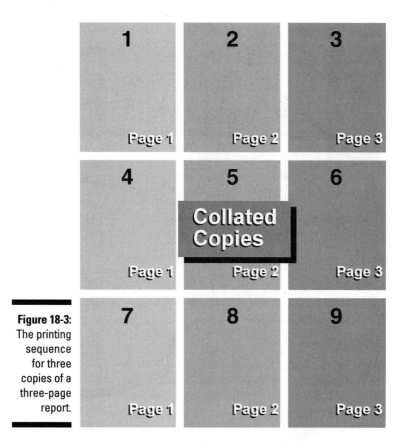

Figure 18-3:
The printing
sequence
for three
copies of a
three-page
report.

The goal in this example is to vary the printing based on which copy is being produced. The key is that each time Access begins a set of copies, the value of the Page property returns to 1.

However, there is another problem to solve. Not only must you recognize when Access begins a new copy of the report, you must keep track of which copy is being printed because the heading in copy 2 is different from the heading in copy 3.

This problem can be solved by placing a variable in the declarations section of the report's Access Basic module. Recall that a variable defined in the declarations section maintains its value for as long as the form is open. The following example defines *Copies* as an Integer type variable:

```
Option Compare Database    'Use database order for string comparisons
Dim Copies As Integer
```

This variable will be used to keep track of which copy is being printed.

To ensure that each printing cycle begins with the correct setting for the variable *Copies*, you can set a default value for the variable in the Open event procedure of the report, as shown in the following code:

```
Sub Report_Open (Cancel As Integer)
    Copies = 1
End Sub
```

In the following code, the value of *Copies* is used to alter the appearance of the printed form:

```
Select Case Copies
    Case 1
        [Invoice Heading].Caption = "Invoice"
    Case 2
        [Invoice Heading].Caption = "Customer Copy"
    Case 3
        [Invoice Heading].Caption = "Office Copy"
End Select
```

In this example, the text of a Label control called *Invoice Heading* is changed based on the value of *Copies* so that it reads differently depending on which copy is being printed. Because the changes caused by this section involve the value of the control, this structure could be used in either the Format procedure or the Print procedure for the section that contains the control — that is, *PageHeader0_Format* or *PageHeader0_Print*.

If you want to change the layout of the section — for example, the position or size of the control, whether it is visible, the font size and style — you must use the Format event rather than the Print event. If a statement that modifies a layout attribute is placed in a Print event procedure, Access generates an error message, *Can't set property... after printing has started*, when you try to print the report.

The next example expands on the structure you use to produce different versions of the same page. This example alters the appearance of a Line type control, *Line50*, as well as the text in *Invoice Heading*. The line is printed at different thicknesses on copies 1 and 3 and it isn't printed on copy 2.

The statements that refer to the Visible and Borderwidth property mean that this code *must* be placed in a Format procedure — for example, *PageHeader0_Format*:

```
Select Case Copies
    Case 1
            [Invoice Heading].Caption = "Invoice"
    Case 2
            [Invoice Heading].Caption = "Customer Copy"
    Case 3
            [Invoice Heading].Caption = "Office Copy"
End Select
```

One more statement is needed in this procedure to control the value of *Copies*. This can be accomplished fairly simply by using the Page and Pages properties. Each time the value of Page is equal to Pages, you know that you have completed one printing. For example, if you are printing 10 invoices, the value of Page and Pages will be 10 when the last invoice is printed. This can be expressed with the following statement:

```
If Page = Pages Then Copies = Copies + 1
```

This statement increments the value of *Copies* each time Access prints a new copy of the report.

This statement uses a shortened form of the If...Then structure. Because no Else segment is involved, the statement *Copies = Copies + 1* can be placed on the same line as If...Then. In this form, no End If statement is required.To execute several statements after Then, separate the statements with colons. ∎

When you put the pieces together, you get the following procedure, which is associated with the Print event of the Page Header section:

```
Sub PageHeader0_Print (Cancel As Integer, PrintCount As Integer)
    Select Case Copies
            Case 1
                    [Invoice Heading].Caption = "Invoice"
                    [Line50].Visible = True
                    [Line50].Borderwidth = 1
            Case 2
                    [Invoice Heading].Caption = "Customer Copy"
                    [Line50].Visible = False
            Case 3
                    [Invoice Heading].Caption = "Office Copy"
                    [Line50].Visible = True
                    [Line50].BorderWidth = 3
        End Select
        If Page = Pages Then Copies = Copies + 1
End Sub
```

The Print event is used because the procedure doesn't change any of the layout characteristics of the section.

Keep in mind that this procedure will work *only* if a control on the report contains the Page and Pages properties. If you don't include this control, Access won't calculate values for these properties and Access Basic will treat them as null values. An example of the required control is as follows:

Name	**Control Source**	**Visible**
PageValues	= [Page] & [Pages]	No

Note that you can use any type of expression for the Control Source property. The only requirement is that it must include both Page and Pages. In this example, the Visible property is set to No so that the control doesn't print on the report. This doesn't affect the value of Page and Pages. Access calculates these values even though the control is invisible because it is possible that a macro or event procedure that executes during the printing process might change the control to Visible.

It's best to insert this control in the Page Header section of the report because this is the first section evaluated on each page.

Printing Multiple Copies of Reports

The printing of reports is always executed either manually or with macro actions. Access Basic has no direct printing commands, but the macro actions can be executed from Access Basic with the DoCmd statement.

To produce multiple copies of a report, you must perform the print operation in two steps:

1. **Open the report in the Print Preview mode**. The OpenReport action allows you to access a stored report for design, direct printing, or preview. In this case, you can't use direct printing because it doesn't support multiple copies. Instead, you need to open the report in the Print Preview mode. Then you can use a Print action to generate the desired number of copies.

2. **Print collated copies**. After opening the report in the Print Preview mode, you can use the Print action to output the desired number of copies of the report. The Print action is equivalent to the dialog box displayed by the File | Print command.

Note that you *must* print the copies using Collated copies (the default). Collated copies means that Access prints all of the pages of the first copy and then starts again with the first page of the second copy.

If Collated is turned off, Access generates multiple copies of each page on a page-by-page basis — that is, three copies of page 1, followed by three copies of page 2, and so on.

However, the method used to produce non- collated copies varies from printer to printer. Some printers, such as laser printers, can produce multiple copies of a page by automatically duplicating the last page received from the computer. This is similar to the way that a copy machine works. In such cases, Access no longer controls the format of each copy, and the procedures described in this section won't work because only the first page in each copy is formatted by Access.

When you use Collated copies, Access specifically formats each page of each copy. This means the Format and Print procedures can alter the appearance of the report based on which copy is printing. For example, if you print three copies of a three-page report using the Collated copies method, the *PageHeader0_Print* procedure is executed nine times. If you use non-collated printing, this may be reduced to three times, depending on the type of printer you are using.

The following procedure prints three copies of a report named *Invoice 3 Ply*:

```
Function InvoiceCopies ( )
    DoCmd OpenReport "Invoice 3 Ply", A_PREVIEW
    DoCmd Print A_PRINTALL, , , , 3, True
    DoCmd Close
End Function
```

The *3* in the Print action specifies the number of copies. *True* specifies collated copies.

Chapter 19

Bean Counting

• •

In This Chapter

▶ Creating an inventory system

▶ Updating inventory when an item is sold

▶ Confirming inventory updates

▶ Replacing items returned to inventory

▶ Updating raw materials inventory when manufactured items are sold

• •

The title of this chapter, *Bean Counting,* refers to using a database to keep track of physical items. The most common example of this type of application involves maintaining an inventory of the items used by a business.

Most accounting tasks are considered open- ended because they keep track of events — for example, financial transactions. In theory, you can make an unlimited number of sales or purchases. You account for the receipt or expenditure of money by adding one or more records to the appropriate table in the database.

However, when you refer to activities as *bean counting,* you imply that the data in the database corresponds to physical items. If a record is added to one table, it implies that something else must be taken from another table.

This chapter shows how Access Basic is used to set up an inventory system in which changes to a financial table (an invoice table) are reflected in another table (an inventory table).

The Basic Inventory Problem

Suppose you want to keep track of your inventory as part of your invoicing and billing system. By tracking inventory, you know how much of each item is still in stock, and more important, how much money you have tied up in inventory.

However, integrating inventory information with an invoicing and billing system raises some new logical and technical problems that I refer to as the *inventory problem*. Why is inventory different?

Most database relationships are referential. *Referential* means that records are associated by some common data item or value. For example, when you create an invoice, the invoice number links all the records that are related to the sale. One important characteristic of referential relationships is that they are open-ended. There is no predefined limit to the number of records that can be related to each invoice. A single invoice might have one item or a hundred items. It makes no difference whether you add or subtract items related to an invoice.

When you add inventory to this type of system, it is no longer open-ended. The Inventory problem resembles a zero-sum game. The mathematician John Von Neumann, often credited as the father of the modern computer, defined zero-sum games as those in which any gain for one player results in an equal loss for the other player. Each item on an invoice is an item that must be removed from inventory. In general terms, the number of items that you can add to an invoice is limited by the number of items in inventory.

Invoice operations directly affect the information contained in the inventory. When an item from inventory is used on an invoice, you must update the inventory table to reflect that change.

When a change occurs in the quantity value of any invoice item — new or old — it may require a corresponding change to the inventory record set. Access event procedures allow you to create a system in which any changes to the invoice are immediately reflected in the inventory.

Immediate Inventory Updates

The simplest way to implement an inventory system is at the point of entry. In other words, the inventory is updated when you enter items in the invoice. The essence of this type of inventory operation is the multiple column drop list, which is shown in Figure 19-1. The list is composed of the information stored in the Inventory table. It shows the part number, part name, and price. For each item stored in inventory, it also lists the current quantity.

The control pictured in Figure 19-1 has the following properties:

Name	**Part Number**
Control Source	Part Number
Row Source Type	Table/Query
Row Source	Select [Part Number],[Part Name],[Quantity], [Price] From Inventory Where [Quantity]>0;

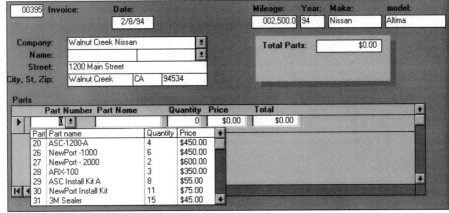

Figure 19-1:
A multiple
column drop
list shows
inventory
information.

Column Count:	4
Column Heads:	Yes
Column Widths:	0.25 in; 1.5 in; 0.5 in; 0.75 in
Bound Column:	1
List Rows:	8
List Width:	3 in

When multiple columns are displayed in a drop list, the Bound Column property determines which value is entered into the field. In this example, the Bound Column is column 1. As a result, when a selection is made, the data from the first column, Part Number, is inserted into the control.

By default, the List Width property is set to Auto. This means that the width of the drop list matches the control width. In this example, the drop list should be wider than the control from which it is dropped. The value 3 inches is simply the total width of the four displayed columns. Note that you must manually calculate the correct width and enter that value.

The part number is a critical element of this system because it must be a unique method for identifying each inventory item. In this example, the *Part Number* field is a Counter type field. The key point is that it must be a unique value for each inventory item.

After creating the multiple column drop list, you need to create Access Basic procedures that perform the following operations:

✔ **Filling in related values.** When you select an item from the inventory drop list, Access fills the current control with the data from the column specified in the Bound Column property. However, Access doesn't save the information from the other columns displayed in the list, such as part name and price. You need to create a procedure that updates the other controls with this information based on the selected part number.

✔ **Updating inventory.** Once you make a selection, you need to subtract the item from the inventory so that the inventory list is accurate.

✔ **Revising inventory when the quantity changes.** The user may want to increase or decrease the invoice quantity. In this case, you need to update the inventory for any additional parts that are removed or returned.

The Access Basic code for this inventory system is entered in the form module for the parts details subform that appears on the invoice.

Filling In Related Items

After the *Part Number* field has been updated, you can use an AfterUpdate event procedure to insert values, such as the part name and price, into the corresponding controls. This procedure includes two object variables for the current database control:

```
Dim D As Database, C As Control, R As Recordset
Set D = DbEngine.Workspaces(0).Databases(0)
Set C = Screen.ActiveControl
```

There is also a record set variable that contains the inventory table information. You can use a shortcut to create the inventory record set. Recall that the Row Source property of the current control, *Part Number,* is the SQL statement that's used to create the multiple column drop list:

```
Select [Part Number],[Part Name], [Quantity],[Price] From Inventory
          Where [Quantity]>0;
```

You can avoid entering this lengthy SQL statement by simply referring to the RowSource property of the current control, defined here by the variable *C.* The following statement opens a record set that duplicates the one that appears in the drop list:

```
Set R = D.OpenRecordset(C.RowSource)
```

Next, you need to locate the inventory item that matches the current part number. This is done using a MoveFirst method:

```
R.FindFirst "[Part Number] = " & C
```

Once the correct part is located, the name and price can be inserted into the controls:

```
[Part Name] = R.[Part Name]
[Price] = R.Price
```

If no *Quantity* value has been entered, an additional operation is needed to set the default value for *Quantity* to 1. You can also calculate *Total* by multiplying the price and quantity:

```
If Quantity = 0 Then Quantity = 1
[Total] = [Quantity] * [Price]
```

Updating the Inventory Table

At this point in the procedure, you need to update the inventory record for the part that is being sold. Because this action makes a permanent change in the Inventory table, you should display a message box that allows the user to accept or cancel the Inventory update. Figure 19-2 provides an example of this message box.

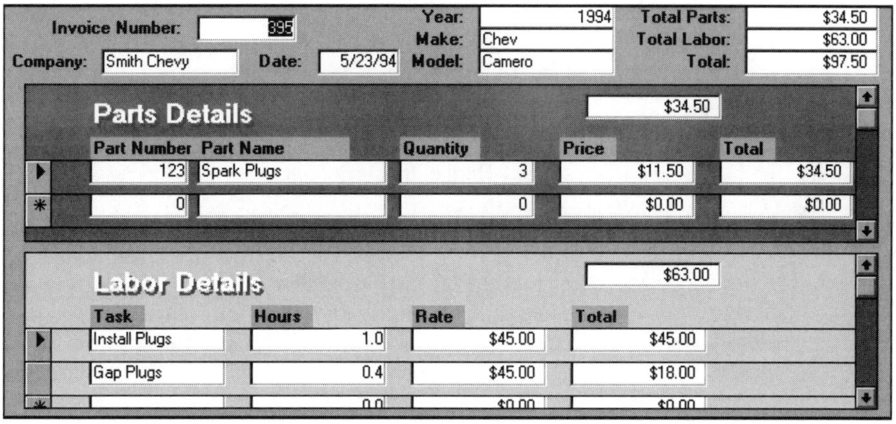

Figure 19-2: The message box allows the user to decide whether the inventory table should be updated.

First, the text of the message box is assigned to the variable *MsgText*. The message asks whether the user wants to remove the specified quantity of the selected item from inventory. The message is displayed with the function form of *Msgbox( )*. In this form, the function returns a value of either True or False, depending on which button is selected to close the message box:

```
MsgText = "Remove " & Quantity & " " & [Part Name] & " from
          inventory?"
OK = MsgBox(MsgText, 33, "Inventory Update")
```

The value 33 determines the style of the message box. The number is a composite value based on the values listed in Table 19-1. In this case, you want a two-button display — OK and Cancel — and a ? icon. The values for these two styles are 1 and 32 respectively, which makes a total of 33.

Table 19-1: Values for message box styles

Value	Meaning
0	Display OK button only
1	Display OK and Cancel buttons
2	Display Abort, Retry, and Ignore buttons
3	Display Yes, No, and Cancel buttons
4	Display Yes and No buttons
5	Display Retry and Cancel buttons
0	Display no icon
16	Display Critical Message icon
32	Display Warning Query icon
48	Display Warning Message icon
64	Display Information Message icon
0	First button is default
256	Second button is default
512	Third button is default

If OK is true (that is, if the user selects the OK button in the message box) the inventory record set R is updated to reflect the change. The following code includes an *If* structure that alters the *Quantity* field of the current record in record set R (the record located with the previous FindFirst is still the active record):

```
If OK Then
   R.Edit
   R.Quantity = R.Quantity - [Quantity]
   R.Update
   DoCmd DoMenuItem 0, 0, 4
End If
```

The DoCmd DoMenuItem action is used to save the record in the form. This action forces Access to update the parts details record set at the same time the inventory record set is updated. The completed procedure is as follows:

```
Sub Part_Number_AfterUpdate ()
   Dim D As Database, C As Control, R As Recordset
   Set D = DbEngine.Workspaces(0).Databases(0)
   Set C = Screen.ActiveControl
   Set R = D.OpenRecordset(C.RowSource)
   R.FindFirst "[Part Number] = " & C
```

```
            [Part Name] = R.[Part Name]
            [Price] = R.Price
            If Quantity = 0 Then Quantity = 1
            [Total] = [Quantity] * [Price]
            If OK Then
                    R.Edit
                    R.Quantity = R.Quantity - [Quantity]
                    R.Update
            End If
    End Sub
```

By selecting Cancel instead of OK in the message box, the user can cancel the inventory update. This feature is included because it's difficult to write a set of procedures that covers all possible circumstances. For example, the Cancel button allows users to override the inventory update in cases where they simply want to change the invoice but not the inventory. The user can also, enter items on the invoice that don't appear in inventory. If you omit the part number and enter a part name, quantity, and price, the inventory procedures simply ignore that entry.

Changing the Quantity

After an item is added to the invoice, the user might need to enter a correction or change the quantity of the item. This can affect inventory in three ways:

- ✔ **Removing the item from inventory.** If the new value for *Quantity* is greater than the current value, you may want to remove the corresponding item from the inventory.

- ✔ **Adding the item to inventory.** If the new quantity is less than the current value, you may want to return the item to inventory.

- ✔ **No change.** You may want to change the quantity without updating the inventory.

The OldValue property

To account for a change in quantity, you need to know the old value entered into the control and the new value that is replacing it. Thus you must execute the procedure with the BeforeUpdate event rather than the After Update event. This lets you access both the old and new values for the control.

When the BeforeUpdate event is triggered, Access maintains a copy of the previous value for each control on the form. This value can be accessed with the OldValue property. The following expression refers to the old value of the Quantity control:

```
Quantity.OldValue
```

Note that the OldValue doesn't appear on the screen. The current value of the control is the value of the newly entered data that caused the BeforeUpdate event. As shown in the following expression, you can calculate the change in quantity by subtracting the old value from the new:

```
Change = Quantity - Quantity.OldValue
```

The Quantity_BeforeUpdate() procedure is built around the difference, if any, between what was stored in the control and the new value. The procedure begins by calculating that difference:

```
Sub Quantity_BeforeUpdate (Cancel As Integer)
   Change = Quantity -Quantity.OldValue
```

Access considers a control to be edited if any changes are made in the control, even though the edits might not cause a substantive change. For example, re-entering the existing value in the *Quantity* control could still generate BeforeUpdate and AfterUpdate events. For this reason, you need to determine whether the change actually makes a difference in the quantity:

```
If Change <> 0 Then
```

If there is a change, you need to open a record set so that you can access the inventory record that corresponds to the current part number. In the following example, the record set is defined by a SQL statement. This means that the record set will contain only the record that matches the current part number.

```
Dim D As Database, R As Recordset
Set D = DbEngine.Workspaces(0).Databases(0)
SQLText = "Select * From Inventory Where [Part Number] = " & [Part
          Number]
Set R = D.OpenRecordset(SQLText)
```

It would be helpful to inform the user whether the inventory change removes or adds items. You can use the following *If* structure to specify different messages, depending on whether *Change* is greater than or less than 0:

```
If Change > 0 Then
   MsgText = "Remove " & Abs(Change) & " " & [Part Name] & " From
             inventory?"
Else
   MsgText = "Add " & Abs(Change) & " " & [Part Name] & " To
             inventory?"
End If
```

Remember that you have already eliminated the possibility that *Change* equals 0.

Note that this code uses the *Abs()* function. This function returns the *absolute value* of a number, which essentially deletes the minus sign from any negative number. This function is needed because the value of *Change* may be a negative number if you are returning a part to inventory instead of taking one out. If *Abs(Change)* isn't used to eliminate the minus sign, the user might see a message such as *Add -1 to inventory*, which doesn't make much sense.

The next step is to display the message box and allow the user to decide whether the inventory should be updated:

```
OK = MsgBox(MsgText, 33, "Inventory Update")
```

If the user chooses to update the inventory record set — that is, to select OK in the message box — the following statements perform that operation:

```
If OK Then
    R.Edit
    R.Quantity = R.Quantity - Change
    R.Update
End If
```

Note that if *Change* is a negative number, the inventory quantity increases, because subtracting a negative number is arithmetically equivalent to addition. The entire inventory update procedure looks like this:

```
Sub Quantity_BeforeUpdate (Cancel As Integer)
    Change = Quantity - Quantity.OldValue
    If Change <> 0 Then
        Dim D As Database, R As Recordset
        Set D = DbEngine.Workspaces(0).Databases(0)
        SQLText = "Select * From Inventory Where [Part Number] = " &
                [Part Number]
        Set R = D.OpenRecordset(SQLText)
        If Change > 0 Then
        MsgText ="Remove "&Abs(Change)&" " &[Part Name]&" From
                inventory?"
        Else
            MsgText = "Add " & Abs(Change) & " " & [Part Name] & " To
                inventory?"
        End If
        OK = MsgBox(MsgText, 33, "Inventory Update")
        If OK Then
            R.Edit
            R.Quantity = R.Quantity - Change
            R.Update
        End If
    End If
End Sub
```

Saving a record after the quantity changes

To ensure that inventory updates use the correct value for the quantity whenever a change in inventory is needed, the record must be saved after the *Quantity* control is updated. This is done in the parts details subform.

As shown in bold, the DoMenuItem action is inserted in the AfterUpdate procedure for the *Quantity* control:

```
Sub Quantity_AfterUpdate ()
    Total = Quantity * Price
    DoCmd DoMenuItem 0, 0, 4
End Sub
```

The values 0, 0, 4 correspond to the **File** | **Save** | **Record** command. The procedure already contains a statement that automatically calculates the total value when there is a change in *Quantity*.

These procedures create a system in which all invoice activity is reflected in the inventory table. The process of selling goods is now linked to the purchase of goods for resale.

Job Batch Inventory

The inventory problem described earlier in this chapter depicts a business in which inventory items are a *direct* part of a sale. For example, if the item listed on a sales invoice is a sunroof for a car, the item taken out of inventory is a sunroof. To account for this change, the item that appears on the invoice is simply subtracted from the inventory.

However, not all businesses view sales in this way. Suppose your business sells custom-designed cabinets that you manufacture to order. Your physical inventory consists of sheets of plywood and particleboard. However, when you write up an invoice, you record the model of the cabinet that the customer has requested.

For example, if the customer orders a model 100 cabinet, you know that four sheets of two different types of plywood are needed to fill the order. There is an *indirect* connection between the items that appear on the invoice and the items in inventory. How do you set up an inventory system when there isn't a direct connection between the inventory stock and the items sold?

The answer is to use an intermediate table that links each invoice item to the item or items in inventory. I call this intermediate table a *job batch table* because it relates each sale item to the inventory items used to manufacture that item.

You use the job batch table to connect the sales items to the inventory items. This connection allows your Access Basic program to update the inventory correctly when a manufactured item is sold.

A jobs table

Job batch inventory differs from normal inventory because it involves an indirect rather than a direct connection. A direct connection means that the items that appear on the sales form or invoice correspond directly to items in inventory. Indirect inventory means that the item you sell to a customer must be manufactured or assembled from items that you have in inventory.

Figure 19-3 shows a sales form that records sales of items. The item shown in the subform labeled *Items* is called *A100 4 draw*.

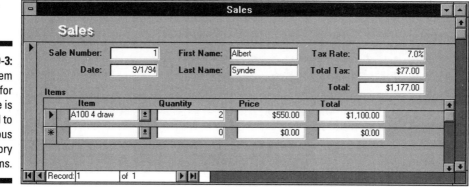

Figure 19-3:
The item selected for sale is related to numerous inventory items.

The name refers to a particular style of cabinet with four drawers, made from white laminated board. However, these cabinets aren't already manufactured. They must be created by using inventory items as raw materials. Table 19-2 lists the inventory items used to create each *A100 4 draw* cabinet.

Table 19-2: The raw materials used to create the item *A100 4 draw*

#	Job	Part	Quantity
1	A100 4 draw	White Lan 4x8	2
2	A100 4 draw	A-100 Hinges	8
3	A100 4 draw	A-1000 Rails	8

One solution is to list the raw materials directly on each sales form or invoice. But this may be confusing to both the customer and the salespeople. A better solution is to create a jobs table.

Figure 19-4 shows a table called Jobs that lists the raw materials used to create each of the sales items. This table can be used to update the raw materials inventory each time a sales item, such as the *A100 4 draw* cabinet, is sold.

Figure 19-4:
The Jobs
table relates
raw
materials
inventory to
sale items.

Id	Job	Part	Quantity
1	A100 4 draw	White Lan 4x8	2
2	A100 4 draw	A-100 Hinges	8
3	A100 4 draw	A-1000 Rails	8
4	A100 6 draw	White Lan 4x8	3
5	A100 6 draw	B-200 Hinges	12
6	A100 6 draw	A-1000 Rails	12
[Counter]			0

Table: Jobs
Record: 7 of 7

Linking jobs with inventory

The key to a job batch inventory is to use the Jobs table as the link between the sales items — for example, the *A100 4 draw* cabinet — and the inventory items, such as *White Lan 4x8*.

You do this by writing a procedure for the AfterUpdate event of the Items subform. This procedure is executed each time an item is added to the Items subform on the sales form.

The procedure uses two record sets. *J* is used to access information from the Jobs table and *I* is used to update the Inventory table:

```
Sub Form_AfterUpdate ()
    Dim D As Database, J As Recordset, I As Recordset
    Set D = DbEngine.Workspaces(0).Databases(0)
```

The record set J is defined as all the records that match the item entered into the current record. The *A100 4 draw* cabinet involves three inventory items that should be included in the J record set. In the following code, the text of the SQL statement is defined as the variable *SQLText*. Then, that variable is used with the OpenRecordSet method. Because *Item* is text, Chr(34) is used to insert quotation marks within the SQLText string:

```
SQLText = "Select * From Jobs Where Job = " & Chr(34) & Item &
          Chr(34) & ";"
Set J = D.OpenRecordset(SQLText)
```

The next set of statements displays the message box shown in Figure 19-5. This message box lists the items to be removed from inventory.

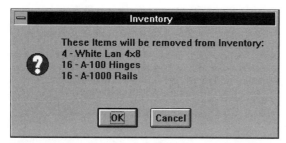

Figure 19-5: The message box shows the items to be removed from the inventory.

Unlike direct inventory operations, adding a single item to this sales form may result in changes to any number of different inventory items. The text of the message box is created by starting with a single line of text, which is assigned to the *MessText* variable. The procedure then loops through the J record set, adding one additional line for each inventory item used to create the sale item. The quantity of each item is calculated by multiplying the job quantity times the number of items sold. This calculation uses the *Quantity* control on the Items subform. The new lines within the text are created by inserting ASCII characters 10 and 13 at the end of each line. Because this technique is used more than once, the variable *Nl* is assigned to the new line characters:

```
Nl = Chr(10) & Chr(13)
MessText = "These Items will be removed from Inventory:" & Nl
Do Until J.Eof
    MessText=MessText & (J.Quantity*Quantity)&"-" & J.Part & Nl
    J.MoveNext
Loop
OK = MsgBox(MessText, 33, "Inventory")
```

The procedure uses the function form of MsgBox. Style 33 displays a ? icon with two buttons — OK and Cancel. The procedure then tests the value of the *OK* variable to determine whether the user has chosen to update the inventory. If the value of *OK* is 1, the inventory should be updated. This requires access to a second record set, which is associated with the Inventory table:

```
If OK = 1 Then
    Set I = D.OpenRecordset("Inventory")
```

Once the Inventory record set is opened, the J record set is repositioned to the beginning:

```
J.MoveFirst
```

The inventory is updated by a loop that uses each item in the J record set to locate the matching part in the inventory record set. This is accomplished with a FindNext method. The criteria for the FindNext method uses the value of

J.Part to determine which inventory item needs to be updated. When the item is located in inventory (record set I), the inventory quantity is reduced by the number of items needed to fill the order:

```
Do Until J.Eof
   I.FindFirst "Part = " & Chr(34) & J.Part & Chr(34)
   I.Edit
   I.Quantity = I.Quantity - J.Quantity * Me.[Quantity]
   I.Update
   J.MoveNext
Loop
```

When the entire J record set has been processed, the inventory update is finished. The complete procedure is as follows:

```
Sub Form_AfterUpdate ()
   Dim D As Database, J As Recordset, I As Recordset
   Set D = DbEngine.Workspaces(0).Databases(0)
   SQLText = "Select * From Jobs Where Job = " & Chr(34) & Item &
             Chr(34) & ";"
   Set J = D.OpenRecordset(SQLText)
   N1 = Chr(10) & Chr(13)
   MessText = "These Items will be removed from Inventory:" & N1
   Do Until J.Eof
      MessText=MessText & (J.Quantity*Quantity)&"-" & J.Part & N1
      J.MoveNext
   Loop
   OK = MsgBox(MessText, 33, "Inventory")
   If OK = 1 Then
      Set I = D.OpenRecordset("Inventory")
   J.MoveFirst
   Do Until J.Eof
      I.FindFirst "Part = " & Chr(34) & J.Part & Chr(34)
      I.Edit
      I.Quantity = I.Quantity - J.Quantity * Me.[Quantity]
      I.Update
      J.MoveNext
   Loop
   End If
End Sub
```

The job batch method of inventory updating allows you to update your inventory even when the items sold are manufactured or assembled from raw materials kept in inventory. This chapter uses a manufacturing business as an example. However, the job batch approach can also work for a business that assembles or bundles different premanufactured parts and sells them as a single unit — for example, computer systems.

Chapter 20

The Attendance Problem

*I*n many industries, employee attendance at various seminars, classes, or training sessions is required by federal or state law or professional associations. For example, people who work with certain chemicals or operate various types of manufacturing equipment are required to attend safety classes to be eligible for state worker's compensation coverage or private insurance programs. This chapter helps you ensure that workers attend the required classes by providing techniques for creating an attendance tracking application.

Maintaining Attendance Records

Suppose you manage a small business that produces custom furniture. You are required to keep track of which employees have safety training on the various types of equipment used in your workshop. How would you go about keeping these records?

Ideally, you would have a form similar to the one shown in Figure 20-1. This form includes a list of employees and check boxes that indicate whether each employee attended the class, workshop, or seminar. Each time you conduct a new class, a new checklist is displayed so you can record attendance for that session.

Although I'm using the form shown in Figure 20-1 as a solution to the attendance problem, the techniques involved in creating a working attendance form can be applied to a wide range of database applications.

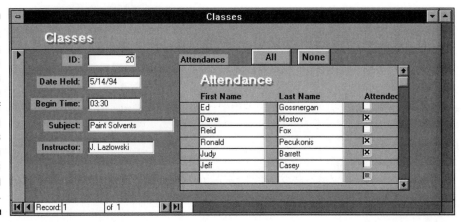

Figure 20-1:
This
attendance
form allows
you to
check off
which
workers
attended a
specific
training
session.

The solution to this problem involves a special type of *many-to-many* relationship between two sets of records. Many-to-many relationships arise when either of the record sets involved is related to more than one item in the other record set.

The attendance problem involves two record sets: one for events such as classes, workshops, or training sessions; and the other for individuals who attend a specific event. As shown in Figure 20-2, you can have a one-to-many record relationship in either direction. The top of the diagram shows that any given event — for example, *Training Session #1* — may be attended by one or more people. Conversely, the bottom portion of the diagram shows that any individual may attend one or more sessions.

Figure 20-2:
Two
record sets
can have
one-to-many
relationships
in either
direction.

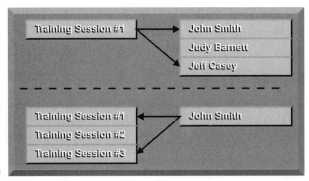

As shown in Figure 20-3, the solution is to relate the two record sets by using a third record set that records attendance — that is, a record set that includes one record for each unique combination of events and individuals.

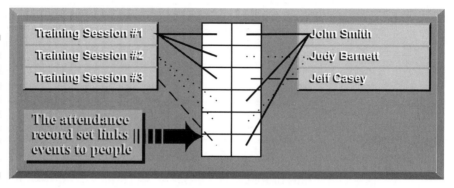

Figure 20-3:
A third record set is used to record the many-to-many relationships.

I called this a special type of many-to-many relationship. I used the term *special* because of another complication of the attendance problem, which I call *negative* information. For example, the fact that Judy Barnett *did not* attend Training Session # 2 is just as important as the fact that John Smith *did* attend.

In terms of record sets, each new record that is added to the Classes record set requires an additional set of attendance records, which correspond to the individuals who may have attended the event. You can then use a form like the one in Figure 20 -1 to check off who actually attended the class. To get that checklist, however, the attendance record set must already include a record for each employee who *might* have attended the class.

Defining Many-to-Many Links

Solving the attendance problem requires three tables that are similar in structure to the ones listed in Table 20-1. To solve the attendance problem, the Classes (event) and Workers (people) tables must contain a field that uniquely identifies each record. The simplest way to accomplish this is with Counter type fields. In this example, a field called *ID* is used in both tables.

The Attendance table links records in the other two tables by storing the ID from the Classes table in *Class Code* and the Workers ID in *Worker Code*. *Attended* is a Yes/No field that records either positive or negative information — that is, the person did or did not attend the event. Regardless of the value of Attended, the Attendance table must include one record for each possible combination of event and person.

Table 20-1: Tables and fields used in the attendance problem

Classes	Workers	Attendance
ID*	ID*	Class Code*
Date Held	Last Name	Worker Code*
Begin Time	First Name	Attended
Subject	...	First Name
Instructor		Last Name

---

* key fields

The Workers table doesn't need to be specifically dedicated to the attendance problem. In many cases, another table already includes the list of people who are involved in the events for which you are recording attendance. For example, it's likely that the company already maintains a personnel information table.

At a minimum, the Workers table must contain the fields listed in Table 20-1. In practice, the table probably contains a great deal more information about the individuals involved.

I should also note that the *First Name* and *Last Name* fields in the Attendance table are not strictly required. In theory, you could look up the name of the worker by using the Worker Code with a function such as *DLookUp( )*. In practice, however, it's best to store the names along with the code. This helps to avoid delays when displaying the records in the form.

In terms of Access Basic techniques, the solution to the attendance problem requires procedures that perform two tasks:

- **Appending a full set of records**. The procedures must automatically add an entire set of attendance records each time an event record (a class, training session, or seminar) is added to the Classes record set.
- **Triggering the append.** Each time a new record is added to one table — for example, Classes — a full set of records must be appended to another table. As you will see, the timing of these coordinated events can be complicated.

Creating a Class Attendance Form Layout

As with most of the Access techniques discussed in this book, forms play a fundamental role as the objects that combine the various elements into a single system. In the attendance problem, attendance information is entered on a form that is based on the Classes table.

The attendance information is inserted into this form by means of the subform shown in Figure 20-4.

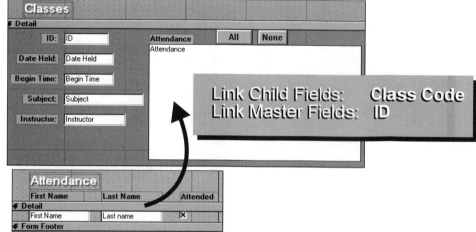

Figure 20-4:
The Class form displays attendance records in a subform.

As mentioned, the subform is based on the Attendance table. A tabular layout is used so that when multiple records are displayed they form a list. The form and subform are linked by the *ID* field from the Classes table and the *Class Code* field from the Attendance table.

Appending a Set of Records

The heart of the solution to the attendance problem is a procedure that adds a set of new records to the Attendance table each time a new record is added to the Classes table. For now, I'm going to sidestep the question of how this action is triggered.

Because each worker might or might not attend any class, the number of records that must be added to the Attendance table is determined by the number of records in the Workers table. As a result, you will be working with three record sets:

✔ **Classes.** The class record is determined by the current form. The key value in this record is the *ID* field, which uniquely identifies the class for which attendance is to be recorded.

✔ **Workers.** This table supplies the name and ID number of each worker who does or does not attend the class. In this example, the Workers table functions as a resource table. In other words, it supplies a list of names and ID numbers, but it isn't altered by the procedure. As such, it can be used in read-only mode.

✔ **Attendance.** A new set of records will be added to this table. The number of records that are added is determined by the number of names supplied by the resource table, Workers.

The procedure starts by defining four objects: *D* is the current database, *F* is the information from the record on the currently displayed form, *W* is the Workers resource table, and *A* is the Attendance table into which the new records will be appended:

```
Dim D As Database, W As Recordset, A As Recordset, F As Form
Set D = DBEngine.Workspaces(0).Databases(0)
Set F = Screen.ActiveForm
Set W = D.OpenRecordset("Workers", DB_OPEN_DYNASET, DB_READONLY)
Set A = D.OpenRecordset("Attendance", DB_OPEN_DYNEST,
            DB_APPENDONLY)
```

The two *OpenRecordSet( )* methods use special options to limit the methods that can be applied to the record sets. Because the Workers records are used only to provide a list of names, this record set is opened in *read-only* mode. In addition, because only new records will be added to the Attendance record set, it is opened in *append-only* mode. These options aren't required for the procedure to operate correctly. They are used to eliminate in advance the need to monitor record sets for actions that won't take place, such as editing changes to existing records. This allows for maximum performance by Access.

Once the record sets are opened, a DoUntil loop is used to add the new records to the Attendance table:

```
Do Until W.Eof
    A.AddNew
    A.[Worker Code] = W.[ID]
    A.[Class Code] = F.[ID]
    A.[First Name] = W.[First Name]
    A.[Last Name] = W.[Last Name]
    A.Update
    W.MoveNext
Loop
```

It's worthwhile to take a close look at these statements, because they involve the exchange of information among three different sources.

First, the loop is controlled by the resource record set W so that one record is added to A (*A.AddNew*) for each record in W. Once the record is added to A, it is linked to a specific worker by copying the *ID* field from W into the *Worker Code* field of A. A similar link is made between the new record in A and the ID of the class, which is found in the *ID* control on the form F.

The first and last names of the worker are also inserted into the new record. This isn't logically required because the ID numbers actually link the records. However, it's easier to recognize people by their names instead of an arbitrary number. The form is easier to use if the names are displayed in the subform.

Although you can accomplish the same thing with a lookup expression such as *DLookup "[Last Name]", "Workers", "ID = [Worker Code]"*, this is more trouble than it's worth. First, the lookup expression is far more complicated than the statement that inserts the name — *A.[Last Name] = W.[Last Name]*. Second, performing lookups for each record in each subform each time they are displayed will cause annoying delays that are easily avoided. In other words, it doesn't always pay to get too fancy.

One final action is needed. Recall that the record set that is to be displayed in the subform portion of the current form was chosen before the new records were added. To display these new records in the subform, you must perform a Requery method on the subform control. In this example, the subform control is named *Attendance*:

```
F.[Attendance].Requery
```

You can add the full procedure to the form's module as a subroutine called UpdateWorkerList:

```
Sub UpdateWorkerList ( )
    Dim D As Database, W As Recordset, A As Recordset, F As Form
    Set D = DBEngine.Workspaces(0).Databases(0)
    Set F = Screen.ActiveForm
    Set W = D.OpenRecordset("Workers", DB_OPEN_DYNASET, DB_READONLY)
    Set A = D.OpenRecordset("Attendance", DB_OPEN_DYNASET,
            DB_APPENDONLY)
    Do Until W.Eof
        A.AddNew
        A.[Worker Code] = W.[ID]
        A.[Class Code] = F.[ID]
        A.[First Name] = W.[First Name]
        A.[Last Name] = W.[Last Name]
        A.Update
        W.MoveNext
```

continued

```
      Loop
F.[Attendance].Requery
End Sub
```

You can add this Sub procedure to the form's module by using the **Edit | New Procedure** command or by entering **sub Update Worker List** anywhere in the code window.

Triggering the New List

Although the UpdateWorkerList procedure will perform the required operation, you still haven't associated it with an event property that will trigger its execution. You know that you want to add a new set of attendance records each time you add a new class record. It might seem logical that the BeforeInsert event will do the trick. This event is triggered immediately *after* you enter the first character into a new record.

However, BeforeInsert runs into trouble because of the way Counter fields (and controls bound to Counter fields) operate in Access. When you open a new record in a table or form that contains a Counter field, the counter will show *(Counter)* rather than an actual value. The counter value isn't established until after you enter at least one character into a field or control. In other words, the counter's value is triggered by an event similar to the BeforeInsert event. Which comes first?

Unfortunately, the BeforeInsert event takes place *before* Access establishes the value of the counter. As a result, you can't execute the UpdateWorkerList procedure with the BeforeInsert event because the required ID value (*F.[ID]*) won't be available.

What you need is essentially a new event that occurs as soon as possible after the counter value is actually inserted into the form. Because the counter value isn't established until at least one character is entered, you can eliminate from consideration all of the events that take place before that happens.

To find the answer, you need to examine in detail what happens when you start an entry in a new record. At least one character must be entered into a control, and you can assume that an AfterUpdate event takes place when you leave that control. In the current example, the first character is probably entered into the *Date Held* control.

Should you trigger the UpdateWorkerList procedure with the AfterUpdate event of the *Date Held* control? The answer is a definite maybe. Yes, you want to execute UpDateWorkerList if this is a new record. No, you don't want to execute UpdateWorkerList if you are merely revising an existing record.

This means you need a mechanism by which a procedure can determine whether this is a new record or an existing record. Access doesn't provide an *IsNewRecord* property or function, so you need to invent one.

To implement this technique, let's go back to the BeforeInsert event. This event is important because it is triggered by one and only one event — that is, the entry of the first character into a new record. BeforeInsert comes too early for the UpdateWorkerList procedure. However, instead of directly executing UpdateWorkerList, the BeforeInsert event can indicate to the events that follow whether this record is a new record.

This can be accomplished with a *module-level* variable. A module-level variable is defined with a Dim statement in the declarations section of the form's Access Basic module. As a result, it is available for as long as the form remains open. For this example, you could define a variable called *IsNewRecord* as a module-level variable:

```
Options Compare Database  'Use database order for string comparisons
Dim IsNewRecord As Integer
```

By default, this value is a null, or a False value. To indicate that the current record is a new record, the BeforeInsert event changes the value to True:

```
Sub Form_BeforeInsert (Cancel As Integer)
    IsNewRecord = True
End Sub
```

You can use this variable with the AfterUpdate event procedure for the first control on the form, *Date Held*, to perform UpdateWorkerList as soon as the date for the class is entered:

```
Sub Date_Held_AfterUpdate ( )
    If IsNewRecord Then
            UpdateWorkerList
            IsNewRecord = False
    Endif
End Sub
```

The last action in this procedure is to set the *IsNewRecord* value back to False. With this action, you avoid adding another set of workers for the same class.

With these procedures, as soon as the date of the class is entered, a full list of workers appears in the subform so you can check off who attended the session.

Marking and Unmarking All

When you are using a checklist, it's often handy to be able to check or uncheck all the items with a single command. For example, if eight of ten workers attend a class, it's easier to start with all the names checked and then uncheck two, rather than specifically checking eight names. The *ChangeAll* procedure can be used to change all the *Attended* values to True or False, depending on which value is passed as an argument to the variable *V*:

```
Sub ChangeAll (V)
    Dim D As Database, R As Recordset
    Set D = DBEngine.Workspaces(0).Databases(0)
    SQLText = "Select * From Attendance Where [Class Code] = " & [ID]
        & ";"
    Set R = D.OpenRecordset(SQLText)
    Do Until R.Eof
            R.Edit
            R.Attended = V
            R.Update
            R.MoveNext
    Loop
    Screen.ActiveForm![Attendance].Requery
End Sub
```

The procedure uses the ID displayed in the form to select the records that need to be changed. The procedure also requires the subform control *Attendance* to ensure that it displays the records accurately.

You can also convert the ChangeAll procedure to a toggle procedure. A *toggle* procedure doesn't change all the items to one value. Instead, it simply reverses the current value — for example, True to False and False to True. The bold section of the following procedure shows how a toggle is implemented.

```
Function ToggleAll ()
    Dim D As Database, R As Recordset
    Set D = DBEngine.Workspaces(0).Databases(0)
    SQLText = "Select * From Attendance Where [Class Code] = " & [ID]
        & ";"
    Set R = D.OpenRecordset(SQLText)
    Do Until R.Eof
            R.Edit
            If R.Attended Then
                    R.Attended - False
            Else
                    R.Attended - True
            Endif
            R.Update
            R.MoveNext
    Loop
    Screen.ActiveForm![Attendance].Requery
End Function
```

Taking the Opposite View

When you work with a linking record set such as the Attendance table in this example, you can apply the same basic method to view the data from the opposite direction. In other words, this example could have a form that displays a worker and then uses a subform to list all the classes that person has attended. This reverse view is illustrated by the form shown in Figure 20-5.

Figure 20-5:
This form
lists the
classes
attended by
a specific
worker.

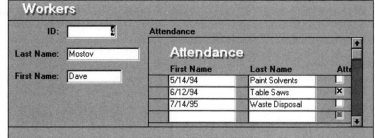

In this case, the link between the form and the subform is based on the *ID* and *Worker Code* fields:

Link Child Fields: **Link Master Fields:**

Worker Code   ID

The only information stored about the class is the *Class Code* ID number. Because the ID number won't make a meaningful display in the subform, *DLookUp()* functions can be used to find information stored in the Classes table, such as the date and subject of each class. The following examples retrieve the corresponding date and subject for each class:

Name	Control Source
Date	=DLookup("[Date Held]", "Classes", "ID = [Class Code]"),
Subject	=DLookup("[Subject]", "Classes", "ID = [Class Code]"),

The form pictured in Figure 20 -5 also supplies negative information about attendance. In other words, it also shows which classes were not attended by the worker.

Part IV
Practical
Problem Solving

In This Part...

*N*ow you get to apply the general ideas you've learned to solve specific practical problems that occur when you use databases in business. The chapters in the rest of the book cover the production of form letters, printing special forms such as bills and invoices, accounting, inventory control, and scheduling.

In addition to addressing specific problems, the techniques explored in these chapters will help you get a feel for the varied ways you can use Access programming to streamline many types of jobs.

Chapter 21

Schedules and To-Do Lists

· ·

In This Chapter

▶ Scheduling appointments

▶ Separating workdays and weekends

▶ Accounting for holidays

▶ Rounding dates

▶ Generating a to-do list

· ·

*T*he techniques described in the preceding chapter are not limited to solving the attendance tracking problem. They can be applied to a broad range of problems involving coordination between multiple tables. In this chapter, you learn how you can apply these techniques to create a scheduling form.

Creating the Scheduling Form

A scheduling form automatically projects a schedule of events based on some initial event. For example, suppose your business processes applications for home mortgage loans. Each client you work with must complete a specific series of tasks. These tasks usually appear on a checklist so you can easily tell what's been done and what needs to be done.

You can use Access Basic to create a scheduling form that replaces the paper checklist. Figure 21-1 shows a sample layout for this form.

The main form lists the client information. A subform lists the tasks that must be completed before the client's loan application can be presented to the loan committee for approval.

One way to approach this type of database is by creating a table that lists the standard tasks that are performed for each client. Figure 21-2 displays a form you might fill out for each of the tasks.

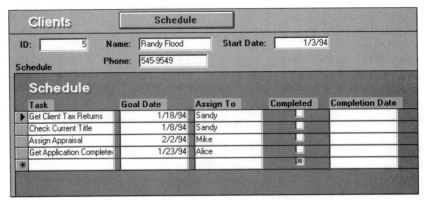

Figure 21-1: The Schedule form lists client information, required tasks, deadlines, assignments, and status.

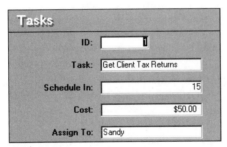

Figure 21-2: The Tasks table contains descriptions of the tasks that are needed to process one client.

The Tasks table includes such fields as:

- **Schedule In.** In most cases, you can estimate a completion date for the various tasks related to a client. For example, you may want to schedule an appraisal within 5 days, and receipt of the appraisal report within 30 days of starting the client's file. You can enter these day values in the Tasks table and automatically calculate the actual dates for each client.

- **Cost.** You can attach a cost value to each task, and use this information to obtain the actual cost of processing each client.

- **Assign To.** You can enter the name of the person responsible for performing or monitoring each task. This name can function as a default value that can be replaced later if necessary.

Similar to the attendance form from the previous chapter, the scheduling application should automatically generate a complete set of tasks for each client. You can use this list to verify if and when each task is completed. Like the attendance form, the schedule also provides the negative information — that is, which tasks are not yet completed. The tables used in this example are listed in Table 21-1.

Table 21-1: Client scheduling tables

Clients	*Tasks*	*Schedule*
ID*	ID*	Class Code*
Start Date	Task	Client ID*
Name	Schedule In	Attended
...	Cost	First Name
	Assign To	Last Name

*key fields

In this example, the Tasks table functions as a resource table. The information in the Tasks table defines the standard tasks that must be scheduled whenever a new record is added to the Clients table. The actual schedule is created by adding records to the Schedule table based on the setup information stored in Tasks.

The approach used to solve the scheduling problem is similar to the one you used in the attendance problem. In this case, the scheduling of events is triggered by a button on the Clients form. When the button is selected, it activates a procedure that sets up a schedule of activities for the current client based on the activities in the Tasks table.

The procedure begins by creating three object variables — *F*, *T*, and *S* — that correspond to the three record sets — the client shown in the form, the tasks stored in the Tasks table, and the events stored in the Schedule table:

```
Sub Button22_Click ()
    Dim D As Database, F As Form, S As Recordset, T As Recordset
    Set D = DBEngine.Workspaces(0).Databases(0)
    Set F = Screen.ActiveForm
    Set T = D.OpenRecordset("Tasks")
    Set S = D.OpenRecordset("Schedule")
```

The heart of the procedure is a *Do Until* loop that processes the events stored in the resource table, Tasks. The loop adds a new record to the Schedule table for each record in Tasks. The schedule events are linked to each client by means of the client's ID, as shown in the active form:

```
Do Until T.Eof
    S.AddNew
    S.[Client ID] = F.ID
    S.[Task] = T.Task
    S.[Goal Date] = F.[Start Date] + T.[Schedule In]
    S.[Assign To] = T.[Assign To]
    S.Update
    T.MoveNext
Loop
```

The final step is to update the subform control, which is called *Schedule*, to show the newly scheduled events for this client:

```
    F.Schedule.Requery
End Sub
```

The result is a subroutine that generates a checklist of events for each new client.

Accounting for Weekends

One noteworthy aspect of the scheduling procedure is the way the dates for each activity are calculated. Each client form contains a field called *Start Date* which indicates when the client's file becomes active. The Tasks table contains a field called *Schedule* In, which the procedure uses to calculate the *Goal Date* for each scheduled task.

As shown in the following statement, the *Goal Date* is determined by adding the *Schedule In* value to the *Start Date*:

```
    S.[Goal Date] = F.[Start Date] + T.[Schedule In]
```

However, this could result in a weekend goal date. It would be more logical to exclude weekend dates from the schedule. Thus, if the goal date is a Saturday or Sunday, it can be pushed ahead to Monday.

This type of adjustment is made by creating a new function called *WorkDay*:

```
Function WorkDay (d)
If Weekday(d) = 1 Then
    d = d + 1
ElseIf Weekday(d) = 7 Then
    d = d + 2
End If
WorkDay = d
End Function
```

This function uses the built-in Access function *WeekDay( )* to determine the day of the week for the specified date. If the value is 1 (Sunday), the date is increased by one day to Monday. If the value is 7 (Saturday), two days are added to the date to change it to the following Monday.

You can then use the following function to ensure that no tasks are scheduled for completion on a weekend:

```
S.[Goal Date] = WorkDay(F.[Start Date] + T.[Schedule In])
```

By default, Access assumes day 1 of each week is Sunday. You can change day 1 of each week to another day — for example, Monday — by changing the First Weekday property on the General list in the **View** | **Options** dialog box. ■

Another variation on the working days idea is to create a function that counts only working days. For example, if a task is supposed to be scheduled in 15 days, the following function ensures that only working days are counted:

```
Function WorkingDays (Sdate, i)
    k = 0
    Do Until k = i
            Sdate = Sdate + 1
            If Weekday(Sdate) > 2 And WeekDay(Sdate) < 7 Then
                    k = k +1
            End If
    Loop
    Working Days = Sdate
End Function
```

The *WorkingDays* function uses two arguments Sdate is the starting date, and *i* is the increment for the number of days. The procedure contains a loop that repeats until the value of *k* (counter) equals (increment). The trick is that *k* increases by 1 only if the date specified by the variable *Sdate* is a weekday. If *d* is a weekend, *k* remains the same.

When performing date arithmetic, this function counts only the workdays, not weekends. Without this function, if you add 15 days to a starting date of 1/5/94, you arrive at 1/20/94. Using *WorkingDays( )*, however, the same starting values yield 1/26/94 because six weekend days (8, 9, 15, 16, 22, and 23) fall within that range.

As shown in the following statement, you can use the *WorkingDays()* function in the Schedule procedure:

```
S.[Goal Date] = WorkingDays(F.[Start Date], T.[Schedule In])
```

Note that the starting date and increment values are separate arguments for the function.

Skipping Holidays

In addition to accounting for weekends when you make date calculations, you may also want to account for other nonworking days such as holidays. Holidays can't be calculated directly, but you can factor them into date calculations if you create a resource table that lists holiday dates.

Figure 21-3 is an example of a resource table that lists the holidays you want to treat as nonworking days.

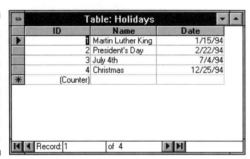

Figure 21-3:
The
Holidays
resource
table lists
additional
nonworking
days.

The Holidays resource table is integrated into the *WorkingDays( )* function by adding the statements shown in bold in the following. The variable *R* is defined as a record set drawn from the Holidays table. Each of the dates that qualifies as a working day is tested with a FindFirst method to determine whether it appears in the list of holidays. If the *NoMatch* value is True, the date is assumed to be a working day and it is counted. If the *NoMatch* value is False, the date is ignored. The revised code for the *WorkingDays( )* function is as follows:

```
Function WorkingDays (Sdate, i)
    Dim R As RecordSet
    Set R = DBEngine.Workspaces(0).Databases(0).OpenRecordSet("Holidays")
    k = 0
    Do Until k = i
        Sdate = Sdate + 1
        If Weekday(Sdate) > 2 And WeekDay(Sdate) < 7 Then
                R.FindFirst "[Date] = #" & Sdate & "#"
                If R.NoMatch Then
                        k = k +1
                End if
        End If
    Loop
    Working Days = Sdate
End Function
```

This procedure includes a shortcut that I haven't used before. Record sets are usually defined in two steps. First, the source database is assigned to a variable — usually *D* — and then the *OpenRecordSet( )* method is applied to the *D* variable to create the record set:

```
Dim D As Database, R As RecordSet
Set D = DBEngine.Workspaces(0).Databases(0)
Set R = D.OpenRecordSet("Holidays")
```

However, in the revised version of *WorkingDays( )*, I used only a single variable, *R*. The *OpenRecordSet( )* method is applied directly to the *DBEngine.Workspaces( ).Databases( )* object, rather than a variable assigned to that object. This method is functionally equivalent to the two-step method used throughout this book and in the Access manual and help examples.

The primary reason for using two steps rather than one is that once *D* is defined, you can use it in several Set commands. This eliminates the need to repeat *DBEngine.Workspaces( ).Databases( )* each time. Even when you're defining only a single record set, you might still prefer the two-step method. As you can see, applying the *OpenRecordSet( )* method directly to the database object creates a long and complicated statement that is best avoided.

Date Rounding

The *WorkingDays( )* function can select any day of the week based on the addition of a specified number of working days to a given date. In practice, you may prefer target dates that are *rounded* to a larger unit of time — perhaps a week. For example, if you are given the date 7/13/94, you might set the goal as the *week of 7/11/94 – 7/15/94*, or a single date such as Friday of that target week, *7/15/94*.

This idea is expressed as a single statement in the following *WeekOf( )* function. The function takes two arguments: *SDate*, which is any date value; and *WkDay*, which is the weekday value 1– 7 for the day of the week that you want to round to:

```
Function Weekof(SDate,WkDay)
   Weekof = Sdate + WkDay - Weekday(Sdate)
End Function
```

As shown in bold in the following code, a modified version of the WorkingDays function uses the *WeekOf( )* function to convert the value returned by *WorkingDays( )* to the nearest Friday (weekday value 6):

```
S.[Goal Date] = WeekOf(WorkingDays(F.[Start Date], T.[Schedule In]), 6)
```

To-Do Lists

As with the data used in the attendance example, you can examine your schedule data from several different points of view. For example, the tasks are originally scheduled on a client-by-client basis, but it's also useful to retrieve the data as *to-do lists* that show all the tasks scheduled for a given worker in the current week. Figure 21-4 shows an example of a to-do list.

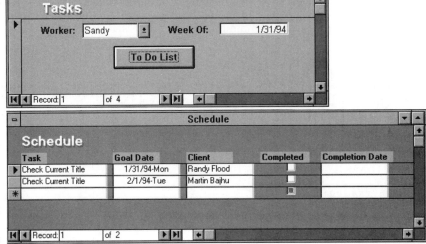

Figure 21-4:
This form
retrieves a
to-do list for
a specific
worker for
the current
week.

In this example, two forms operate in conjunction with each other. The Tasks form allows you to select the name of a worker and enter a date (this could default to today's date). The To Do List button opens a second form that displays all the tasks scheduled for the worker in the current week.

The Tasks form has three controls:

✔ **Worker**. This is a drop list control that allows you to choose the name of a worker. The list contents can be gathered from the Schedule table by using the following SQL statement as the Row Source for the control:

```
Select Distinct [Assign To] From Schedule;
```

✔ **Week Of.** This control shows the date that will be used to select scheduled tasks. Typically, this date might default to today's date. This is accomplished by setting the *Default* property to the expression =*Date( )*.

✔ **To Do List.** This is a command button that opens the To Do list form and applies the *Worker* and *Week Of* values as criteria for selecting schedule items.

The following procedure uses the OpenForm action to apply a rather complicated criteria to the record set of the form. In this case, the criteria is created in several steps. First, *SQLText1* sets up a criteria to select by worker name. *SQLText2* sets up a criteria to select for the week that matches the selected date. The two criteria are combined with an And operator to form a single selection criteria:

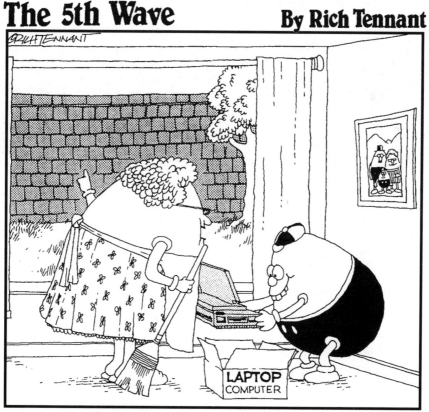

The 5th Wave   By Rich Tennant

"WHY DON'T YOU TAKE THAT OUTSIDE, HUMPTY, AND PLAY WITH IT ON THE WALL?"

```
Sub Button50_Click ()
    SQLText1 = "[Assign To] = " & Chr(34) & [Assign To] & Chr(34)
    SQLText2 = "WeekOf([Goal Date],2) = #" & WeekOf([Week Of], 2) &
        "#"
    DoCmd OpenForm "To Do", , , SQLText1 & " And " & SQLText2
End Sub
```

By dividing the criteria into two separate phrases, you can easily test each one separately if you encounter problems with the entire criteria argument.

You can use the To-Do List technique to produce a printed list by either printing the forms as they appear on the screen, or creating a report form that prints the same information in another layout.

Why a Subform Won't Work

In terms of understanding which Access technique to use to solve a problem, it is useful to see why, in this particular case, it is necessary to use two separate forms rather than a single form/subform combination.

The form/subform approach works if the criteria for selecting schedules uses a direct match between items on the Tasks form and fields in the Schedule table. This is the case when workers are selected by name, for example, *[Assign To] = [Assign To]*. If you had chosen to use a subform to display the task list, you would simply enter [Assign To] in the Master and Child Link properties of the subform's property sheet.

The same would be true if the date criteria was simply a matter of matching a specific date, that is, selecting all scheduled tasks for 1/31/95. However, in practice, selecting records based on exact date matches may be too inflexible.

The solution here is to always choose a week's worth of tasks. You can use other date functions to set a month's worth of tasks. The key problem is once you decide to use a calculated value as the criteria to retrieve a set of records, you can no longer accomplish that using the Master and Child Link properties. They work only with fields in the underlying record sources.

The solution in this example gets around this limitation by opening the retrieved records in a different form rather than in a subform. This allows you to apply any type of valid SQL *Where* clause to the selection process.

A second solution is to alter the record source so it contains the values you want to select by. You could add an extra field to the underlying table that contains the chronological value (for example, week or month) you wanted to match. Or you could create a query with a calculated field that yields the desired values and use that as a record source for the subform.

Which approach you choose is determined primarily by subjective factors —
which one makes the most sense or seems easiest. For example, I avoid adding
query forms to the database because it's awkward later when I've forgotten why
I created the query. In contrast, looking at Access Basic code is more efficient
because it shows information rather than referring to the details stored in
another form (the query). I'm not saying my way is the right way. I may feel that
my way makes more sense, but others will feel just the opposite — they are
more comfortable with queries than with Access Basic code.

Many readers will find solutions that look different from the ones shown here,
but the underlying process of analyzing the problems will be similar.

Chapter 22

Calendars

• •

• •

*B*y using the clock/calendar that's built into your computer and the chronological functions that are built into Access, you can create powerful tools for performing time- and date-related operations, some of which have already been illustrated in the preceding chapters. For the most part, chronological values are expressed in written form, such as *1/25/95*.

This chapter shows you how to use Access to create forms that look like the calendar displays most people are familiar with. The techniques presented in this chapter also reveal how you can use Access Basic to dynamically alter the appearance of objects such as forms and controls.

A Perpetual Calendar

Tacked on the wall of almost every office in the world is a monthly calendar, and at year-end they all have to be replaced. Several popular software programs do nothing but print calendars. However, calendars follow a cyclical pattern that repeats over a long period of time — like the 29-year calendar cycle.

The *serial* date functions built into Access provide a means of generating calendar information based on these complicated calendar cycles. For example, Figure 22-1 shows a form that displays the monthly calendar for any month and year entered into the boxes at the top of the form. Figure 22-1 shows the monthly calendars for that troublesome month, February, of 1995 and 1996.

How do you create such a display? Surprisingly, the answer is a lot less complicated than you would imagine. It also illustrates, once again, how much you can accomplish with a little bit of Access Basic.

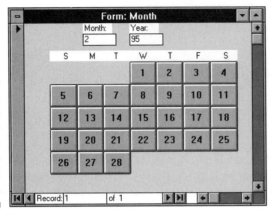

Figure 22-1:
This
calendar
form
displays any
selected
month.

Setting up the calendar form

The first and most important step in creating the calendar form shown in Figure 22-1 involves the layout. You need a command button for each day that can be displayed on the calendar. You begin the layout process by opening a new, blank form in the Form Design mode. The layout process involves the following steps:

1. **Create a command button.** Starting with a new, blank form, place a Command button control near the upper left corner (the placement is not critical). As shown in Figure 22-2, you can use the mouse to drag the button handles and change the shape of the button from a rectangle to a square. The button should be about .5 inches on each side. If you have trouble with the mouse, simply enter .5 in the Width and Height properties.

Figure 22-2: Changing the shape of a command button.

2. **Erase the caption.** By default, this button has the name and caption of *Button0.* Erase the Caption property (but not the name) to display the button as a blank, gray square.

3. **Duplicate the button.** With the button still selected, use the **Edit | Duplicate** command to create a duplicate of the first button. As shown in Figure 22-3, this button is assigned the name *Button1.* This assignment is important because the procedure you write will take advantage of the sequential names that are automatically generated by Access. Your goal is to create

buttons named *Button0* to *Button41*. Note that adding other controls to the form disrupts the automatic sequence. In that case, you would have to manually name each of the button controls.

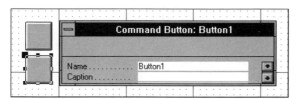

Figure 22-3: The duplicate button has the name Button1.

4. **Place the duplicate button.** Drag the new button to the right of *Button0*. Align the tops of the two buttons. As shown in Figure 22-4, repeat the **Edit** | **Duplicate** process until you have seven buttons (Button0 to Button6) in a row.

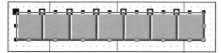

Figure 22-4: Seven buttons should be aligned in a row.

5. **Duplicate a row of buttons.** Select all seven buttons shown in Figure 22-4 and use the **Edit** | **Duplicate** command to create a second row of seven buttons. Drag this row so that it is positioned directly under the first row of buttons. Repeat this process until you have six rows of seven buttons, as shown in Figure 22-5. If you do this correctly, the buttons will be named *Button0* through *Button41*.

Figure 22-5:
The calendar is composed of 42 buttons arranged in six rows and seven columns.

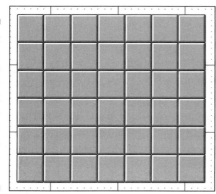

6. **Add other controls.** After placing the 42 buttons on the form, you need to add three more controls. As shown in Figure 22-6, two text boxes called *Month* and *Year* are used to set the month and year for the calendar. The third control is simply a text label that places the letters S, M, T, W, T, F and S over the columns of buttons.

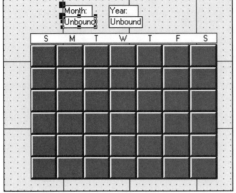

Figure 22-6: The completed calendar form.

Changing the form's appearance

Once the form is laid out, most of the work is done. The changes in the appearance of the form based on the selected month and year are performed by a single procedure called *Cal*. The function requires two arguments: *m* for the month value and *y* for the year value. The first two statements define the object *F* as the current form:

```
Function Cal (m, y)
    Dim F As Form
    Set F = Screen.ActiveForm
```

Because this procedure modifies the properties of the button controls, you need to be sure that the focus isn't on any of the buttons. Access doesn't allow changes to some control properties if the object is selected. The following statement places the focus on the *Month* control:

```
F.[Month].SetFocus
```

The next step in the procedure is to make all the buttons on the form invisible. This is easily accomplished because of the names Access generated for the buttons in the design mode — Button0, Button1...Button41. The following statements use a *For...Next* loop to cycle through the numbers 0 to 41. As the value of *k* changes, the expression *"Button" & k* equals all 42 button names. The expression sets the Visible property of each button to False, which removes the button from the form's display:

```
For k = 0 To 41
    F("Button" & k).Visible = False
Next
```

Next, to create a calendar, you must go back through the command buttons and turn on the ones that represent days in the specified month. Then, you need to change the captions of the buttons to show the days of the month. Before you can do all this, however, you need to determine where to start. Button0, which is positioned in the upper left corner of the form, is the first day of the month only if the month begins on a Sunday.

To know how to fill out the month's calendar, you need to figure out which button represents the first day of the month and how many days (buttons) should be displayed for the month.

You can use the built-in Access function *WeekDay( )* to calculate the day of the week on which the month starts:

```
WeekDay(#7/1/94#)
```

In this example, the value returned is 6, because 7/1/94 is a Friday. But what button does that value correspond to? On the form, the first Friday is Button5, the sixth button on the row. The weekday value for the first day of the month is an *offset* value that affects the location of all the other days in the month. For example, which button should display 7/15/94, the 15th day of the month? To calculate this, start with the day — 15 — then add the offset value of the first day of the month — 6 — to make 21, then subtract 2 to make 19. In other words, Button19 represents the 15th day of the month. You can express this calculation with the following formula:

```
Day of the Month + Starting Offset - 2
```

The *-2* is needed to correct for two factors: first, the buttons begin with 0, not 1. Second, because the weekday values start with 1 instead of 0, the number of buttons you need to offset is one less than the starting day of the week. For example, if a date falls on a Sunday, its *WeekDay( )* value is 1. However, because each row begins with a Sunday, you don't need to advance, so the actual offset is 0.

You can solve the second problem — determining the number of days in the month — by creating the *LenMonth( )* function:

```
Function LenMonth (d)
    Start = DateValue(Month(d) & "/1/" & Year(d))
    Finish = DateAdd("m", 1, Start)
    LenMonth = Start - Finish
End Function
```

The function begins with the argument *d,* which can be any valid date. It doesn't have to be the first day of the month. Based on date *d, Start* is then set as the first day of the month and year.

The function then uses the built-in Access function *DateAdd( )* to increment the date by one month. The number of days between *Start* and *Finish* is the number of days in the specified month. (You can't use *End* as a variable name because it's part of various Access Basic commands, such as End Sub and End Function.)

With these two concepts, you can return to the problem at hand. Two values are calculated based on these concepts. *DayOne* represents the first day of the month. *Offset* is the value used to adjust between the day of the month and the number of the button that represents it:

```
DayOne = DateValue(m & "/1/" & y)
OffSet = Weekday(DayOne) - 2
```

The next set of statements creates a temporary table of values stored in an array called *Days.* The total number of days in the month is calculated using the *LenMonth( )* function:

```
ReDim Days(LenMonth(DayOne))
For k = 1 To LenMonth(DayOne)
    Days(k) = "Button" & k + OffSet
Next
```

The loop is repeated using the names stored in the *Days( )* array to change the Visible and Caption properties of the buttons. Note that the value of *k* — that is, numbers from 1 to the end of the month — functions as the caption for each button:

```
For k = 1 To LenMonth(DayOne)
    F(Days(k)).Visible = True
    F(Days(k)).Caption = k
Next
```

The completed Cal and LenMonth procedures are as follows:

```
Function Cal (m, y)
    Dim F As Form
    Set F = Screen.ActiveForm
    F.[Month].SetFocus
    For k = 0 To 41
        F("Button" & k).Visible = False
    Next
    DayOne = DateValue(m & "/1/" & y)
    Offset = Weekday(DayOne) - 2
    ReDim Days(LenMonth(DayOne))
```

```
        For k = 1 To LenMonth(DayOne)
            Days(k) = "Button" & k + Offset
        Next
        For k = 1 To LenMonth(DayOne)
            F(Days(k)).Visible = True
            F(Days(k)).Caption = k
        Next
    End Function

    Function LenMonth (d)
        Start = DateValue(Month(d) & "/1/" & Year(d))
        Finish = DateAdd("m", 1, Start)
        LenMonth = Start - Finish
    End Function
```

The *Cal( )* function can be executed by placing it in the AfterUpdate property of both the *Month* and *Year* controls:

Name	AfterUpdate
Month	=Cal([Month],[Year])
Year	=Cal([Month],[Year])

The result is that the form shows the month calendar for the specified month and year.

If you look carefully at the code used for the *Cal( )* function, you'll notice that it's a bit longer than necessary. To make the function easier to understand, the button names are first stored in an array and then used to change the properties of the buttons. You can reduce the number of statements in the procedure by eliminating the steps that store the names of the buttons and inserting the expression used for that purpose — *"Button" & k + Offset* — in the parentheses form of the control name — *F("Button" & k + Offset)*. This reduces the length of the procedure by four lines:

```
    Function Cal (m, y)
        Dim F As Form
        Set F = Screen.ActiveForm
        F.[Month].SetFocus
        For k = 0 To 41
            F("Button" & k).Visible = False
        Next
        DayOne = DateValue(m & "/1/" & y)
        Offset = Weekday(DayOne) - 2
        For k = 1 To LenMonth(DayOne)
            F("Button" & k + Offset).Visible = True
            F("Button" & k + Offset).Caption = k
        Next
    End Function
```

However, it isn't essential that you make your procedures as short as possible. It's more important to make sure that the statements are correct and that you understand what each one does. For this reason, you may find it better to write more, albeit simpler, statements instead of trying to create a single complex statement that does the same job.

Using the Calendar as a Menu

Many forms, such as the To-Do List form described in the preceding chapter, use date values as selection criteria. You usually enter a date into a text box. However, it may be useful to select dates from the calendar display instead of a visual menu. In such cases, the date is selecting by clicking on the button that represents a specific day of the month.

Figure 22-7 shows a modified version of the Calendar form in which the dates for scheduled events appear in white, while open dates appear in black. This form allows you to see at a glance which dates have been included in the Schedule table.

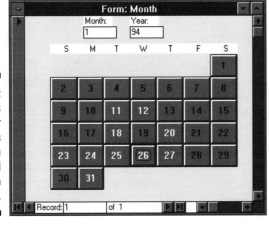

Figure 22-7:
This calendar shows dates with scheduled events in white.

A procedure called *Appoint( )* changes the basic calendar into one that supplies information about the records stored in a table. This procedure determines whether any appointments are scheduled for a given date.

The procedure requires a date, *SelectedDay*. The procedure opens a record set — in this example, from a table called Schedule — and searches for records matching that date. If the *NoMatch* value is True, the function returns a False value to indicate that no events are scheduled for that date. If not, the opposite value is returned. The code for the *Appoint( )* function is as follows:

```
Function Appoint (SelectedDay)
    Dim D As Database, R As Recordset
    Set D = DBEngine.Workspaces(0).Databases(0)
    Set R = D.OpenRecordset("Schedule")
    R.FindFirst "[Goal date] = #" & SelectedDay & "#"
    If R.NoMatch Then
        Appoint = False
    Else
        Appoint = True
    End If
End Function
```

The *Appoint( )* function performs a test — that is, it returns a True or False value, depending on which tasks are stored in the Schedule table. You can use this function to control some aspect of the calendar's appearance and thereby distinguish between dates with appointments or tasks, and those without.

The following modified version of the *Cal( )* procedure uses *Appoint( )* to determine the color of the caption for each button. The *RGB( )* function sets the ForeColor to white (255) if *Appoint( )* returns a True value, or black (0) if the function returns False. The result is a calendar that shows, at a glance, the active dates:

```
Function Cal (m, y)
    Dim F As Form
    Set F = Screen.ActiveForm, C As Control
    F.[Month].SetFocus
    For k = 0 To 41
        F("Button" & k).Visible = False
    Next
    DayOne = DateValue(m & "/1/" & y)
    Offset = Weekday(DayOne) - 2
    For k = 1 To LenMonth(DayOne)
        Set C = F("Button" & k + Offset)
        C.Visible = True
        C.Caption = k
        CurDate = m & "/" & k & "/" & y
        If Appoint(CurDate) Then
            C.ForeColor = RGB(255, 255, 255)
        Else
            C.ForeColor = RGB(0, 0, 0)
        End If
    Next
End Function
```

Note that one change in *Cal( )* isn't related to the use of the *Appoint( )* function. The variable *C* is used as a control variable. It is assigned the button name that is derived from the expression *"Button" & k + Offset*. This change doesn't affect the logic of the procedure but it does simplify the statements that change button properties, because the name *C* can be used in place of the identifier *F("Button" & k + Offset)*.

Showing the Appointments

You can take the calendar concept one step further by making the buttons on the form open up a To-Do list showing the scheduled tasks or appointments. You do this by setting up a function — *ShowAppoint( )* — that uses the same To Do form that you used for the To-Do list example earlier in this book. The only difference is that now the records selected are represented by the date of the selected button. In this case, the function requires three arguments: *m* for the month value, *d* for the date value, and *y* for the year value:

```
Function ShowAppoint (m, d, y)
    DoCmd OpenForm "To Do",,,"[Goal Date] = #" & m & "/" & d & "/" &
            y & "#"
End Function
```

To use this function, set the OnClick event property of each of the buttons to the following expression:

```
=ShowAppoint([month],Screen.ActiveControl.Caption,[Year])
```

Note that the day of the month value is supplied by using the Caption property of the active control. In other words, when you click on a button, the caption — which is the day of the month — is passed as an argument to the *ShowAppoint( )* function.

However, for this example, you need to enter the same expression into the event property of 42 command buttons — a lot of tedious editing. You can avoid all of this editing by setting the property from Access Basic at the same time that you display the calendar. Keep in mind that the *OnClick* property can be set from Access like other control properties.

The following statement inserts the text that is not in bold into the OnClick property of the control. This sets up any of the white labeled buttons to execute the *ShowAppoint( )* function if the user selects the button:

```
C.OnClick = "=ShowAppoint([month],Screen.ActiveControl.Caption,[Year])"
```

With this addition to the *Cal( )* procedure, if the user selects any of the buttons with white captions, the procedure opens an additional window that shows all the tasks or events for that date stored in the Schedule table. This new window is shown in Figure 22-8.

The following procedure shows the new line (in bold) that sets up the OnClick property of the white captioned buttons to execute the *ShowAppoint( )* function when selected:

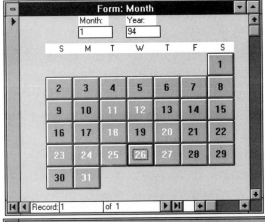

Figure 22-8:
The calendar form displays tasks or appointments for the selected day.

```
Function Cal (m, y)
   Dim F As Form
   Set F = Screen.ActiveForm, C As Control
   F.[Month].SetFocus
   For k = 0 To 41
      F("Button" & k).Visible = False
   Next
   DayOne = DateValue(m & "/1/" & y)
   Offset = Weekday(DayOne) - 2
   For k = 1 To LenMonth(DayOne)
      Set C = F("Button" & k + Offset)
      C.Visible = True
      C.Caption = k
      CurDate = m & "/" & k & "/" & y
      If Appoint(CurDate) Then
         C.ForeColor = RGB(255, 255, 255)
         C.OnClick = "=ShowAppoint([month],
         Screen.ActiveControl.Caption,[Year])"
      Else
         C.ForeColor = RGB(0, 0, 0)
      End If
   Next
End Function
```

Index

• E •

• F •

Notes

Notes

Notes

Notes

Notes

Notes

IDG BOOKS WORLDWIDE REGISTRATION CARD

RETURN THIS REGISTRATION CARD FOR FREE CATALOG

Title of this book: **Access Programming For Dummies**

My overall rating of this book: ☐ Very good [1] ☐ Good [2] ☐ Satisfactory [3] ☐ Fair [4] ☐ Poor [5]

How I first heard about this book:

☐ Found in bookstore; name: [6] _____

☐ Advertisement: [8] _____

☐ Word of mouth; heard about book from friend, co-worker, etc.: [10] _____

☐ Book review: [7] _____

☐ Catalog: [9] _____

☐ Other: [11] _____

What I liked most about this book:

_____

_____

What I would change, add, delete, etc., in future editions of this book:

_____

_____

Other comments:

_____

Number of computer books I purchase in a year: ☐ 1 [12] ☐ 2-5 [13] ☐ 6-10 [14] ☐ More than 10 [15]

I would characterize my computer skills as: ☐ Beginner [16] ☐ Intermediate [17] ☐ Advanced [18] ☐ Professional [19]

I use ☐ DOS [20] ☐ Windows [21] ☐ OS/2 [22] ☐ Unix [23] ☐ Macintosh [24] ☐ Other: [25]_____
(please specify)

I would be interested in new books on the following subjects:
(please check all that apply, and use the spaces provided to identify specific software)

☐ Word processing: [26] _____

☐ Data bases: [28] _____

☐ File Utilities: [30] _____

☐ Networking: [32] _____

☐ Other: [34] _____

☐ Spreadsheets: [27] _____

☐ Desktop publishing: [29] _____

☐ Money management: [31] _____

☐ Programming languages: [33] _____

I use a PC at (please check all that apply): ☐ home [35] ☐ work [36] ☐ school [37] ☐ other: [38] _____

The disks I prefer to use are ☐ 5.25 [39] ☐ 3.5 [40] ☐ other: [41]_____

I have a CD ROM: ☐ yes [42] ☐ no [43]

I plan to buy or upgrade computer hardware this year: ☐ yes [44] ☐ no [45]

I plan to buy or upgrade computer software this year: ☐ yes [46] ☐ no [47]

Name: _____ Business title: [48] _____ Type of Business: [49] _____

Address (☐ home [50] ☐ work [51]/Company name: _____)

Street/Suite# _____

City [52]/State [53]/Zipcode [54]: _____ Country [55] _____

☐ **I liked this book!** You may quote me by name in future
IDG Books Worldwide promotional materials.

My daytime phone number is _____

**IDG
BOOKS**

THE WORLD OF
COMPUTER
KNOWLEDGE